C for Interviews

Concepts, Code & Common Questions

By

Sayam

ISBN: 978-93-5469-458-5

About the Author

Sayam was born in 2005 in Kamptee, Nagpur. At the age of three, his family relocated to his maternal hometown. From a young age, he developed a strong fascination for technology, beginning as early as five.

He is an aspiring author in the field of engineering and is currently pursuing a Bachelor's degree in Computer Science and Engineering. With over five years of writing experience, Sayam focuses on creating practical and clear guidance for learners. He has also completed a summer internship at the National Institute of Technology, Delhi, further strengthening his academic and professional foundation.

Through his books, he aims to share his programming insights and experiences, helping students and professionals deepen their understanding of technology.

He can be reached at: *sayampradhan07@outlook.com* .

ABBREVIATIONS

Abbrev.	Full Form / Description
AI	Artificial Intelligence
API	Application Programming Interface
ASan	AddressSanitizer — detects memory errors
ATS	Applicant Tracking System
B.Tech	Bachelor of Technology
CSE	Computer Science and Engineering
CPU	Central Processing Unit
DBMS	Database Management System
DSA	Data Structures and Algorithms
EOF	End of File
F-Pattern	Eye-scanning pattern used by recruiters
GD	Group Discussion
GCC	GNU Compiler Collection
GDB	GNU Debugger
Git	Version control system
HR	Human Resources
IDE	Integrated Development Environment
I/O	Input / Output
IT	Information Technology

Abbrev.	Full Form / Description
LLD / HLD	Low-Level / High-Level Design
malloc()	Memory allocation function in C
free()	Memory deallocation function in C
realloc()	Memory resizing function in C
argc	Argument Count (CLI parameter in C)
argv	Argument Vector (CLI argument array in C)
ML	Machine Learning
MCQ	Multiple Choice Question
NIT	National Institute of Technology
O0 / O1 / O2 / O3	Compiler optimization levels
OOP	Object-Oriented Programming
OS	Operating System
PDF	Portable Document Format
REST API	Representational State Transfer — API
SQL	Structured Query Language
STAR	Situation–Task–Action–Result (HR method)
STL	Standard Template Library (C++)
UI	User Interface
URL	Uniform Resource Locator
VS Code	Visual Studio Code
Valgrind	Runtime memory debugging tool (Linux)
WSL	Windows Subsystem for Linux
DoS	Denial of Service (security context)
CPU Cache	High-speed memory inside CPU

This list covers key technical and interview-related abbreviations used throughout the book for quick reference.

Contents

Phase 1

Getting Started with the Interview Journey

"Every great journey begins with a single step — and a bit of patience."

Understanding how interviews work and how to prepare smartly

Chapter 1

INTRODUCTION TO THE JOURNEY

If you have ever sat in front of a C program and wondered where to start, you are not alone. We have all been there – staring at the first *#include <stdio.h>* line, trying to make sense of it. This book is here to walk with you through that journey – understanding how C works to cracking real interviews with confidence.

Maybe you're preparing for your first job, or you are in college and simply want to strengthen your C fundamentals before facing an interview. Whatever your reason, this book will help you think like an interviewer, write code like professional, and stay calm when the real questions come.

This book is divided into 5 sections. We'll begin by revisiting the foundations of C – the simple things that most people rush through. Then, step by step, we'll move toward practical questions, real interview puzzles, and problem-solving techniques. By the end, you'll not only know C – you'll know how to talk about it, explain it, and use it confidently in interviews.

As a third-year computer science student, I'm still on my own journey of learning and preparing for interviews. Along the way, I realized that mastering C isn't just about knowing syntax — it's about building logic, understanding how things work behind the code, and staying calm when solving real problems. This book is my way of sharing what I've learned so far — not as a professional, but as someone who's walking the same path as you, learning, exploring, and growing every day.

So, take a deep breath, open your mind, and let's start building from the very first line of C code.

Together, we'll go from basics to brilliance — and prepare you not just for interviews, but for your journey as a confident programmer.

Chapter 2

WHY THIS BOOK?

The idea for this book came from own experiences as a student preparing for interviews. I noticed that while there are many books that teach C syntax, very few actually help you think like an interviewer – how to approach problems, how to explain your logic, and how to stay confident under pressure.

This book aims to bridge that gap. It combines concepts, examples, and real interview-style questions that reflect what companies actually ask. My goal is to make learning C both practical and purpose-driven – not just to pass exams, but to clear interviews and build real problem-solving skills.

Every concept here is written in simple language, supported by examples, and followed by practice questions that gradually challenge your understanding.

Wheather you're revising for a technical test or building your confidence for an interview, this book is designed to be your companion through that process.

Chapter 3

WHO SHOULD READ THIS BOOK?

This book is written especially for students, beginners, and interview aspirants who want to strengthen their understanding of the C programming language and prepare for technical interviews with confidence.

If you are a college student like me – currently exploring C as part of your syllabus – this book will help you go beyond your classroom knowledge. It will showyou how the same concepts are tested in interviews, how to explain your thought process clearly, and how to handle tricky questions calmly.

If you're someone preparing for your first job or internship, you'll find practical interview tips, coding questions, and real problem-solving approaches that can make a difference during your selection process.

Even if you're just beginning your programming journey, this book will guide you from the very basics – step by step – toward thinking like a developer and answering like a problem-solver.

You don't need prior interview experience to start. All you need is curiosity, consistency, and the willingness to learn. Together, we'll build that foundation and the confidence that comes with it.

Chapter 4

WHY C LANGUAGE STILL MATTERS IN INTERVIEWS

When I graduated from school in 2023, I still remember how the syllabus for Computer Science had just changed. CBSE had replaced C++ with Python, and my batch was only the second one to follow the new curriculum. I was excited to learn Python — it felt modern, simple, and beginner-friendly. But somewhere along the way, I kept hearing people say, "You should still learn C."

That made me curious. Why C? It looked old. It didn't have all the shortcuts and built-in features Python offered. If newer languages were easier, why would anyone still go back to C?

If you're thinking the same thing right now, trust me — I've been there too. But here's what I discovered along the way: C is the language that builds your logic from the ground up. It doesn't hide the inner workings of the computer — it lets you see what's really happening under the hood.

That's exactly why companies still love asking C-based questions in interviews. When you can write clean, efficient code in C, it shows that you understand the **core** of programming — how memory works, how logic flows, and how a program actually talks to the machine.

So yes, while Python and other languages are amazing tools for development, C remains the ultimate test of a programmer's foundation. Mastering it gives you confidence, discipline, and problem-solving skills that shine through in every technical interview.

By the time you reach the later chapters of this book, you'll see how learning C isn't just about syntax — it's about thinking like an engineer. And that's what makes all the difference when you sit across from an interviewer.

Chapter 5

IS C STILL BEING USED IN THE INDUSTRY?

In the summer of 2024, I had the incredible opportunity to spend two months at the National Institute of Technology (NIT) Delhi, as a research intern. Those weeks turned out to be among the best experiences of my student life. I got to explore advanced tools, learn from brilliant minds, and see how real-world projects are built beyond textbooks.

One afternoon, while our team was working in the lab, our professor came in to review everyone's progress. One of the groups was facing issues related to networking, and our professor decided we'd visit the Indian Institute of Technology (IIT) Delhi to discuss the problem with Professor Sirohi, a Professor of Practice there.

The next day, we boarded the air-conditioned institute bus around noon, passing through Delhi's busy streets and lively scenes. After a quick lunch at a South Indian restaurant called "Naivedyam," we reached the Bharti

School of Telecommunication and Management inside IIT Delhi, where Professor Sirohi welcomed us warmly. He even gave us a tour of some of their research labs.

In one of the labs, Professor Huzur Saran explained their work — cutting-edge research aimed at reducing internet latency and improving network efficiency. The concepts were so advanced that most of us were left speechless, trying to keep up. Except for one of my colleagues, Sayan, who was in his final year and confidently discussed the technical details with the professor. Watching that exchange made me realize how deep the world of technology truly goes.

But what surprised me the most was the programming language they were using to develop and test their complex network models. It wasn't Python, Java, or any flashy modern language — it was **C**.

That moment changed my perspective. Even at one of the country's top research labs, where the latest technologies were being developed, C was still the foundation. It reminded me that while languages evolve, the systems that run the world — operating systems, networks, embedded systems, and high-performance tools — still rely on C.

So, the next time you wonder whether learning C is worth it, remember this: the world's most advanced technologies still depend on it. C might be old, but it's far from outdated — it's timeless.

Chapter 6

WHY COMPANIES STILL ASK C?

These days, we have a whole sea of programming languages — Python, Java, C++, Go, Rust — and the list keeps growing every year. So, you might wonder: *"If there are so many newer languages, why do companies still ask questions in C during interviews?"*

I used to have the same question. But here's what I realized — C isn't just a language you code in; it's a language that teaches you how computers actually work. When you write in C, you're not just telling the system *what* to do — you're understanding *how* it does it. You get to work with memory directly, manage variables efficiently, and understand how data moves inside the machine.

And that's exactly why companies still value C so much. It reveals how strong your fundamentals are. It's not about syntax; it's about logic, precision, and problem-solving — the things every good programmer must master. Once you can handle C, learning other languages becomes a piece of cake because you already understand what's happening under the hood.

That's why C is often called the "mother of all programming languages." It has shaped how modern languages like C++, Java, and even Python work today. So, when companies test you in C, they're not testing whether you can memorize syntax — they're checking whether you truly understand programming.

Now, you got the answer — **why companies still ask C?**

With that understanding, let's take things one step further. You now know why C matters and how it builds your foundation. But how does this translate into real interviews? What exactly do companies look for when they test your skills?

In the next chapter, we'll walk through the **Overview of the IT Interview Process** — exploring each stage, what to expect, and how to prepare smartly for every step ahead.

Chapter 7

OVERVIEW OF IT INTERVIEW PROCESS

If you've ever imagined what really happens inside an IT interview, you're not alone. Most of us start preparing for interviews without actually knowing what the full process looks like. We just hear terms like "technical round" or "HR round" and jump straight into solving questions. But trust me, understanding the *structure* of the process makes your preparation ten times easier.

When you know what to expect, you stop fearing the unknown. You start focusing your energy on what actually matters — and that's what this chapter is all about. I'll walk you through each stage of a typical IT interview — from the first online test to the final HR interaction. You'll see what interviewers really look for at each step, what kind of questions to expect, and how your mindset can make all the difference.

So, before we pick up our compilers and start coding,

let's take a calm, clear look at how the entire interview journey unfolds — one step at a time.

7.1 Your First Step — The Online Test

You open your laptop, log into the company's test portal, and there it is — the timer is ticking down from 90 minutes. Your heart beats a little faster. That's your first real step towards your dream job — the **Online Test**.

The online test isn't just about getting the right answers — it's about how you *think* when the clock is ticking. Recruiters want to see if you can stay logical, calm, and efficient when every second counts. They're not just testing your memory — they're testing your mindset. So, what exactly are they looking for? Well, they want to see if you can think like a problem solver under pressure, apply your programming fundamentals (especially C and DSA), and manage your time wisely even when the questions get tough.

Every company designs its online test a little differently, but the overall idea stays the same. No matter where you apply, you'll usually find a few common sections that show up again and again. Don't worry — I've broken them down for you in the next part so you know exactly what to expect.

What the Online Test Usually Includes

- **Aptitude and Logical Reasoning:** Tests your problem-solving and numerical thinking.

- **Verbal Ability:** This section of the online assessment test simply checks your command of the English language. It is one of the most scoring sections of the test.
- **C Programming or Core Concepts:** Checks how well you understand syntax, loops, functions, and pointers.
- **Coding Section:** Often includes one or two small programs to test your logic and approach.

How to Prepare Smartly

- Practice online mock tests regularly.
- Revise key C concepts like arrays, strings, and loops.
- Focus more on logic than memorizing syntax.
- Learn to manage your time — attempt easy questions first.
- After every mock test, analyze your mistakes and improve.

Remember, the online test doesn't define your talent — it only filters for those who prepared with focus. And you're already doing that by reading this book.

Clearing the online test is a big win — but it's just the start. The next step is where real communication, logic, and confidence come into play — the Technical Interview. Let's see what that's all about.

7.2 Where Logic Meets Confidence — The Technical Round

So, you've cleared the online test — that's a great start! But now comes the real test of understanding: the **Technical Round**. This is where interviewers go beyond the surface to see how well you actually understand what you've studied.

Think of it like this — the online test checks what you *know*, but the technical round checks how you *think*. The interviewer isn't just interested in whether your code works; they want to see your approach, how you handle tricky situations, and how clearly you can explain your thought process.

Most of the questions you'll face here revolve around logic building, code tracing, debugging, and real-world problem-solving. You might be asked to find errors in a small C program, explain the output of a code snippet, or optimize an existing piece of logic. Sometimes, they'll even twist a simple concept just to see how calmly and systematically you can untangle it.

A good tip? Don't rush to the answer. Instead, walk the interviewer through your thinking — step by step. Even if your final answer isn't perfect, showing clarity and reasoning leaves a strong impression. Interviewers appreciate candidates who can think aloud and explain their approach confidently.

And remember, it's okay to say, "I'm not sure, but here's

how I'd find out." That's what real engineers do every day — they keep learning.

In short, the technical round is less about perfection and more about problem-solving attitude. Stay calm, stay logical, and show them how you think — not just what you've memorized.

7.3 The Mindset Test — HR and Managerial Round

By the time you reach this round, you've already proved your technical skills and logical thinking. The HR or Managerial round isn't here to test how well you can code — it's here to see how well you can communicate, stay calm, and fit into a team.

Think of it as a conversation, not an interrogation. The interviewer already knows you're capable; now they just want to understand who you are as a person — your attitude, clarity of thought, and how you handle challenges.

You might get questions like:

- "Tell me about yourself."
- "What's your biggest strength and weakness?"
- "How do you handle pressure or conflicts in a team?"
- "Where do you see yourself in the next few years?"

These aren't trick questions. They're designed to check how you think, how honestly you respond, and how confidently you carry yourself.

Here's a simple rule — be genuine. If you don't know something, admit it politely. If you've made a mistake in the past, talk about what you learned from it. Honesty leaves a stronger impression than a perfect but robotic answer ever will.

Also, remember: body language speaks before your words do. Sit upright, maintain eye contact, and smile when appropriate. These little gestures quietly show confidence and positivity.

So, the HR round is really the final check — not of your skills, but of your mindset. It's about showing that you're ready to learn, grow, and work well with others. By the end of this round, they should see you not just as a candidate, but as a future teammate.

And that's the big picture — the full journey of a typical IT interview. From the fast-paced online test to the logical depth of the technical round, and finally, the mindset check in the HR round — each stage has its own purpose and challenge.

Now that you know what to expect, it's time to prepare for it the smart way. In the next phase of this book, we'll go back to the roots — understanding C language from the ground up. We'll rebuild your concepts, strengthen your logic, and get you ready for the kinds of questions that actually come up in interviews.

So, take a deep breath — the real learning journey begins now.

Phase 2

Mastering C Fundamentals

"C teaches you not just to code, but to think like a computer."

Building your foundation for interview success

Chapter 8

GETTING STARTED WITH C

First of all, I want to congratulate you on making it this far. Reaching this point means you have the curiosity and determination to truly learn and grow — qualities that every good programmer needs. This book was written with learners like you in mind, and I'm genuinely glad that we've walked this journey together so far. In the previous phase, we explored why C still holds such importance in interviews and got a clear picture of how companies design their selection process, from online tests to technical and HR rounds. We also understood why top companies continue to rely on C when assessing problem-solving and logical thinking. Now, it's time to move from understanding to application — to open our editor, write our first few lines of C code, and start learning this powerful language from the ground up.

8.1 Setting the Stage

Before we begin typing our first program, let's take a step back and see what this chapter is really about. We'll start by understanding what C is — not just as a language, but as a way of thinking. We'll set up the environment where our programs will run, learn how to write and execute a basic program, and explore what happens behind the scenes when the computer processes our code. By the end of this chapter, you'll not only be able to write your first working C program but also truly *understand* what goes on when it runs.

8.2 What Exactly is C?

C is not just another programming language. It is the foundation on which many modern languages are built — including C++, Java, and even parts of Python. Developed in the early 1970s by **Dennis Ritchie** at **Bell Labs**, C was created to write operating systems, which means it had to be fast, reliable, and close to the hardware. That is still true today.

C lets you see how a computer really works — how data moves, how memory is managed, and how logic turns into performance. Once you understand C, learning any other language becomes much easier, because you'll already know what's happening underneath the surface. That's also why interviewers still value candidates who can think and solve problems in C — it's a sign that they understand computers at a deeper level.

8.3 Setting Up Your Environment

To write and run C programs, you need two main things:

1. A **text editor or IDE** where you'll write your code.
2. A **compiler** that converts your human-readable code into machine instructions the computer can execute.

There are several options depending on your operating system:

- **Windows:** You can use Code::Blocks, Dev-C++, or Visual Studio Code with a GCC compiler extension.
- **Linux / macOS:** Most systems already come with the `GCC` (GNU Compiler Collection) pre-installed. You can check by typing `gcc --version` in your terminal.

To keep things simple and close to what companies often use during online coding tests, we'll use the **GCC compiler** and its debugger companion, **GDB**.

8.4 Understanding GCC and GDB

When you write a C program, the compiler plays a crucial role — it takes your `.c` file and turns it into an executable program that your computer can understand.

Here's what happens step by step when you compile with GCC:

1. **Preprocessing:** Handles all the #include and #define statements.
2. **Compilation:** Converts your code into assembly language.
3. **Assembly:** Turns assembly code into object code (machine instructions).
4. **Linking:** Combines all object files into one final executable.

That final executable is what you run.

In many company coding environments and technical assessments, you'll often find **GCC and GDB** as the default tools.

- **GCC (GNU Compiler Collection)** — compiles your code.
- **GDB (GNU Debugger)** — helps you debug your program and find logical or runtime errors.

Why GDB matters for interviews: When you face a programming question in an online or on-site test, it's not just about getting the output right — it's about how efficiently you can trace what went wrong when it doesn't work. Tools like GDB let you pause your program mid-execution, inspect variable values, and step through your code line by line.

Example: If your code file is named `test.c`, you can compile and debug it as follows:

```
gcc -g test.c -o test
gdb ./test
```

Inside GDB, you can use:

```
break main       // set a breakpoint at main()
run              // start the program
print x          // print value of variable x
next             // go to the next line
continue         // resume execution
quit             // exit GDB
```

Learning to use GDB even at a basic level gives you an edge — it shows interviewers that you know how to think like a problem solver, not just a coder.

8.5 Your First C Program

Now let's write the classic "Hello, World!" program. This is where it all begins.

```
#include <stdio.h>

int main() {
    printf("Hello, World!\n");
    return 0;
}
```

Explanation:

- `#include <stdio.h>` — includes the standard input/output library.
- `int main()` — every C program starts from here.
- `printf()` — prints text to the screen.

- `return 0;` — tells the operating system that the program ended successfully.

To compile and run:

```
gcc hello.c -o hello
./hello
```

Output:

```
Hello, World!
```

That simple line connects you to decades of programmers who began right where you are now.

8.6 What Happens When You Run the Program

When you hit "Run," a fascinating process takes place. Your source code, which is readable by humans, is translated into **machine code** — sequences of 0s and 1s that the processor executes.

The compiler doesn't just convert; it also optimizes — ensuring your program runs as efficiently as possible. The moment you understand this, you stop being a "syntax memorizer" and start thinking like an engineer who speaks the computer's language.

This understanding is what separates an average coder from a great one — and interviewers know that.

8.7 Common Beginner Mistakes

Everyone makes them — and that's okay. Here are some typical early errors and how to fix them:

Mistake	Cause	Fix
Missing semicolon	Each statement in C must end with ;	Add semicolon at the end of each line
Mismatched brackets {}	Forgetting to close a block	Count opening and closing braces carefully
Case sensitivity	`Main` ≠ `main`	Always use lowercase for `main()`
Wrong header file	`#include <studio.h>` instead of `stdio.h`	Use the correct header names

8.8 Quick Recap Before You Move On

Before moving to the next chapter, make sure you can:

- Explain how a compiler and linker work.
- Write and run a basic C program.
- Understand what GDB is and how to use it to debug code.
- Fix common beginner-level syntax errors confidently.

Do-It-Yourself: Practice Zone

Now it's your turn to code! These simple exercises will help you build confidence and get comfortable with the basics before diving deeper. Don't worry if you make mistakes — that's how real learning happens.

1. Write a C program to print your name, age, and college name on separate lines.
2. Modify the "Hello, World!" program to print a personalized message, like "Hello, [Your Name]! Welcome to C programming."
3. Write a C program to add two numbers and print the result.
4. Write a C program that prints the size of different data types (like `int`, `float`, `char`) using the `sizeof()` operator.
5. Challenge: Write a program that asks the user for their name and then prints "Hello, [Name]! Have a great day!".

Remember, every big programmer once wrote their first "Hello, World!" — this is where your journey truly begins.

Chapter 9

DATA TYPES, VARIABLES AND OPERATORS

After writing your first few lines of C code, it's natural to wonder what's really happening behind those curly braces. When we declared something like `int x = 10;`, where did that `10` actually go? How does your computer remember it? What happens if you assign a floating-point value to it? These are small questions that most learners skip—but understanding them deeply is what makes you truly confident in C. And more importantly, it's what helps you think like an interviewer expects you to.

In the previous chapter, we set up our tools and learned to compile and execute our first program. In this one, we're going to peek behind the curtain and see what's going on inside the machine when we declare and manipulate data. By the end of this chapter, you'll understand how C looks at data, how variables are stored, how operators work behind the scenes, and how these tiny details often become the deciding factor in an interview.

9.1 Why Understanding Data Types Matters

Every programming language works with data, but C gives you direct access to how that data is stored and managed. When you declare a variable, you're not just creating a name—you're reserving a specific amount of memory to store information, and you're also defining how that memory should be interpreted.

For example, when you write:

```
int a = 5;
float b = 5.0;
```

you might think both represent "five." But internally, the computer treats them very differently. One occupies four bytes to store an integer value, while the other uses four bytes (or sometimes more) to store a fractional representation in binary form.

Understanding these internal differences is what gives you control over efficiency, memory usage, and precision—three things every interviewer silently tests you for. Most coding questions in C interviews are built to see if you understand **how the com- puter thinks about data**, not just if you can use syntax correctly.

Going One Step Deeper: When you truly grasp data types, you begin to see your program not as lines of code, but as a structured memory layout. Every variable you declare has a size, an address, and a type — three attributes that decide how your program behaves. A well-optimized program isn't about writing fewer lines; it's about choosing the right types for the right tasks. That's why, in interviews, even a small discussion about why you chose an `int` over a `float` can reveal how mature your programming decisions are.

9.2 What is Data? How C Sees the World

To the human eye, data is a number, a character, or a string of text. But to a computer, everything is stored as bits—0s and 1s. What gives meaning to those bits is the data type you associate with them.

When you declare:

```
int num = 10;
```

C allocates a small box in memory—usually 4 bytes—and stores the binary representation of 10 inside it. That's all. The "type" you give it (`int`) simply tells the compiler how to interpret those bits later.

Observation: The same binary pattern can mean different things depending on the data type. The value 01000001 could mean the character 'A' if it's stored in a `char`, or it could represent the number 65 if it's stored in an `int`. C doesn't enforce meaning—it simply gives you tools to interpret memory in a structured way.

This is what makes C both powerful and dangerous.

The language trusts you completely—it assumes you know what you're doing.

Expanding the Perspective: If you could peek into your computer's RAM, you'd find it to be nothing more than a long sequence of bytes. There's no label, no name, no "integer" or "character" — just raw data. What C gives you is a disciplined way to navigate that chaos. It teaches you to treat memory with precision and respect, because one wrong type interpretation can change both logic and output. Once you see data the way the compiler does, debugging stops being guesswork — it becomes detective work.

9.3 Variables — Names for Memory

A variable is nothing but a name given to a particular memory location. When you create a variable in C, you're asking the operating system for a small piece of memory to store data.

```
int age = 20;
```

Here, the variable age is not the number 20 itself—it's a label for the memory space that holds 20. This is why, when you print the address using:

```
printf("%p", &age);
```

you'll see a hexadecimal number—the physical memory address of the variable.

Observation: When an interviewer asks, "What happens to a variable when a function ends?", they're not testing your memory—they're checking if you understand **variable lifetime**. Local variables live in the stack, and once the function exits, that memory is reclaimed automatically. Global and static variables, however, remain in memory throughout the program's execution.

Understanding these concepts now will make pointer handling, recursion, and memory management much clearer later.

Deeper Insight: Every variable you create has a story—it's born when your program starts a block, and it disappears when that block ends. This life cycle determines not just where it's stored, but how safe it is to use. Many beginners unknowingly access variables after their lifetime ends, leading to mysterious bugs. Interviewers love exploring this with questions about local vs global scope, or static vs automatic storage. So, when you see a variable, don't just think of it as a "container." Think of it as a traveler with a limited journey inside your program's memory.

9.4 Constants — The Unchangeable Values

Sometimes, you want data to remain the same throughout the program. That's where constants come in. There are two main ways to define constants in C:

```
#define PI 3.14
const float pi = 3.14;
```

Both look similar but behave differently.

- The `#define` constant is handled during preprocessing—before compilation begins. It's a literal text replacement.

- The `const` keyword, however, allocates memory for the variable and enforces read-only behavior during program execution.

Observation: Many students assume both are the same—but in interviews, the difference between compile-time and runtime constant handling often appears as a subtle question. Understanding this distinction shows that you know what happens behind the scenes.

9.5 Data Types — The Building Blocks

Let's talk about the types of data C understands. Every data type defines three things:

1. How much memory will be used.
2. What kind of data can be stored.
3. How that data will be interpreted.

Type	Size (bytes)	Range (approx.)	Example
char	1	-128 to 127	'A', 'z'
int	4	-2,147,483,648 to 2,147,483,647	100, -42
float	4	3.4e-38 to 3.4e+38	12.56
double	8	1.7e-308 to 1.7e+308	3.1415926

Observation: C doesn't automatically check if your data fits the type. If you assign a value larger than the maximum range, it simply wraps around—creating a logical error known as an overflow. Interviewers often test this behavior because it reveals if you think beyond syntax.

9.6 Type Conversion and Casting

C allows conversion between different data types, but it doesn't always warn you about what's lost in the process. There are two ways this happens:

- **Implicit Conversion (Type Promotion)** — Happens automatically when mixing different data types.
- **Explicit Conversion (Type Casting)** — You instruct the compiler to convert manually.

```
int a = 5;
float b = 2;
float result = a / b;
```

You might expect the answer to be 2.5, but it's actually 2.0. Why? Because both a and b are integers during division. The conversion happens only after the operation, not before.

Observation: Most interview questions on this topic revolve around the timing of conversion—whether the promotion happens before or after an operation.

9.7 Operators — The Logic Makers

Operators are the tools that bring logic to life in C. They allow you to manipulate variables, compare values, and perform operations on data.

C provides several categories:

- Arithmetic operators (+, -, *, /, %)
- Relational operators (==, !=, >, <, >=, <=)
- Logical operators (&&, ||, !)
- Assignment operators (=, +=, -=, etc.)
- Bitwise operators (&, |, ∧, ~, «, »)

Observation: When an interviewer asks about bitwise operators, they're not testing your memory—they're testing how well you can visualize data at the bit level. Bitwise logic is essential in embedded systems, low-level coding, and optimization problems.

Example:

```
int a = 5, b = 3;
printf("%d", a & b);  // Output: 1
```

Why 1? Because in binary, 5 is 0101 and 3 is 0011. The bitwise AND compares each bit and keeps only the ones that match in both positions.

9.8 Common Pitfalls and Interview Traps

C's flexibility is both a gift and a test. Some of the most common interview-level mistakes include:

- `char c = 255;` — Overflow occurs because a signed char can't store 255.
- `float x = 3/2;` — Output is 1.0, not 1.5 (integer division first).
- `printf("%d", 'A');` — Prints 65 because characters are stored as ASCII codes.
- `int i = 5; printf("%d", i++ + ++i);` — Unpredictable because of sequence point violations.

Observation: Interviewers don't expect you to memorize every case—they want to see if you can reason through it. If you understand memory, types, and precedence, you can handle any question calmly.

9.9 Naming Conventions (Identifiers That Read Like Intent)

Good names make code easier to read, review, and debug—especially in interviews where you must explain your logic quickly. In C, a name (identifier) must start with a letter or underscore and can contain letters, digits, and underscores. Beyond the rules, choose names that communicate intent.

Core Rules You Should Never Forget

- **Valid start:** letter `[A_Za_z]` or underscore `_`; then letters/digits/underscores.
- **Case sensitive:** `sum`, `Sum`, and `SUM` are different.
- **Avoid keywords:** don't use `int`, `for`, `return`, etc.
- **Length:** keep names short but clear (~15–30 chars is usually plenty).

Project-Wide Style (Be Consistent)

Pick one style and use it everywhere:

- **snake_case** for variables and functions (common in C): `total_count`, `read_file()`.
- **SCREAMING_SNAKE_CASE** for constants and macros: `MAX_SIZE`, `#define BUFFER_LEN 256`.
- **PascalCase** is uncommon in C; reserve it for module/type names only if your team prefers it.

What to Name *What*

- **Variables:** nouns that describe data: `index`, `line_count`, `sum`.

- **Functions:** verb + object: `open_file()`, `parse_header()`, `compute_average()`.
- **Booleans/flags:** prefix with a question or state: `is_empty`, `has_error`, `enable_log`.
- **Constants/macros:** `MAX_USERS`, `DEFAULT_TIMEOUT_MS`. Avoid magic numbers in code.
- **Enums:** type in `PascalCase` (optional), values in `SCREAMING_SNAKE_CASE`:

```
typedef enum {
    COLOR_RED, COLOR_GREEN, COLOR_BLUE
} Color;
```

- **Structs:** type names as nouns; fields as data names:

```
typedef struct {
    int    id;
    char   name[64];
    size_t size_bytes;
} FileMeta;
```

- **Files/modules:** short, all-lowercase with underscores: `file_io.c`, `file_io.h`.

Scope-Based Hints (Make Life Easier for Future You)

- **Local variables:** short but clear: `i`, `j` are fine as loop indices; prefer `row`, `col` when meaning matters.
- **Static internal symbols:** use `static` and keep names

simple: `static int cache_hits;` in a C file.

- **Global/public API:** use a module prefix to prevent collisions:

```
int  net_connect(...);
void net_close(...);
```

Good vs Bad (Quick Glance)

Bad	Good
`a, b, c`	`width, height, depth`
`doit()`	`compute_checksum()`
`x1_2`	`bytes_read`
`max` (global, ambiguous)	`arr_max` (local) / `stats_max` (module-scoped)
`#define n 100`	`#define MAX_NODES 100`

Operator-Aware Names (Prevent Bugs By Wording)

When code is heavy with arithmetic or bitwise logic, names should reveal units and intent:

- Include units: `timeout_ms`, `speed_kbps`, `size_bytes`.
- Mark inclusive/exclusive bounds: `end_exclusive`, `limit_inclusive`.
- For bit masks, use the `MASK`/`FLAG` suffix and hex constants:

```
#define PERM_READ   0x01
#define PERM_WRITE  0x02
#define PERM_EXEC   0x04
unsigned char perms = PERM_READ | PERM_WRITE;
```

Interview Pointers (What They Listen For)

- Explain decisions out loud: "I'm using `snake_case` for C functions and `SCREAMING_SNAKE_CASE` for macros."
- Rename when confused: if a name confuses you while speaking, it will confuse reviewers too.
- Avoid over-abbreviations: `cfg` is fine; `c` is not. Prefer `config`.

Mini Practice

Rename these to improve clarity:

```
int m; float t; int f(int a, int b);
```

Possible direction: `int month; float temperature_c; int add(int lhs, int rhs);` (or based on your problem domain).

9.10 Quick Recap Before You Move On

In this chapter, you learned:

- How C represents data in memory.
- The meaning of variables, constants, and data types.
- How implicit and explicit conversions affect output.
- The logic and usage of different operators.

If you can now visualize how data is stored, moved, and manipulated in C—you're already ahead of most learners.

Do-It-Yourself: Practice Zone

Try the following small programs to deepen your understanding:

1. Write a program to display the size (in bytes) of all fundamental data types using `sizeof()`.
2. Declare a `char` variable and assign it the value 130. Observe the output and explain why it happens.
3. Print the ASCII values of all uppercase letters using a loop.
4. Write a program to demonstrate the difference between `#define` and `const`.
5. Challenge: Swap two variables without using a third variable.

Understanding how data types and operators work will make you a better programmer—not because you know more syntax, but because you now understand how computers actually think.

Chapter 10

CONTROL STRUCTURES

Up until now, we've learned how data lives and behaves inside memory — how variables store values, how types define interpretation, and how operators let us manipulate that data. But our programs are still following a straight line: one statement after another. Real programs, however, don't just move forward — they make decisions, repeat actions, and respond to different situations. That's where **control structures** come in.

Control structures are the brain of your program. They decide which path your logic takes, when to repeat a set of instructions, and when to stop. Understanding them deeply doesn't just make you a better C programmer — it prepares you to think like an interviewer expects you to: logically, calmly, and with precision.

10.1 What Are Control Structures?

Every C program follows one of three possible flows:

1. **Sequential flow:** The default mode — statements execute one after another.
2. **Selection flow:** Decision-making — the program chooses between alternatives.
3. **Iteration flow:** Repetition — executing a block multiple times until a condition fails.

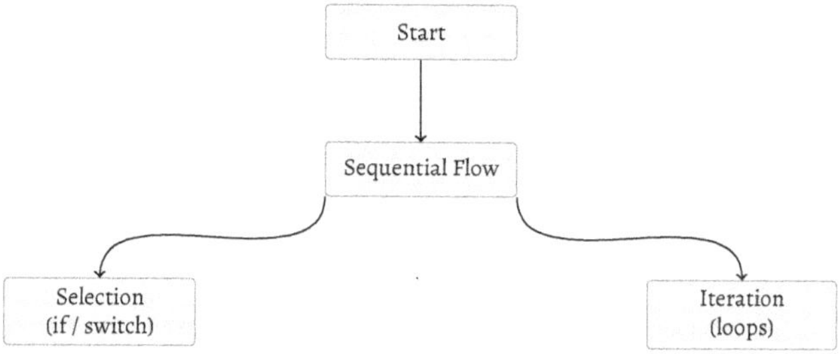

Figure 10.1: *Types of Control Flow in C Programs*

Observation: When an interviewer asks you to trace or predict output, what they're really testing is your understanding of control flow — how your logic moves through these paths step-by-step.

10.2 Decision-Making in C

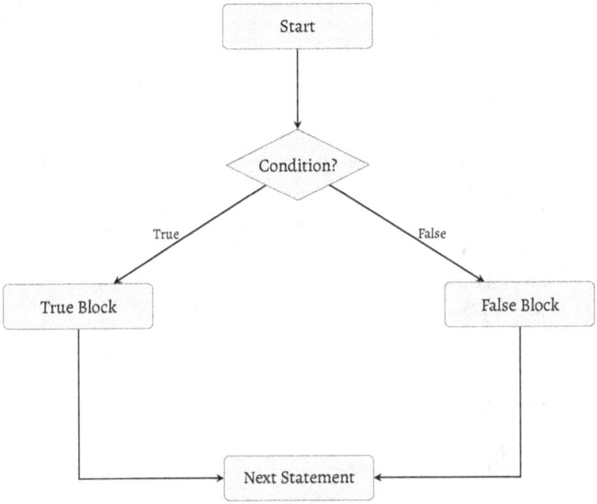

Figure 10.2: *Flow of an if–else Decision in C*

The if Statement

The simplest form of decision-making in C is the `if` statement. It tests a condition — if true, a block of code runs; if false, the program skips it.

```
int num = 10;
if (num > 0) {
    printf("Positive number\n");
}
```

Here, if `num > 0` evaluates to true, the program prints the message. Otherwise, it moves on silently.

Interview Tip: Interviewers often use nested or

combined if statements to test how well you trace conditions. Always follow the program as the compiler would — top to bottom, left to right.

The if–else Ladder

The if–else ladder lets you handle multiple possible conditions in a structured way.

```
if (marks >= 90)
    printf("Grade A\n");
else if (marks >= 75)
    printf("Grade B\n");
else if (marks >= 60)
    printf("Grade C\n");
else
    printf("Grade D\n");
```

Observation: C evaluates each condition in order. As soon as one condition is true, the rest are skipped. In interviews, this concept often appears disguised in "overlapping condition" questions.

Nested if Statements

A nested `if` is simply an `if` inside another. It allows more refined decisions.

```
if (x > 0) {
    if (x % 2 == 0)
        printf("Positive even number");
    else
        printf("Positive odd number");
}
```

Interview Tip: Nested conditions test clarity. If

your indentation and braces are messy, logic errors are inevitable. Keep your structure clean — especially when writing on paper during interviews.

The switch Statement

The `switch` is cleaner for fixed-value conditions.

```
int day = 3;
switch(day) {
    case 1: printf("Monday"); break;
    case 2: printf("Tuesday"); break;
    case 3: printf("Wednesday"); break;
    default: printf("Invalid day");
}
```

Observation: The `break` statement stops fall-through. If you forget it, the next cases execute too — a common interview trap.

10.3 Loops: The Power of Repetition

Loops let your program repeat instructions until a condition changes.

The for Loop

Used when you know how many times to repeat.

```
for (int i = 1; i <= 5; i++) {
    printf("%d ", i);
}
```

Interview

Tip: Trace each iteration carefully. Interviewers often ask for output of nested loops or ask how many times a loop runs.

The while Loop

Used when you don't know how many times to iterate.

```
int i = 1;
while (i <= 5) {
    printf("%d ", i);
    i++;
}
```

The do–while Loop

Executes the block once, even if the condition is false.

```
int i = 1;
do {
    printf("%d ", i);
    i++;
} while (i <= 5);
```

Observation: A do–while always executes at least once. That's why it's often used for menu-driven programs or input validation.

10.4 How the CPU Executes Control Structures

Behind every decision or loop, the CPU uses jumps and branches. - `if` becomes a conditional jump (executed only if true). - Loops are backward jumps — repeat until the condition fails.

Understanding this helps you debug infinite loops and logic errors.

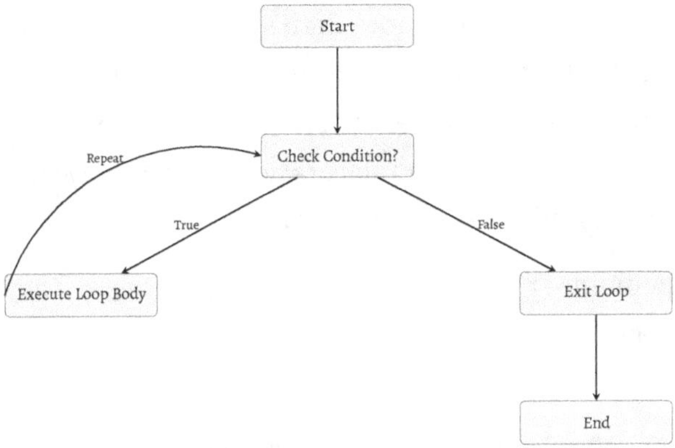

Figure 10.3: *Basic Loop Flow in C*

10.5 Common Mistakes and Interview Traps

- Using = instead of == in conditions.
- Forgetting braces for multi-line `if` or `else`.
- Adding a stray semicolon after `for` or `while`.
- Infinite loops due to unchanged variables.
- Misunderstanding operator precedence in complex conditions.

Observation: These "tricks" are not meant to confuse you — they reveal whether you understand how C actually executes logic. Always trace your code step by step.

10.6 Developing the Right Mindset for Logic Questions

Control structures are more than syntax — they train your logical thinking. When you write code under interview pressure, your calm reasoning is your biggest strength. If you can visualize each branch and loop as it executes, you've already passed the toughest part.

Remember: interviews don't test memory — they test how you think.

10.7 Quick Recap Before You Move On

Before you dive into the next chapter, let's pause for a moment and make sure everything we covered in this one has settled well. Control structures are what give your programs decision-making power — the ability to act differently based on conditions, and to repeat actions when needed.

Here's what you should be comfortable with by now:

- Understanding
  how control flow works in a C program and how it directs the sequence of execution.
- Using `if`, `if-else`, and `nested if` statements to handle decision-making.
- Knowing when to use the `switch` statement for

cleaner multi-condition logic.

- Grasping the purpose of loops (`for`, `while`, and `do-while`) and how they make your programs efficient.
- Understanding how to trace loop flow — when it starts, when it ends, and how it repeats.
- Recognizing how interviewers test your logic using control structure-based questions.

If you can confidently explain these concepts — not just write code, but actually *reason about it* — you're already building the mindset of a strong C programmer.

In the next chapter, we'll take this logic-building further and see how we can use **functions** to make our code modular, reusable, and easier to understand — something interviewers really love to see.

Do-It-Yourself: Practice Zone

Try these small programs to sharpen your logic:

1. Write a program to check whether a number is positive, negative, or zero.
2. Find the largest of three numbers using nested `if`.
3. Write a program to print all even numbers between 1 and 100.
4. Write a program to find the factorial of a number using a loop.
5. Challenge: Write a menu-driven program using `do-while` and `switch` to perform basic arithmetic operations.

Practice is how logic becomes instinct. Each of these questions builds a step toward the kind of calm, clear thinking that defines a confident C programmer.

Chapter 11

FUNCTIONS AND RECURSION

First of all, take a moment to appreciate how far you've come. From learning how C handles decisions and loops, you've now reached a point where your code can make choices and repeat actions automatically. That's a big step! But here's the next question — what if your program grows larger? How do you organize your logic, reuse what you've already written, and make your code easier to manage? That's where functions step in — one of the most powerful concepts in C.

11.1 Why Think in Functions?

When you first start coding, it's easy to write everything in one big block inside the `main()` function. But as your code grows, that approach becomes messy. Imagine trying to run a restaurant alone — cooking, taking orders, serving, cleaning — all by yourself. That's exactly what your `main()` function does when you don't use other functions.

Functions let you divide your code into smaller, logical pieces, each responsible for a specific task. They help you think in modules — and that's exactly what interviewers look for. They often test if you can take a big problem and break it into smaller ones. That's not just programming skill; that's problem-solving ability.

11.2 Understanding Functions in C

A function in C is like a mini-program inside your program. It takes input (parameters), performs a specific task, and gives output (return value). The structure of a function in C looks like this:

```
return_type function_name(parameter_list) {
    // body of the function
}
```

Example:

```
int add(int a, int b) {
    return a + b;
}
```

Here, `int` is the return type, meaning the function sends back an integer value. When you call this function from `main()`, C pauses what it's doing, jumps to the function, executes it, and then returns back to where it left off.

Example usage:

```
int main() {
    int sum = add(4, 5);
```

```
    printf("%d", sum);
    return 0;
}
```

In interviews, candidates are often asked to explain "what happens when a function is called." When that happens, remember this — the compiler creates a temporary space in memory (called a stack frame) for the function, stores all its local variables there, executes the function, and then clears that memory when done.

11.3 Types of Functions

There are mainly three kinds of functions in C:

- **Library functions** – predefined, like `printf()`, `scanf()`, `sqrt()`.
- **User-defined functions** – functions you create for specific tasks.
- **Recursive functions** – functions that call themselves (we'll discuss them soon).

Understanding these helps you write clean, modular code — a skill every interviewer appreciates.

11.4 Why Modular Programming Matters (Interview Insight)

Think of modular programming as "divide and conquer." If your code has separate, well-named functions, it becomes readable and easy to debug. For example, a simple calculator program can be split into:

```
add(), subtract(), multiply(), divide()
```

Each function does just one job — simple and clear.

Interview Tip: Before you start coding a large problem, outline the functions you'll need. Interviewers love when candidates plan before they write.

11.5 How Function Calls Work Internally

When you call a function, several things happen behind the scenes:

1. The program jumps to the function's definition.
2. Space is allocated in memory for that function's local variables.
3. The function executes its code.
4. The program returns to the caller with the result.

Each call gets its own memory space, known as a **stack frame**. When the function ends, that frame is destroyed — this is called "stack unwinding."

This diagram helps you visualize how C "jumps" between functions — and why you can have multiple calls happening in sequence without mixing up data.

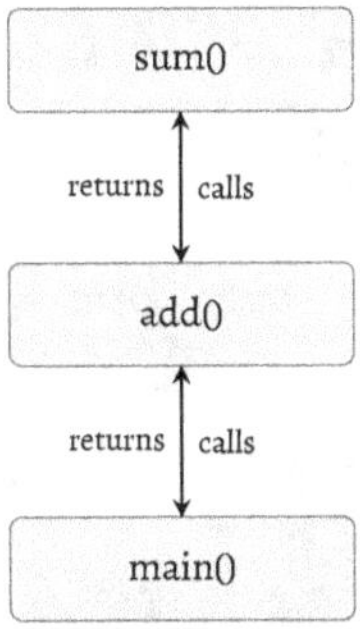

Figure 11.1: *Function Call Flow and Stack Return*

11.6 Parameter Passing and Return Values

When you pass values to a function, C copies them — this is called **pass by value**. That's why changing the value inside a function doesn't affect the variable in `main()`. This concept is tested in interviews often.

Example:

```
void change(int x) {
    x = 10;
}
int main() {
    int a = 5;
    change(a);
    printf("%d", a); // still prints 5
}
```

Understanding this shows interviewers that you know how memory and functions interact.

11.7 Recursion – When a Function Calls Itself

Now comes one of the most fascinating parts of programming — recursion. It's when a function calls itself to solve smaller versions of the same problem.

Example: Factorial using recursion

```
int fact(int n) {
    if(n == 0)
        return 1;
    else
        return n * fact(n-1);
}
```

The key to recursion is having:

- A **base case** – the stopping condition.
- A **recursive case** – where the function calls itself.

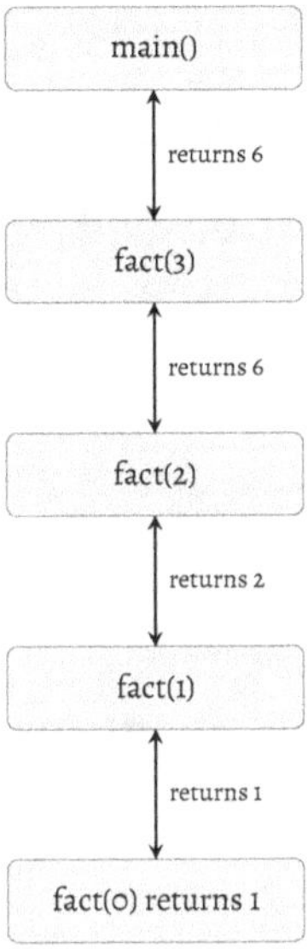

Figure 11.2: *Recursive Function Flow for Factorial*

In interviews, when you're asked to "trace a recursive function," draw something like this. It helps you visualize how recursion moves deeper and then returns step by step.

11.8 When (and When Not) to Use Recursion

Recursion is powerful but not always the best tool. It's best for problems that naturally repeat within smaller sub-problems — like traversing trees, generating Fibonacci series, or exploring paths.

However, recursion uses stack memory, and if not handled properly, can lead to stack overflow. That's why interviewers often ask: > "Can you solve this problem using both recursion and iteration?"

It tests your ability to think logically, not just write code.

11.9 Common Mistakes Beginners Make

Here are some common pitfalls and how to fix them:

Mistake	Cause	Fix
Missing function declaration	Compiler doesn't know about it yet	Add prototype before `main()`
Infinite recursion	Base condition missing	Always define a stopping case
Wrong return type	Function returns incompatible value	Match return type with declaration
Local variable confusion	Reusing variable names across functions	Use meaningful, unique names

11.10 Quick Recap Before You Move On

Let's pause here and check what we've learned:

- Functions divide large problems into smaller, logical parts.
- Each function has its own space in memory — and returns control after finishing.
- C uses "pass by value" for parameter passing.
- Recursion allows a function to call itself for smaller sub-problems.
- Every recursive solution must have a base case to avoid infinite calls.

If you can explain these ideas clearly, you're ready to tackle interview questions involving function design, recursion, and modular problem-solving. In the next chapter, we'll move to another powerful part of C — **Arrays and Pointers**, where we explore how C stores and accesses data efficiently.

Do-It-Yourself: Practice Zone

Now that you've understood how functions and recursion work, it's time to put your knowledge into practice. These exercises will help you strengthen your logic, prepare for technical interviews, and build confidence in writing modular programs.

Remember — don't just aim to get the output right. Focus on understanding ***how*** the function executes, what happens in memory, and how control flows between calls. That's what interviewers really care about.

Part A – Function-Based Questions

1. Write a function named `maxOfThree()` that takes three integers and returns the largest among them. *(Hint: Use simple if-else conditions.)*
2. Write a program to calculate the factorial of a number using a function (non-recursive). *Now try rewriting it using recursion — what differences do you notice in the control flow?*
3. Create a function `swap()` that swaps two integers using a temporary variable. Then, explain why the original values in `main()` do not change after the function call. *(This tests your understanding of "pass by value.")*
4. Write a function named `isPrime()` that returns 1 if a number is prime and 0 otherwise. Use it in `main()`

to print all prime numbers between 1 and 100.

5. Write a modular program to calculate the sum and average of five numbers using separate functions. *One function for input, one for sum, and one for average.*

Part B – Recursion Practice

1. Write a recursive function to calculate the sum of digits of a number. Example: For input 1234, output should be 10.
2. Write a recursive function to find the nth Fibonacci number. Then, rewrite the same logic iteratively — which one runs faster?
3. Write a recursive function to reverse a string. *(Bonus: Try doing it without using any extra array or library function.)*
4. Write a recursive function to calculate the power of a number (a^b) using the formula:

$$a^b = a \times a^{(b-1)}$$

5. Write a recursive function to find the greatest common divisor (GCD) of two numbers using Euclid's algorithm. *(This one is a favorite in interviews!)*

Part C – Interview-Oriented Thought Questions

1. When does recursion become inefficient? Give an example and explain why iteration might be a better choice.
2. What happens in memory when a function calls itself recursively? Explain using the concept of the call stack.
3. How would you explain the difference between a function's declaration and its definition to a beginner?
4. Write down the sequence of steps the compiler follows from function call to return — as if explaining it to an interviewer.
5. If a recursive function lacks a base case, what exactly happens during execution? *(Think about how the stack behaves.)*

Your Challenge

Pick any two problems from above and:

- Write them both using **functions**.
- Rewrite them using **recursion** (if possible).
- Trace their execution manually or using a debugger (like gdb).

By doing this, you'll not only understand the syntax but also master the thought process behind how C handles control flow, stack usage, and logical decomposition — all of which interviewers love to see.

Remember: Programming is not about memorizing syntax — it's about solving problems logically and explaining your approach clearly under pressure. So take your time, think deeply, and experiment confidently with these exercises before moving to the next chapter.

Chapter 12

ARRAYS AND STRINGS

First of all, congratulations on making it to this chapter — you've come a long way! At this point, you've learned how to make your programs think logically using control structures, and how to make your code modular and reusable through functions. You've built the foundation of logical thinking — the skill that every great programmer relies on. But now, it's time to dive deeper — to learn how C truly stores, manages, and organizes data in memory.

If you ask any experienced programmer or interviewer, they'll tell you this truth: *knowing how to think is half the journey—knowing how data lives inside your program is the other half.* And that's exactly what this chapter is about.

When you write a variable like `int x = 10;`, you're not just storing a number—you're asking the computer to reserve a specific block of memory, label it, and remember it. When you write ten such variables, you're actually creating ten different locations, each with its own address.

But what if you wanted to store a hundred values? Or a thousand? Creating a thousand variable names isn't practical — and that's where **arrays** come in.

Arrays and strings form the backbone of every serious program you'll ever write. They are how data truly exists in C — stored contiguously, accessible through precise logic, and efficiently managed at the lowest level of memory. If you've ever wondered how lists, matrices, or even text are handled inside your favorite programming languages, it all starts here — with arrays and strings.

This chapter is all about building that foundation — not just learning how to use arrays and strings, but understanding what's happening *behind the code*. Once you start seeing memory as something you can navigate, not something to fear, you'll begin to think like a real programmer — and that's exactly what impresses interviewers.

By the end of this chapter, you'll not only know how to use arrays and strings effectively but also understand what happens when your program reads, writes, or even crashes because of them. That kind of deep, intuitive knowledge is what interviewers look for — the ability to explain not just *what* your program does, but *why* it works that way. So take a deep breath — you're about to unlock one of the most fascinating parts of C.

12.1 Why Arrays Matter

When you write a program, you often need to store and manage multiple pieces of related information — marks of students, prices of items, or sensor readings. You could, of course, create separate variables for each value:

```
int mark1, mark2, mark3, mark4, mark5;
```

But that's neither efficient nor elegant. Arrays solve this problem.

An **array** is simply a collection of elements of the same type stored in contiguous memory locations. You can access each element using its *index*.

```
int marks[5] = {90, 85, 75, 88, 92};
```

Now, all five marks are stored side by side in memory. If the base address of `marks[0]` is 1000, then:

$$\text{Address of marks[i]} = 1000 + (i \times 4)$$

because each integer takes 4 bytes.

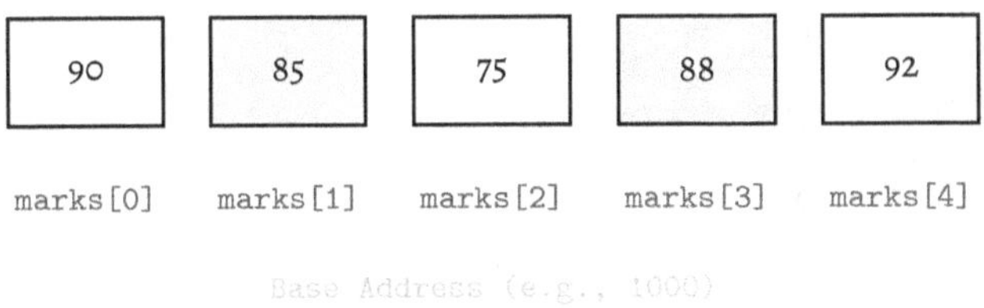

Figure 12.1: *Visualizing an Integer Array in Memory*

Observation: Arrays make memory predictable. The compiler can calculate any element's address instantly because elements are laid out in continuous memory blocks.

Interview Insight: When you explain that arrays are stored contiguously — and how address calculation works — it shows that you understand C at the systems level. This is a great way to stand out in interviews.

12.2 Understanding Memory and Access Time

Each array element sits right next to the previous one in memory. This layout gives arrays a huge advantage in terms of performance — something interviewers often test indirectly.

When you access `marks[2]`, C doesn't have to "search" for it. It simply does:

$$\text{Address} = \text{Base Address} + (2 \times \text{sizeof(int)})$$

That's why array access in C is a constant-time operation, *O(1)*.

```
printf("%d", marks[2]);    // prints 75
```

This is called **direct addressing**. Understanding this helps you write faster and more memory-aware programs

— something companies value deeply.

12.3 Multidimensional Arrays (2D Arrays)

So far, we've seen one-dimensional arrays. But what if you need to store tabular data, like a matrix or a mark sheet with rows and columns?

That's where 2D arrays come in.

```
int matrix[2][3] = {
    {1, 2, 3},
    {4, 5, 6}
};
```

Here, the array has 2 rows and 3 columns. In memory, however, it's stored in **row-major order** — meaning one entire row is stored before moving to the next.

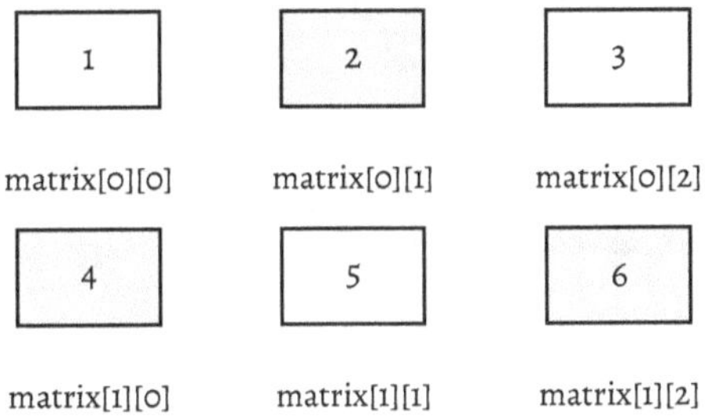

Figure 12.2: *Row-Major Memory Layout of a 2D Array*

Interview Tip: If you're asked how a 2D array is stored, remember this phrase: "All rows are stored back-to-back."

That's the kind of clarity that interviewers look for.

12.4 Arrays and Pointers — The Hidden Connection

One of the most powerful (and tricky) aspects of C is that arrays and pointers are deeply related.

For example:

```
int a[3] = {10, 20, 30};
printf("%d", *(a + 1)); // prints 20
```

The expression `a[i]` is actually just a shorter way of writing `*(a + i)`. That's why both mean the same thing.

Observation: In most cases, arrays *decay* into pointers — they act as if they were the address of their first element. However, arrays and pointers are not exactly the same: - Arrays have fixed size. - Pointers can be reassigned.

12.5 Strings — Arrays with Personality

If arrays are the building blocks of data, strings are the voice of your program. A **string** in C is simply an array of characters ending with the special character `\0` (null terminator).

```
char name[] = "Sayam";
```

Internally, it's stored like this:

```
S | a | y | a | m | \0
```

That last character, \0, tells the compiler where the string ends.

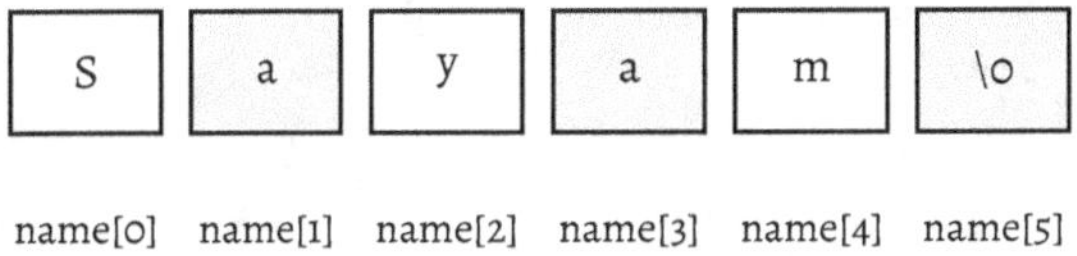

Figure 12.3: *String Representation in Memory (with Null Terminator)*

Interview Insight: A classic question — "What's the difference between `char str[] = "Hi";` and `char *str = "Hi";`?" The first creates a mutable array, the second points to a string literal (stored in read-only memory). If you try to modify the latter, your program crashes.

12.6 Common String Functions — And How They Work Internally

1. `strlen()`

Counts characters until it hits \0.

```
int strlen_manual(char s[]) {
    int len = 0;
    while (s[len] != '\0')
        len++;
    return len;
}
```

2. `strcpy()`

Copies characters one by one until the null terminator.

```
void strcpy_manual(char dest[], char src[]) {
    int i = 0;
    while ((dest[i] = src[i]) != '\0')
        i++;
}
```

3. `strcmp()`

Compares two strings character by character.

```
int strcmp_manual(char s1[], char s2[]) {
    int i = 0;
    while (s1[i] == s2[i]) {
        if (s1[i] == '\0') return 0;
        i++;
    }
    return s1[i] - s2[i];
}
```

Pro Tip: Don't memorize — understand the logic. Interviewers often ask you to "write your own version" of these.

12.7 Common Mistakes and Interview Traps

Mistake	Why It Happens	How to Fix It
Missing \0	String not terminated properly	Always reserve one extra space for null terminator
Array index out of bounds	Accessing elements beyond limit	Use constants or macros for array size
Using `scanf("%s")` for full name	Stops at space	Use `fgets()` for multi-word input
Confusing arrays and pointers	Arrays decay into pointers but aren't identical	Understand how pointer arithmetic works

12.8 Quick Recap Before You Move On

Before you turn the page, take a moment to pause and reflect — this chapter wasn't just about writing syntax. It was about understanding how data truly lives inside your program. If you can explain what's happening in memory while your code runs, you're already ahead of most beginners.

Here's what you've learned:

- **Arrays are stored contiguously in memory** — meaning every element sits right next to the previous one. This predictable layout allows direct, constant-time access to any element, which is why arrays are fast.

- **2D arrays use row-major order.** When you store matrices, one full row is placed in memory before the next begins. Understanding this helps you reason about memory access patterns and performance in larger programs.
- **Arrays and pointers are deeply related but not identical.** An array often "decays" into a pointer when passed to a function, but unlike a pointer, its size and base address are fixed.
- **Strings are character arrays ending with a null terminator (`\0`).** This single invisible character tells C where the string ends — miss it, and your program will read garbage or crash.
- **Standard string functions like `strlen()`, `strcpy()`, and `strcmp()` rely on loops and null termination.** Interviewers often ask you to implement these manually, not to test your memory, but your ability to reason about iteration and memory safety.
- **Interviewers love "memory layout" questions.** They might ask what happens when you access `arr[10]` in a 5-element array or how `char *s = "Hi"` differs from `char s[] = "Hi"`. Be ready to visualize memory — that's the real skill they're looking for.

In short: Arrays and strings are your bridge from logic to memory. They teach you how C truly thinks — not as lines of code, but as precise movements of data in memory. Once you're comfortable here, the next topic — **Pointers** — will no longer feel intimidating; it will feel like a natural next step.

"If you can see your code in memory, you've already started thinking like a real C programmer."

Do-It-Yourself: Practice Zone

Now that you've understood how arrays and strings work at a conceptual and memory level, it's time to put that knowledge into practice. These exercises are designed to help you go from understanding the theory to actually solving problems — the way interviewers expect you to.

Don't just rush for the output; focus on *why* each line of your code works. That's what separates a good coder from a thoughtful one.

Part A – Strengthening the Fundamentals

These problems will help you build confidence with array and string basics.

1. Write a C program to store and display the marks of 5 students using an array.
2. Find the largest and smallest elements in an array of integers.
3. Reverse an array without using another array.
4. Write a program to calculate the average of elements in an array.
5. Declare and initialize a string, then print each character on a new line.

Pro Tip: Try writing your own version of these programs without looking at examples — you'll remember the logic far longer.

Part B – Deepening Your Logic

Now let's apply arrays and strings in slightly more logical or real-world scenarios.

1. Write a program to find the frequency of each element in an array.
2. Accept a string and count the number of vowels, consonants, digits, and spaces.
3. Implement your own version of `strlen()`, `strcpy()`, and `strcmp()`.
4. Write a C program to merge two arrays into a third array.
5. Write a program that checks if a string is a palindrome (e.g., "madam").

Interview Insight: For string questions, most interviewers will ask you to explain how your code identifies the end of a string in memory — make sure you can explain the role of `\0` clearly.

Part C – Interview-Focused Scenarios

These are closer to what you might face in a technical interview. They test not only your syntax but your ability to think through logic and memory flow.

1. Write a function that takes an array and returns the second largest element.
2. Write a program to rotate an array to the left by one position.
3. Reverse a string in place without using any extra array.
4. Write a function that counts duplicate elements in an array.
5. Given a sentence, write a C program to count the number of words.

Pro Tip: During interviews, always be prepared to explain the space and time complexity of your array or string operations — that one step will set you apart.

Your Challenge – Think Like an Interviewer

Now, step into the interviewer's chair. Pick any two problems from above and try the following:

- Rewrite them using **functions** instead of writing all code in `main()`.
- Add **user input** (using `scanf()` or `fgets()`) instead of hard-coded values.
- Trace the flow of execution and memory manually or using a debugger (gdb) — line by line.
- Try to optimize your code: can you make it run faster

or use less memory?

Pro Tip: Interviewers are not impressed by perfect syntax; they're impressed by your ability to debug, adapt, and reason about code. So focus not just on writing correct programs, but on understanding their inner workings.

Remember: Arrays and strings are not just programming topics — they are how data *lives* in memory. Once you understand them deeply, concepts like pointers, dynamic allocation, and data structures will feel far more intuitive.

Something You'll Notice as You Code More

When I first learned arrays, I treated them as just another topic — a list of syntax rules and examples to memorize. But over time, I realized arrays are not just about storing numbers; they are about *understanding how data lives inside your computer*. The moment you visualize memory as a continuous row of boxes — and realize that every variable, every element, every string is just data waiting to be accessed — you begin to think like an engineer, not just a coder.

That's the kind of perspective interviewers are looking for. They don't care if you can write a program to find the largest number; they want to see whether you can explain how your code works in memory, how it moves data, and what happens when it doesn't.

If you've made it this far, you've already started seeing C the way real developers do — from the inside out. Keep that curiosity alive, because the next step is where things get even more exciting: we'll explore how C gives you the power to **directly control memory itself**. That's right — our next stop is **Pointers**.

And once you understand pointers, you'll never look at programming the same way again.

Chapter 13

POINTERS AND MEMORY MANAGEMENT

If you've reached this chapter, you've crossed one of the biggest milestones in C programming. Up to this point, you've learned how C stores groups of values using arrays and how it represents text using strings — but you still haven't taken control of the most powerful concept C has to offer:

Memory itself.

Pointers are the feature that give C:

- its speed
- its flexibility
- its low-level power

...and yes, also its reputation for being "difficult."

But that reputation exists only when pointers are memorized instead of understood.

This chapter is designed to make pointers feel natural. Not mysterious. Not intimidating. Just logical.

We'll approach pointers from both a practical angle (how you use them) and a deeper conceptual angle (how memory works internally). This is exactly what interviewers test — not whether you remember syntax, but whether you understand the *model* behind the syntax.

By the end of this chapter, you'll know:

- how C divides memory into different segments
- how pointers store addresses and allow direct memory access
- how pointer arithmetic works (and why it matters)
- how pointers and arrays are related
- how dynamic memory allocation actually behaves
- how to avoid bugs that interviews love to highlight

Take a deep breath — this chapter is long, friendly, and hands-on. But once you master it, you'll see C like a systems programmer.

13.1 What Exactly Is a Pointer?

Let's start with the simplest definition:

A pointer is a variable that stores the memory address of another variable.

Not magic. Just an address.

Example:

```
int x = 10;
int *p = &x;
```

Here:

- p stores the **address** of x
- *p accesses the **value** at that address

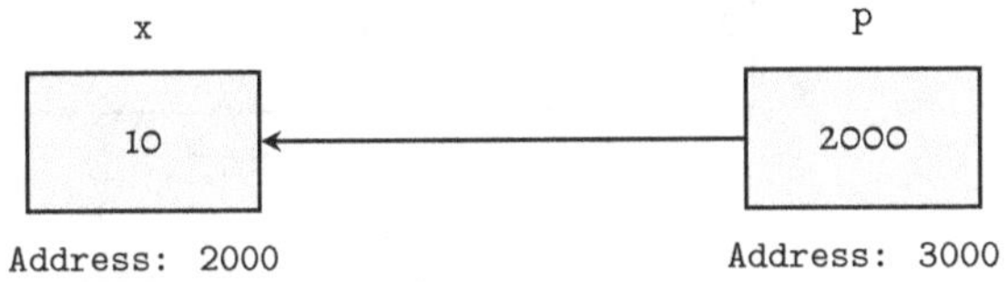

Figure 13.1: *Pointer storing the address of a variable*

Interview Tip: When asked: "What is a pointer?" Say: "*A pointer is a variable that stores a memory address.*"

Short. Sharp. Perfect.

13.2 How Memory Is Organized in C

Understanding pointers requires understanding memory layout.

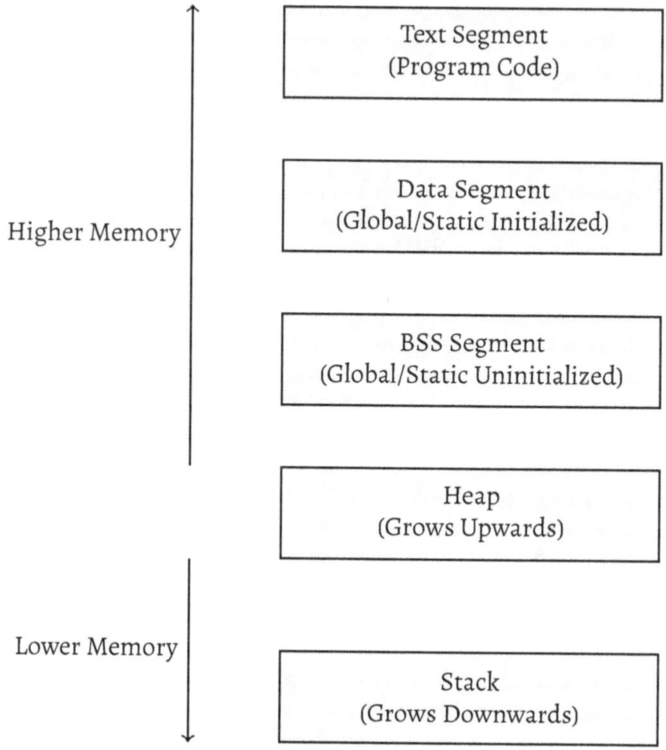

Figure 13.2: *Typical Memory Layout of a C Program*

A typical C program divides memory into regions:

- **Text Segment** — your compiled instructions
- **Data Segment** — global/static initialized variables
- **BSS Segment** — global/static uninitialized variables
- **Heap** — grows upward (dynamic memory)
- **Stack** — grows downward (function calls, locals)

Interview Importance: An alarming percentage of pointer bugs come from confusing stack vs heap memory.

13.3 Declaring and Initializing Pointers

Declaring a pointer:

```
int *p;
```

Initializing it:

```
int x = 10;
int *p = &x;
```

Golden Rule: Always initialize pointers. Uninitialized (wild) pointers cause unpredictable crashes.

13.4 Pointer Arithmetic — The Part That Feels Like Magic

Pointers do not move in bytes — they move in **units of the data type** they point to.

```
int a[3] = {10, 20, 30};
int *p = a;

p++;    // moves forward by sizeof(int) bytes
```

On a typical system, `sizeof(int)` is 4 bytes. So if p initially stores address 1000, after p++ it stores 1004.

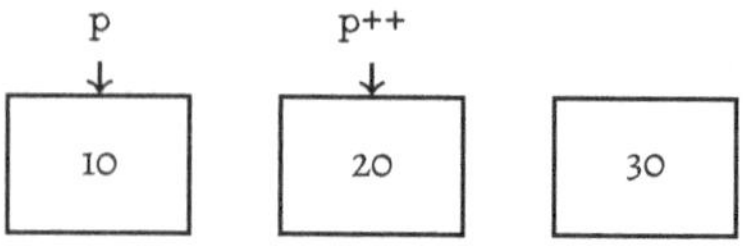

Figure 13.3: *Pointer arithmetic moves by data type size, not bytes.*

Interview Tip: If asked, "Why does p+1 not mean add one byte?" say: *Because pointer arithmetic moves in element-sized steps. That's how C makes array traversal fast.*

13.5 Pointer Arithmetic — Moving Through Memory

Pointers don't just store addresses — they let you **walk through memory**.

```
int a[] = {10, 20, 30};
int *p = a;    // p points to a[0]

p = p + 2;     // now p points to a[2]
```

This allows very efficient iteration over arrays.

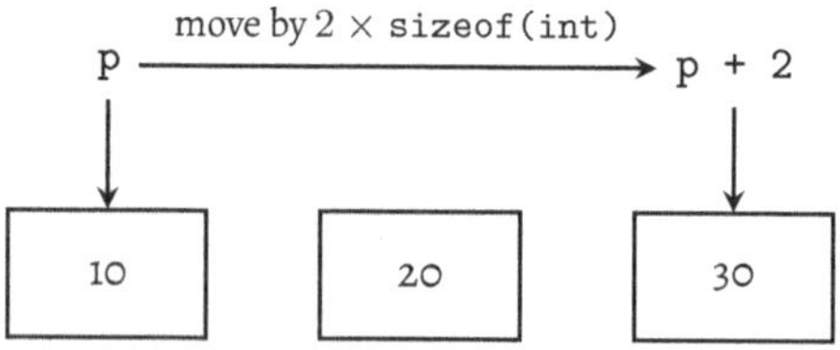

Figure 13.4: *Pointer offset depends on element size.*

Key Insight:

Pointer arithmetic is type-aware. That's why `char *` and `int *` behave differently when incremented.

13.6 Pointers and Arrays — The Deep Connection

Many students memorize that "arrays and pointers are related," but few understand the mechanism.

Let's break it down:

- `arr` is a **constant pointer** to the first element.
- `arr + i` gives the address of `arr[i]`.
- `*(arr + i)` is identical to `arr[i]`.

```
int arr[3] = {10, 20, 30};

printf("%d", arr[1]);          // 20
printf("%d", *(arr + 1));      // 20
```

Both generate the same assembly code.

Arrays "Decay" to Pointers

When passed to a function:

```
void print(int a[]) { ... }
// actually: void print(int *a)
```

The array loses its size information — only a pointer remains.

Interview Question: Why does `sizeof(a)` inside a

function not give the array size?

Answer: Because the array has decayed into an `int *`.

This is one of the most common interview concepts.

13.7 Pointer to Pointer — Multi-Level Indirection

A pointer can store the address of another pointer:

```
int x = 10;
int *p = &x;
int **pp = &p;
```

This is called a **double pointer**.

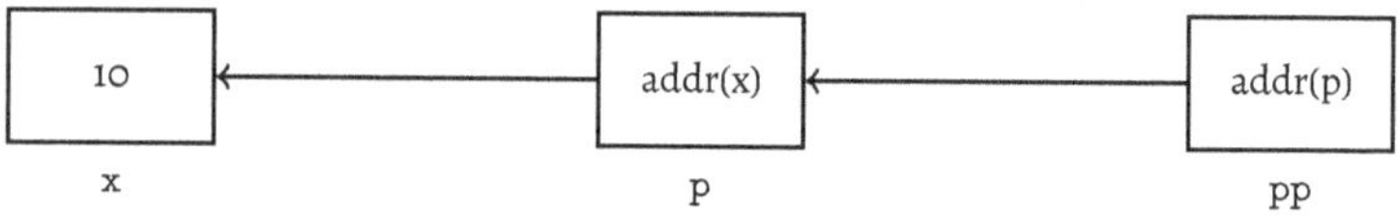

Figure 13.5: *A double pointer stores the address of a pointer.*

Where double pointers appear:

- dynamic 2D arrays
- functions that modify pointer arguments
- linked lists, trees, graphs

Memory relationships:

$$pp = \&p, \quad *pp = p, \quad **pp = x$$

Great interview candidates visualize memory like this.

13.8 NULL, Wild, and Dangling Pointers

These three pointer categories cause the majority of memory bugs.

Wild Pointer

A pointer that has not been initialized.

```
int *p;         // wild pointer
*p = 10;        // dangerous!
```

NULL Pointer

A pointer that intentionally points nowhere.

```
int *p = NULL;
```

Interviewers love this question: **"Why use NULL?"**

Answer: Because it makes failures predictable — dereferencing NULL crashes immediately instead of corrupting random memory.

Dangling Pointer

A pointer that used to point to valid memory but no longer does.

```
int *p = malloc(sizeof(int));
free(p);
*p = 10;    // dangling pointer dereference
```

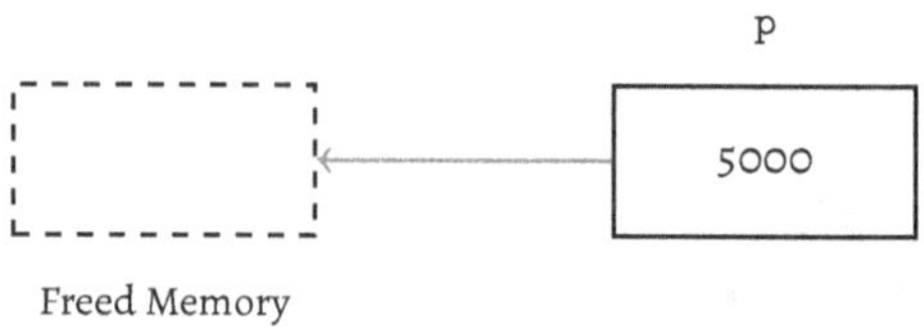

Figure 13.6: *Dangling pointer still referencing freed memory.*

Fix:

```
free(p);
p = NULL;
```

Setting to NULL prevents accidental reuse.

13.9 Introduction to Dynamic Memory

Static arrays have a fixed size determined at compile time:

```
int arr[100];    // always 100 elements
```

But real programs don't always know their memory needs beforehand. Sometimes you need memory that grows, shrinks, or is created on demand.

That is where the **heap** comes in — and with it, four powerful functions:

- `malloc()` — allocate raw, uninitialized memory
- `calloc()` — allocate and zero-initialize
- `realloc()` — resize previously allocated memory

- `free()` — release memory back to the OS

Once you understand these four, you unlock the ability to build:

- dynamic arrays
- dynamic strings
- linked lists
- trees, graphs
- custom memory pools

Let's explore them one by one.

malloc() — Allocate Memory Without Initialization

```
int *p = malloc(5 * sizeof(int));
```

`malloc()` returns a `void *` that points to a block of uninitialized heap memory.

If malloc fails, it returns NULL — always check.

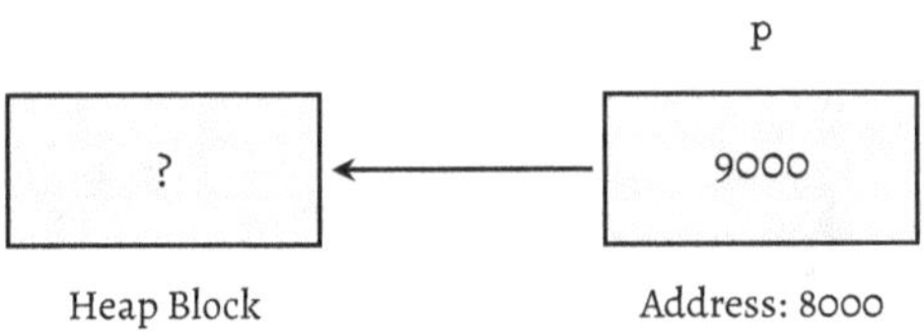

Figure 13.7: *`malloc()` allocates uninitialized memory from the heap.*

Interview Tip: Why use `sizeof(int)` instead of

hardcoding 4? Because the size of an int varies across systems. Good C code is portable.

calloc() — Allocate & Zero-Initialize

```
int *p = calloc(5, sizeof(int));
```

Unlike `malloc()`, which leaves memory uninitialized, **calloc sets all bytes to zero**.

This makes it ideal for:

- arrays
- hash tables
- initializing structures to a known state

Interview Tip: Be prepared to explain the difference: *malloc leaves garbage values; calloc initializes to zero.*

realloc() — Resize Memory Without Losing Data

`realloc()` is extremely powerful — and extremely misunderstood.

```
p = realloc(p, 10 * sizeof(int));
```

What does this do?

- Tries to expand the existing block if possible
- Otherwise allocates a new larger block
- Copies old data to the new block automatically
- Frees the old block internally

But there is a catch.

If `realloc()` fails, it returns `NULL` — and your original pointer is LOST if you assign directly:

```
p = realloc(p, newSize);    // risky!
```

Correct, safe usage:

```
int *temp = realloc(p, newSize);
if (temp != NULL)
    p = temp;
```

This is a favorite interview pattern — master it.

free() — Release Heap Memory

Anything you allocate using `malloc`, `calloc`, or `realloc` **must** be freed.

```
free(p);
p = NULL;
```

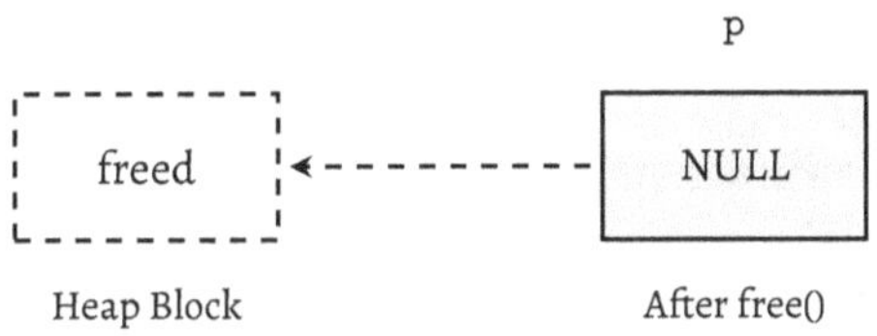

Figure 13.8: *After freeing memory, set the pointer to NULL.*

Setting the pointer to NULL after freeing prevents dangling pointer bugs.

Interview Insight: Many memory bugs come from

freeing something twice. Setting pointers to NULL protects against double frees.

13.10 Common Dynamic Memory Mistakes (Interview Gold)

1. Forgetting to free memory

Memory leak. Your program's memory usage grows forever.

2. Freeing memory twice

Double free. Leads to crashes or security vulnerabilities.

3. Using memory after freeing it

Dangling pointer. One of the hardest bugs to track.

```
int *p = malloc(sizeof(int));
free(p);
*p = 20;     //   invalid write
```

4. Using realloc unsafely

Never overwrite your only pointer with realloc's return value.

This is one of the most repeated mistakes in interviews.

5. Mixing allocations and frees

Never free memory you didn't allocate. Never call free on stack memory:

```
int x;
free(&x);    //  undefined behavior
```

13.11 How Memory Errors Are Detected

Tools interviewers expect you to know:

- **Valgrind (Linux)** — detects leaks, invalid reads, invalid writes
- **AddressSanitizer (ASan)** — detects out-of-bounds, UAF, double frees

Example command:

```
valgrind --leak-check=full ./a.out
```

These tools are lifesavers — mention them in interviews.

13.12 Different Types of Pointers in C

By now, you understand what pointers are and how they behave. But in real programs — and definitely in interviews — you will run into several **special pointer types**.

Mastering these shows depth, confidence, and clarity.

We'll explore:

- `void *`
- constant pointers vs. pointer to constant

- NULL, wild, and dangling pointers
- pointers to arrays
- arrays of pointers
- legacy pointer types (near, far, huge)

These appear constantly in interviews, so pay close attention.

13.12.1 Void Pointers (`void *`) — The Generic Pointer

A `void *` can store the address of **any** data type.

```
void *p;
int x = 10;
p = &x;      //  valid
```

But since a `void *` has no type information, you must cast it before dereferencing:

```
printf("%d", *(int*)p);
```

Where interviewers expect you to mention it:

- `malloc()`, `calloc()`, `realloc()`
- `qsort()` and function callbacks
- implementing generic data structures

Interview Tip: Explain that `void *` is flexible but sacrifices type safety.

13.12.2 Constant Pointers vs. Pointer to Constant

Many beginners confuse these. Here's the trick that never fails:

- `const before *` → value is constant
- `const after *` → pointer is constant

1. Pointer to a Constant Value

```
const int *p = &x;
```

You cannot change the value through the pointer:

```
*p = 20;    //  NOT allowed
```

But you CAN change where the pointer points:

```
p = &y;     //  allowed
```

2. Constant Pointer

```
int * const p = &x;
```

Here:

- pointer cannot change
- value it points to can change

```
*p = 99;    //  allowed
p = &y;     //  NOT allowed
```

3. Constant Pointer to Constant Value

```
const int * const p = &x;
```

Neither
the pointer nor the value can change. Interviewers LOVE this one.

13.12.3 NULL Pointer

A pointer that explicitly points "nowhere."

```
int *p = NULL;
```

You will almost always write NULL checks:

```
if (p == NULL) {
    // handle error
}
```

NULL is safer than an uninitialized pointer.

13.12.4 Wild Pointer

A wild pointer is uninitialized:

```
int *p;     // wild pointer
*p = 10;    //  unpredictable behavior
```

Interviews often ask: "How do you avoid wild pointers?"

Answer: *Always initialize pointers — set them to NULL if nothing else.*

13.12.5 Dangling Pointer

A pointer becomes "dangling" when the memory it points to is freed.

```
int *p = malloc(sizeof(int));
free(p);
*p = 10;     //  dangling pointer dereference
```

Fix:

```
free(p);
p = NULL;    //  safe
```

13.12.6 Legacy: Near, Far, and Huge Pointers

These appeared in **16-bit architectures** (DOS era) where memory was segmented. Modern systems do NOT use these.

Perfect interview answer:

"They were used to address more than 64 KB memory in 16-bit segmented models. Modern flat-memory systems no longer use them."

13.12.7 Pointer to an Array

This often confuses students because of the parentheses.

```
int arr[3] = {1, 2, 3};
int (*p)[3] = &arr;
```

Here:

- p points to the ENTIRE array
- *p is the array itself

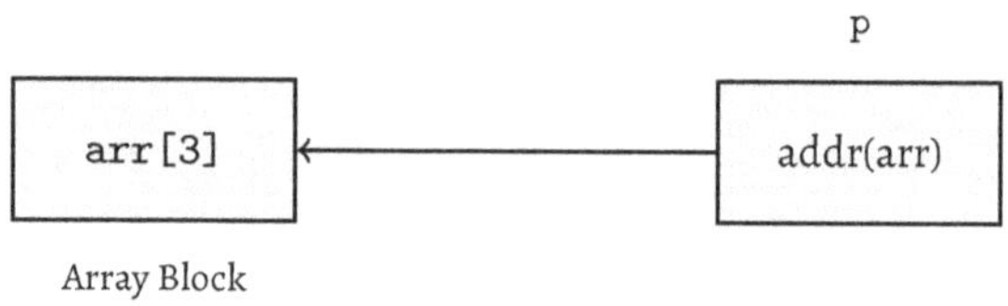

Figure 13.9: *Pointer to an entire array.*

Interview Tip: They ask this to check if you deeply understand declaration syntax.

13.12.8 Array of Pointers

Instead of pointing to a full array, this array stores multiple individual pointers.

```
int x=1, y=2, z=3;
int *arr[3] = { &x, &y, &z };
```

This is extremely useful for:

- arrays of strings
- function pointer tables
- storing nodes in dynamic structures

13.12.9 Pointer-Type Diagram

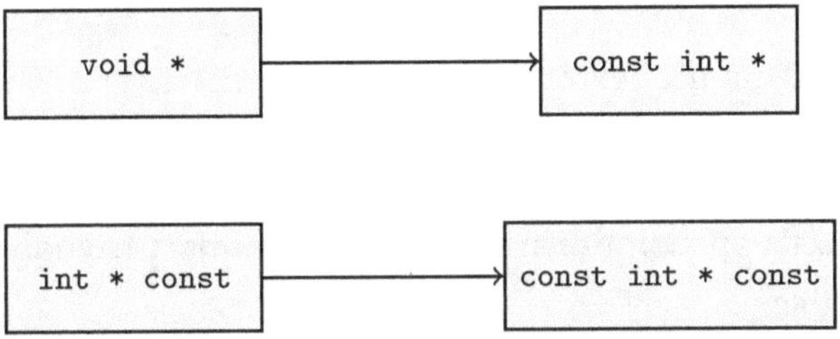

Figure 13.10: *Common pointer types and their relationships.*

Interview Insight: When an interviewer asks about pointer types, they want to know if you can interpret complex declarations confidently.

13.13 Function Pointers — Executing Code Through Addresses

You've seen pointers that store the address of variables and memory blocks. But C lets you do something even more powerful:

You can store the address of a FUNCTION inside a pointer.

This is a major interview topic because it shows that you truly understand how C executes code behind the scenes.

Function pointers power:

- callbacks

- event-driven systems
- flexible APIs
- dynamic behavior (selecting functions at runtime)
- library functions like `qsort()`

Let's break it down in the simplest, most friendly way possible.

13.13.1 Why Interviewers Ask About Function Pointers

Because function pointers reveal:

- whether you understand how code and memory relate
- if you can write flexible, re-usable logic
- whether you can work with system-level C
- if you can follow complicated declarations under pressure

If you master this section, many C interviews suddenly become easier.

13.13.2 Declaring a Function Pointer

Here's a normal function:

```
int square(int x) {
    return x * x;
}
```

A pointer that can store the address of this function looks like this:

```
int (*fp)(int);
```

Breakdown:

- `(*fp)` → fp is a pointer
- `(int)` → accepts an int
- `int` → returns an int

Assign the function:

```
fp = square;
```

Call the function through the pointer:

```
int result = fp(5);    // 25
```

Both forms work:

```
fp(5);
(*fp)(5);
```

13.13.3 Function Pointer Diagram

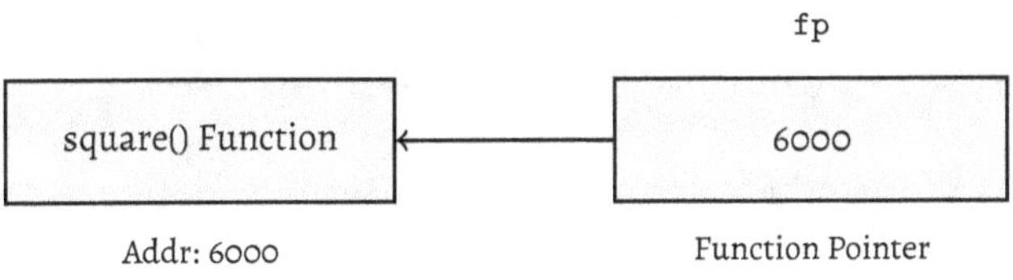

Figure 13.11: *A Function Pointer Holding the Address of a Function*

13.13.4 Callbacks — Passing Logic to Functions

A callback is simply a function passed as an argument to another function.

Example:

```
void greet(void (*printer)()) {
    printer();      // call the passed function
}

void hello() {
    printf("Hello!\n");
}

int main() {
    greet(hello);    // passing a function as argument
}
```

This technique is used everywhere:

- GUI event handlers
- sorting, searching
- asynchronous systems
- custom library hooks

Interview Line: "A callback lets a function receive behavior as a parameter."

13.13.5 `qsort()` — The Most Famous Use Case

`qsort()` uses a function pointer to let YOU define sorting logic.

```
int cmp(const void *a, const void *b) {
    return (*(int *)a - *(int *)b);
```

```
}

qsort(arr, n, sizeof(int), cmp);
```

This is extremely common in interviews.

Breakdown:

- 1st arg → array
- 2nd arg → number of elements
- 3rd arg → element size
- 4th arg → comparison function

Why this matters: It tests your understanding of:

- pointer casting
- void pointers
- function pointer syntax
- sorting logic

13.13.6 Using `typedef` to Simplify Function Pointers

Function pointer syntax is ugly. `typedef` makes it readable.

Original:

```
int (*op)(int, int);
```

Cleaner:

```
typedef int (*mathop)(int, int);
```

Now use it like a normal type:

```
mathop addPtr;
```

Example

```
int add(int a, int b) { return a + b; }
int sub(int a, int b) { return a - b; }

typedef int (*mathop)(int, int);

void compute(mathop f) {
    printf("%d\n", f(10, 5));
}

int main() {
    compute(add);
    compute(sub);
}
```

Interviewers love when candidates use `typedef` — it shows maturity.

13.13.7 Function Pointer Tables — "Jump Tables"

You can create an array of function pointers, allowing dynamic selection of functions.

```
int add(int a, int b) { return a + b; }
int mul(int a, int b) { return a * b; }

int (*ops[2])(int, int) = { add, mul };

printf("%d", ops[0](3,4));    // 7
printf("%d", ops[1](3,4));    // 12
```

This technique is used in:

- interpreters
- menu-driven programs
- state machines
- virtual function tables

Interview Tip: Mention function pointer tables when asked how C implements polymorphism-like behavior.

13.13.8 Common Interview Questions

- How do callbacks work in C?
- Why does `qsort()` need a comparator function?
- Declaring a pointer to a function returning int and taking two floats?
- Can any function be assigned to any function pointer?

Correct answer: **No. Signatures must match exactly.**

Function Pointer Pitfalls

1. Wrong Signature

```
int (*fp)(float);
fp = square;    //  incompatible
```

2. Forgetting Casts in qsort() Comparators

3. Returning Function Pointers Without Matching Type

Why Interviewers Love This Topic

Because it demonstrates:

- memory understanding
- calling conventions
- abstraction ability
- real-world coding skill

Once you understand function pointers, **you're ready for dynamic data structures, callbacks, and advanced C APIs.**

13.14 Advanced Pointer Techniques

By now, you understand how pointers store addresses, move through memory, and interact with arrays and functions. This section goes deeper — into the rules interviewers use to separate beginners from serious C programmers.

We'll cover:

- memory alignment
- strict aliasing
- safe vs. unsafe casting
- when pointer comparison is allowed
- pointer subtraction rules

Mastering these takes you from "knowing pointers" to

"thinking like the compiler."

13.14.1 Alignment — Why Some Addresses Are "More Correct"

Most architectures prefer (or even require) that data be stored at addresses divisible by its size.

Examples:

- `int` (4 bytes) → address divisible by 4
- `double` (8 bytes) → address divisible by 8

Poor alignment can cause:

- slower memory access
- extra CPU instructions
- crashes (on strict CPUs like ARM)

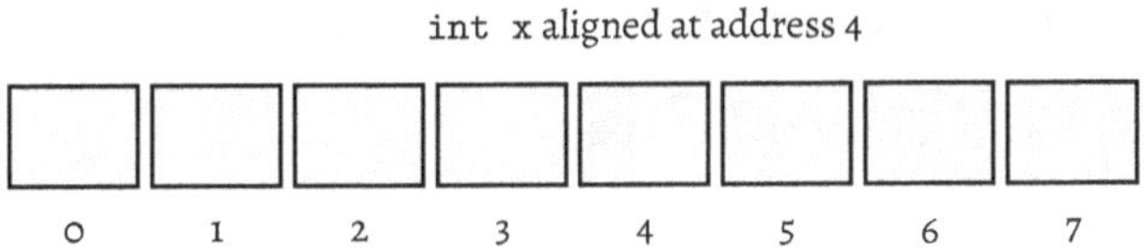

Figure 13.12: *Aligned 4-byte integer: stored at an address divisible by 4*

Interview Tip: If asked "Why does alignment matter?", say: *"Aligned access lets the CPU read data in one operation. Some CPUs fault on misaligned reads."*

13.14.2 Strict Aliasing — The "Don't Pretend" Rule

Strict aliasing says:

You may not access the same memory through two different, unrelated pointer types.

Example of undefined behavior:

```
int x = 10;
float *fp = (float*)&x;    //  violates strict aliasing
```

The compiler assumes that pointers of different types do NOT point to the same memory, so it may reorder or optimize code in surprising ways.

Safe exceptions:

- `unsigned char *` — allowed to access any memory byte-by-byte
- same type (e.g., `int*` aliasing `int`)
- compatible struct types

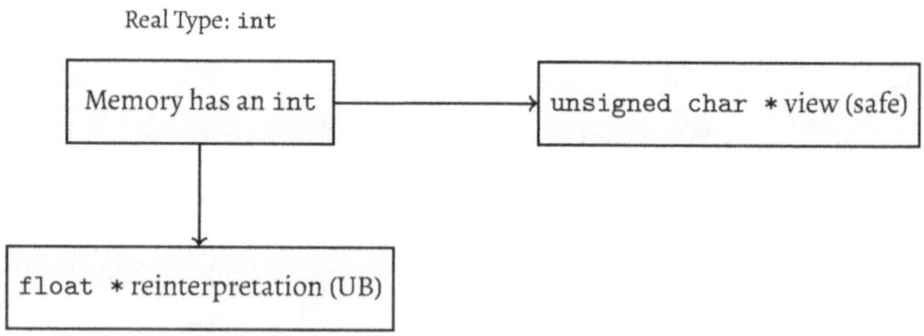

Figure 13.13: *Strict aliasing: only `unsigned char *` may safely alias any object.*

Interview Line (gold): *"When you need to reinterpret bits safely, use memcpy, not casts."*

13.14.3 Pointer Casting — When It's Safe

Safe cast:

- casting `void*` from `malloc` to a typed pointer
- casting between compatible struct types
- casting to `unsigned char*` to inspect raw bytes

Risky cast (may cause undefined behavior):

- casting to unrelated types to reinterpret memory
- ignoring alignment requirements

Golden rule: If you're changing the interpretation of stored bits → use `memcpy`.

13.14.4 Pointer Comparison Rules

Pointer comparison is only defined when:

- both pointers point into the SAME array
- or one-past-the-end of the same array

Example (valid):

```
int a[5];
int *p = &a[1], *q = &a[4];
printf("%d", p < q);   // well-defined
```

Invalid (undefined behavior):

```
int *p = malloc(4);
```

```
int *q = malloc(4);
printf("%d", p < q);    //  Undefined behavior
```

Interview Tip: Explain that comparing pointers from different allocations is "meaningless" in C.

13.14.5 Pointer Subtraction

Pointer subtraction is defined only for pointers into the same array.

```
int arr[] = {10,20,30,40};
int *p = &arr[1];
int *q = &arr[3];

printf("%td\n", q - p);
// prints 2 (element distance)
```

This is an extremely common interview exercise.

13.14.6 Element-Based vs Byte-Based Arithmetic

Correct:

```
p = p + 2;    // moves 2 elements
```

Incorrect:

```
(char*)p + 8;     // moves 8 BYTES, not 2 ints
```

Interview Tip: Element-based arithmetic is portable; byte-based arithmetic is not.

13.15 Building Dynamic Data Structures with Pointers

Up to this point, you've used pointers to access memory and move through arrays. Now we'll use them to build structures that grow, shrink, and link together — the foundation of data structures.

Interviewers LOVE this part because it shows whether you truly understand how pointers model relationships in memory.

We'll build:

- singly linked lists
- doubly linked lists
- dynamic 2D arrays
- pointer-based stacks and queues

These aren't just academic ideas — they're the building blocks of real-world systems.

13.15.1 Singly Linked List — The Classic Interview Starter

A linked list is a chain of nodes. Each node stores:

- a value
- a pointer to the next node

```
struct Node {
    int data;
    struct Node *next;
```

```
};
```

Insert at Head (Most Common Interview Pattern)

```
struct Node* push_front(struct Node *head, int val) {
    struct Node *n = malloc(sizeof *n);
    n->data = val;
    n->next = head;
    return n;    // new head
}
```

Visual Representation

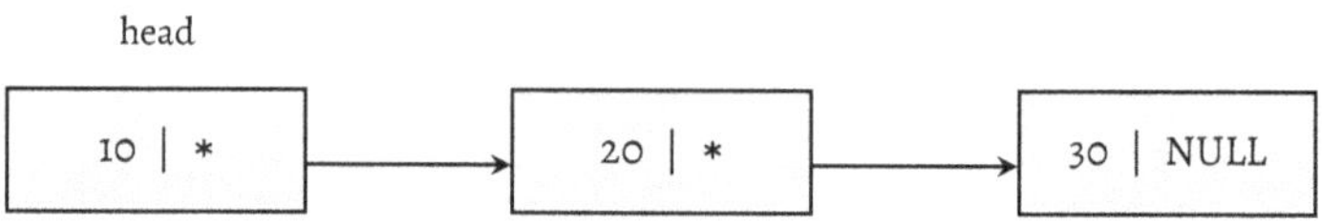

Figure 13.14: *Singly Linked List: each node points to the next.*

Interview Tip: Linked list reversal is one of the top 5 pointer interview problems — practice it thoroughly.

13.15.2 Doubly Linked List — When You Need Both Directions

Each node stores:

- pointer to previous node
- pointer to next node

```
struct DNode {
    int data;
    struct DNode *prev, *next;
};
```

Diagram

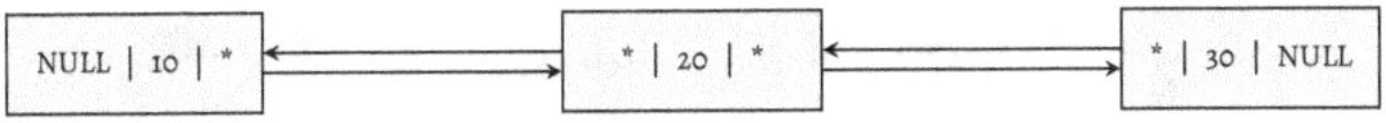

Figure 13.15: *Doubly Linked List: navigation in both directions.*

Interview Tip: Explain when doubly linked lists are better: *"When deletion in the middle must be O(1) without a previous pointer."*

13.15.3 Dynamic 2D Arrays — Two Real Interview Approaches

Interviewers LOVE asking this because it tests:

- memory layout knowledge
- pointer-to-pointer understanding
- dynamic allocation skills

Approach A — Array of Pointers (Rows Allocated Separately)

```
int **m = malloc(R * sizeof *m);
for (int i = 0; i < R; ++i)
    m[i] = malloc(C * sizeof **m);
```

Easy, but memory becomes fragmented.

Approach B — Single Contiguous Block (Most Efficient)

```
int *data = malloc(R * C * sizeof *data);
int **row  = malloc(R * sizeof *row);

for (int i = 0; i < R; ++i)
    row[i] = &data[i * C];
```

Best for performance (cache-friendly). Interviewers prefer this one.

Diagram (Approach B)

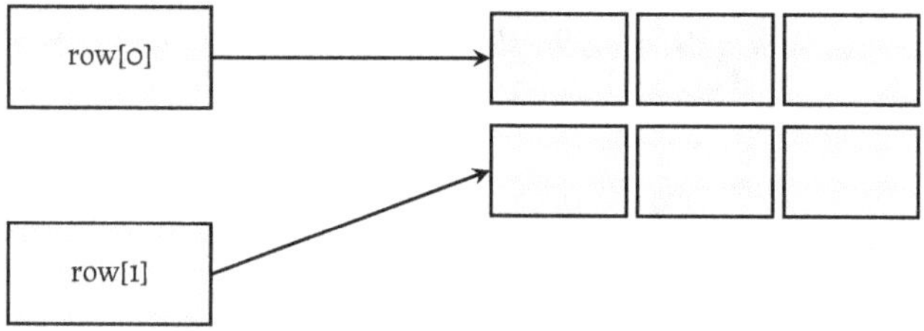

Figure 13.16: *Contiguous 2D array with row-index pointers.*

13.15.4 Stacks and Queues Using Pointers

Stack Using Linked List (Push/Pop at Head)

Push:

```
head = push_front(head, value);
```

Pop:

```
int pop(struct Node **head) {
    struct Node *temp = *head;
    int val = temp->data;
    *head = temp->next;
    free(temp);
    return val;
}
```

Queue Using Linked List

Keep two pointers:

- `front` — dequeue here
- `rear` — enqueue here

```
void enqueue(struct Node **front, struct Node **rear, int v)
    {
    struct Node *n = malloc(sizeof *n);
    n->data = v;
    n->next = NULL;

    if (*rear == NULL)
        *front = *rear = n;
    else {
        (*rear)->next = n;
        *rear = n;
    }
}
```

Interview Tip: Queues test your pointer-updating discipline — especially handling the "empty queue" state.

13.15.5 Why This Section Matters for Interviews

Data structures reveal your true pointer expertise. When interviewers see you write:

- correct memory allocation
- correct pointer updates
- correct cleanup (`free`)

—they know you understand C beyond syntax.

Be sure to practice:

- reversing a linked list
- detecting cycles (Floyd's algorithm)
- dynamic 2D array allocation
- queue operations
- stack operations with linked lists

These are go-to interview problems.

13.16 Debugging Memory Errors (Valgrind & ASan)

By now you understand how pointers work, how memory is structured, and how to allocate it dynamically. But here's the uncomfortable truth:

Even experienced C programmers accidentally write memory bugs.

The real skill — and one interviewers deeply respect — is knowing how to **detect** and **debug** these bugs.

This part introduces two professional tools:

- **Valgrind** — runtime memory checker (Linux)
- **AddressSanitizer (ASan)** — compiler-based memory error detector

Master these tools and you instantly stand out in interviews.

13.16.1 Classic Memory Bugs (and How They Look)

These five errors show up in almost every C interview:

- **Use-after-free** — using memory after freeing it
- **Memory leaks** — freeing too little or not freeing at all
- **Double free** — freeing the same pointer twice
- **Out-of-bounds access** — writing past array limits
- **Uninitialized memory access** — reading garbage

Let's visualize one of the most dangerous issues: **use-after-free**.

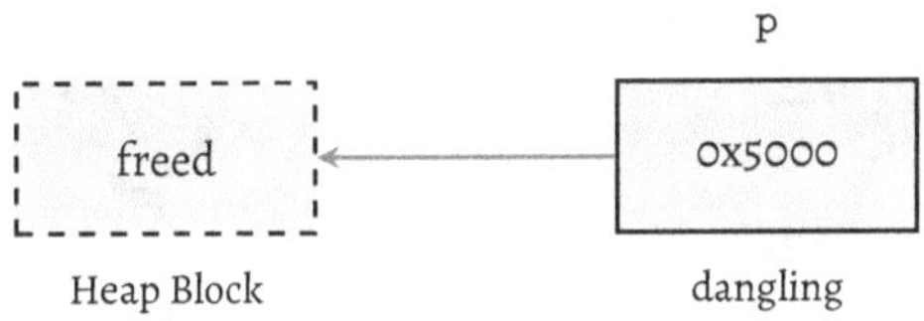

Figure 13.17: *Use-after-free: p still points to memory that no longer belongs to you.*

Interview Tip: When asked "How do you avoid use-after-free?" Say: *"Always set the pointer to NULL immediately after freeing."*

13.16.2 Valgrind (Linux): The Memory Detective

Valgrind runs your program in a special monitored environment that tracks:

- invalid reads/writes

- memory leaks
- use-after-free
- double frees
- uninitialized usage

How to use Valgrind

Compile with debug info:

```
gcc -g program.c -o program
```

Run under Valgrind:

```
valgrind --leak-check=full ./program
```

Sample Output (Simplified)

```
==1234== Invalid write of size 4
==1234==    at 0x401234: main (program.c:10)
==1234==  Address 0x5204040 is 0 bytes after a block
of size 16
```

Valgrind points directly to:

- the error type
- the line number
- the allocation site

This is incredibly powerful during debugging.

13.16.3 AddressSanitizer (ASan): Fast, Built Into Compilers

ASan is a compiler feature available in GCC and Clang. It instruments your code with "red zones" around each memory allocation.

Compile with ASan

```
gcc -fsanitize=address -g file.c -o program
```

ASan catches:

- out-of-bounds reads/writes
- use-after-free
- stack buffer overflows
- global buffer overflows

ASan is faster than Valgrind and shows beautifully detailed stack traces.

13.16.4 A Tiny Buggy Program (Used in Interviews)

Here's a classic question:

```
int *p = malloc(4 * sizeof(int));
for (int i = 0; i <= 4; ++i)    // Off-by-one bug
    p[i] = i;

free(p);
```

Bug:

- Allocated space for 4 elements (indices 0–3)

- Loop writes 5 elements (indices 0–4)

What Valgrind reports:

```
Invalid write of size 4
Address 0x... is 0 bytes after a block of size 16
```

What ASan reports:

```
ERROR: AddressSanitizer: heap-buffer-overflow
WRITE of size 4 at ...
```

Interviewers LOVE this example because it checks whether you take memory limits seriously.

13.16.5 Debugging Strategy (Used by Professionals)

When something crashes:

1. **Compile with AddressSanitizer**

```
gcc -fsanitize=address -g main.c
```

2. **Run under Valgrind (if using Linux)**
3. **Check all pointer operations, especially:**

- array indexing
- pointer arithmetic
- dynamic memory loops
- `realloc()` usage

4. **Check for missing `free()` calls**
5. **Check for NULL checks after malloc**

6. **Check for off-by-one loops**

Interview Tip: If an interviewer asks, "How would you debug a memory bug?" — describe this exact workflow. It immediately demonstrates maturity as a C developer.

13.17 Pointer Safety Checklist: Proven Habits

Even if your logic is perfect, a single careless pointer mistake can break your program in ways that are hard to trace. This is why great C programmers follow a set of disciplined habits — habits that interviewers immediately recognize.

Use this checklist as your personal safety guide whenever writing pointer-heavy code.

- **Always initialize pointers.** Uninitialized pointers (wild pointers) are one of the biggest sources of crashes.
- **Set pointers to `NULL` after freeing.** This prevents accidental use-after-free and makes debugging easier.
- **Check every allocation.**

```
p = malloc(n * sizeof *p);
if (!p) { /* handle error */ }
```

- **Use a temporary pointer with `realloc()`.** Never

overwrite the original pointer directly — you could lose it on failure.

```
int *tmp = realloc(p, new_size);
if (tmp) p = tmp;
```

- **Never perform pointer arithmetic across different allocations.** Only compare or subtract pointers that point into the *same* object or array.
- **Prefer `size_t` and `%zu` for sizes.** Using the correct type avoids overflow issues and makes code portable.
- **Avoid casting away `const`.** Doing so without a strong reason almost always leads to undefined behavior.
- **Avoid raw type-punning (strict aliasing).** If you need to reinterpret memory, use `memcpy()` or unions safely.
- **Do not index beyond array bounds.** Even a single off-by-one write can corrupt the heap.
- **Use sanitizers and tools.** Run with:

  ```
  gcc -fsanitize=address -g file.c
  ```

  or:

  ```
  valgrind --leak-check=full ./a.out
  ```

- **When passing arrays to functions, always pass the size too.** Arrays decay to pointers, losing size information.

- **Document ownership.** In larger programs, clearly indicate who is responsible for freeing memory.

Interview Tip: If asked, "How do you write safe pointer code?", mention at least 4–5 points from this list. It conveys experience, discipline, and awareness of real-world issues — exactly what interviewers look for.

13.18 Interview Preparation Zone (Pointers & Memory)

This section is designed exactly the way interviewers think. These are the patterns, traps, and reasoning questions that companies use to test whether you truly understand pointers and memory — not just the syntax, but the mindset.

Use these questions for revision, mock interviews, and handwritten practice. If you can comfortably solve these, you're ready for pointer-heavy technical rounds.

Conceptual Questions

1. Explain why pointer arithmetic is based on `sizeof(type)` instead of raw bytes. (Interviewers expect more than "because that's how C works.")
2. What does it mean when we say "arrays decay to pointers"? What information is lost?
3. Difference between:

```
char *s = "hello";
```

```
char  s2[] = "hello";
```

(This is one of the most frequently asked questions!)

4. What is a dangling pointer? Give two situations where it occurs.

5. Why is `void *` important in functions like `malloc()` and `qsort()`?

6. Explain strict aliasing. Why does accessing an `int` through a `float *` cause undefined behavior?

7. When is it legal to compare pointers using <, >, ==? Interviewers love this question because most candidates get it wrong.

8. Why does `sizeof` a pointer NOT depend on the data type it points to?

9. Why is it dangerous to write:

   ```
   int *p;
   *p = 10;
   ```

10. Why must dynamic memory allocation always be paired with `free()`? What happens if you forget?

Trace the Code (Short)

Trace these carefully — small pointer movements change everything.

```
int a[] = {10, 20, 30, 40};
int *p = a + 1;
printf("%d", *(p + 2));
```

Expected Output: 40

—

```
int x = 5;
int *p = &x;
int **pp = &p;
printf("%d", **pp);
```

Expected Output: 5

—

```
int arr[] = {3, 6, 9};
int *p = arr;
p++;
printf("%d", *p);
```

Expected Output: 6

Find the Bug

```
int *p = malloc(3 * sizeof *p);
for (int i = 0; i <= 3; ++i) {
    p[i] = i;
}
```

Bug: Out-of-bounds write (last valid index is 2). **Fix:** Change loop to `i < 3` or allocate 4 elements.

—

```
int *p = malloc(sizeof(int));
free(p);
printf("%d", *p);
```

Bug: Dereferencing a dangling pointer. **Fix:** Use `p = NULL;` immediately after `free(p);`.

—

```
int a = 10, b = 20;
const int *p = &a;
*p = 50;
```

Bug: Writing through pointer-to-const. **Fix:** Remove `const` or use a normal `int *`.

Short Coding Drills

1. Write a function that returns how many elements apart two pointers are in the same array.
2. Implement a custom `memset()` using `unsigned char *` only.
3. Write a function that prints an array in reverse using pointer arithmetic only (no indexing).
4. Implement a safe `realloc()` wrapper that prevents losing the original pointer on failure.
5. Implement `swap(int *a, int *b)` using pointers only.

Interview Tip: A strong interviewer will not care as much about syntax as your reasoning. Explain *why* each pointer step works. Show clarity. Show confidence. Show understanding.

13.19 Quick Recap Before You Move On

Before you jump to the next chapter, pause for a moment and make sure these ideas feel clear and natural. If you understand these confidently, you're already ahead of most candidates walking into an interview.

- **Pointers store addresses**, not values. Dereferencing with *p is how you read or modify the value stored at that address.
- C memory is organized into clear regions: **text**, **data/BSS**, **heap**, and **stack**. Most pointer bugs come from mixing up the last two.
- **Pointer arithmetic moves in units of the datatype.** `p + 1` means "next element", not "next byte."
- **Arrays decay to pointers** when passed to functions. The size information is lost — this is why functions must also accept the length.
- **Dynamic memory** comes from the heap via `malloc`, `calloc`, `realloc`, and must be returned with `free`. Forgetting to free causes leaks; freeing twice is a bug.
- **Common pointer failures:** wild pointers (uninitialized), dangling pointers (freed memory), double frees, out-of-bounds writes, forgetting NULL checks.
- **Tools like Valgrind and ASan** are your best allies

when debugging memory errors. Interviewers appreciate when candidates know how to verify code correctness.

- Advanced topics like **alignment, strict aliasing**, and safe casting are frequent differentiators in tougher interviews.

If all of this makes sense, congratulations — you're thinking about memory the way real C developers do. You're now ready to tackle deeper challenges.

Do-It-Yourself: Practice Zone

Now that you've completed one of the most important chapters in the entire book, it's time to strengthen your understanding the way real interview preparation works — through thoughtful, targeted practice.

These exercises are split into three parts. Each part helps you build confidence in a different layer of pointers and memory. Try them without rushing; the goal is to develop clarity, not speed.

Part A — Fundamentals

1. Write a function that returns the distance (in elements) between two pointers within the same array.
2. Implement a simple version of `memset()` using an `unsigned char *` pointer.
3. Given an array `int a[5]`, print its elements in reverse using only pointer arithmetic—no indexing allowed.
4. Explain what happens when you do:

   ```
   int *p = NULL;
   *p = 10;
   ```

   Why is this dangerous? What is a safer alternative?
5. Show

how `arr[i]` and `*(arr + i)` behave identically by printing elements of an array both ways.

Part B — Dynamic Memory

1. Allocate a dynamic 2D array using the **contiguous block + row pointers** method. Fill it with `row * col` and print it neatly. Free all memory correctly.
2. Write a function `resize_int_array(int **p, size_t *n)` that doubles the array size using `realloc` safely. (Hint: use a temporary pointer to avoid losing memory on failure.)
3. Implement a stack using a dynamically resizing array. Support: `push`, `pop`, `top`, `is_empty`. Ensure it never overflows and never leaks memory.
4. Use `calloc()` to create a zero-initialized buffer. Verify by printing each element before writing to it.
5. Demonstrate a memory leak intentionally, then fix it. (Interviews love these "identify the bug" style questions.)

Part C — Linked Structures

1. Build a singly linked list with:
   - insert at head
   - insert at tail
   - delete a given value

- free the entire list

2. Implement a queue using linked nodes. Test it with at least 100 enqueue/dequeue operations.
3. Reverse a singly linked list using pointer rewiring (iterative method). Draw a small diagram in your notebook to understand the transitions.
4. Create a simple hash table with chaining using linked lists. You don't need resizing — focus on pointer relationships.
5. Implement a "deep copy" function that clones an entire linked list.

Your Challenge — The Memory Navigator

Design a small program that acts like a tiny "memory explorer." Your program must:

- Dynamically allocate an integer buffer using `malloc()`.
- Maintain a **current pointer** within this buffer.
- Provide the operations:
  - `move_left()`
  - `move_right()`
  - `read()`
  - `write(int v)`
- Prevent moving out of bounds and print a warning.

- Work cleanly with Valgrind/ASan (no leaks, no invalid reads/writes).

This challenge is extremely close to what real interviews test. If you can build this confidently, you're well on your way to mastering pointers.

Chapter 14

STRUCTURES, UNIONS, AND ENUMS

If you've mastered pointers, then congratulations — you've unlocked the hardest part of C. Now it's time to take that foundation and use it to build more powerful data models.

Welcome to **structures**, **unions**, and **enums** — the three features that let you create custom data types in C. These are the tools interviewers expect you to know when dealing with real programs: linked lists, trees, records, configuration tables, file formats, network packets — all of them rely heavily on these constructs.

This chapter will help you understand:

- What structures really are and how memory is laid out inside them
- How to work with nested structures and pointers to structures
- How unions share memory and why that's useful

(and dangerous)

- How to use enums to make your code safer, clearer, and interview-ready
- How padding and alignment affect structure size
- How to build real interview-level data models using these concepts

By the end of this chapter, you'll be able to model data the way real C programmers do — with clarity, control, and confidence.

14.1 Why C Needs Structures

C gives you the basic built-in data types: `int`, `char`, `float`, `double`. But real-world data is rarely that simple.

Imagine modelling:

- an employee record (name, ID, salary)
- a point in 2D space (x, y)
- a student (roll number, marks, grade)

Using separate variables is messy. Using arrays is worse. What you need is a **custom data type**.

That's exactly what a structure provides.

Definition: A `struct` is a user-defined type that groups multiple variables into a single logical unit.

Example:

```
struct Student {
    int roll;
    float marks;
    char grade;
};
```

Now you can create objects of this type:

```
struct Student s1;
```

Interview Tip: When asked "Why do we need structures?", respond: *"Structures let us create composite data types that package related information together. They make code cleaner and model real entities directly."*

14.2 Memory Layout of a Structure

Every structure has a well-defined memory layout. Consider:

```
struct Point {
    int x;
    int y;
};
```

If `int` is 4 bytes, then:

$$\text{sizeof(struct Point)} = 8 \text{ bytes}$$

A simple diagram:

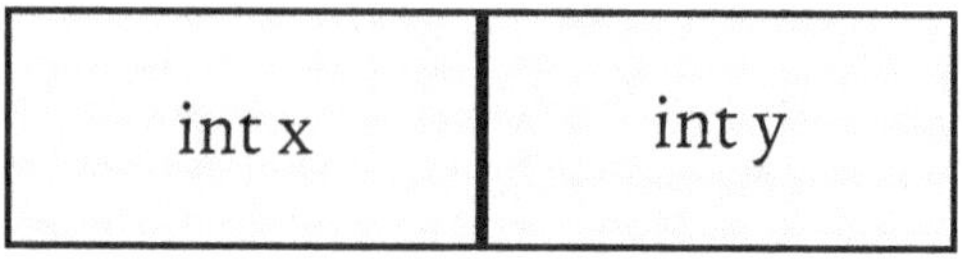

Figure 14.1: *Memory layout of a simple structure.*

Accessing members

```
struct Point p = {10, 20};
printf("%d", p.x);    // 10
```

14.3 Padding and Alignment — Why Structure Size Isn't Always Obvious

This is one of the most common interview topics. C aligns structure members for faster CPU access. That means a structure might be larger than the sum of its fields.

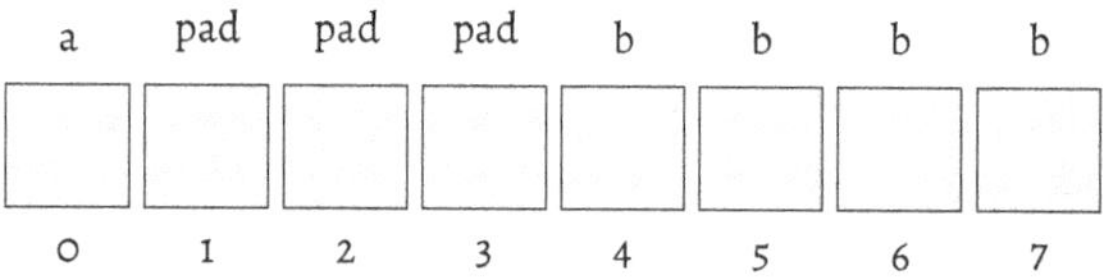

Figure 14.2: *Padding inserted to align* `int` *on a 4-byte boundary.*

Example:

```
struct Test {
    char a;    // 1 byte
    int b;     // 4 bytes
};
```

At first glance, you'd think the size is 5 bytes. But on a typical system:

$$\text{sizeof(struct Test)} = 8$$

Why? Padding.

Interview Tip: If asked why padding exists, say: *"Most CPUs can access aligned data faster or only at aligned boundaries. Padding ensures correct alignment."*

14.4 Pointers to Structures

Structures combine beautifully with pointers and dynamic memory.

```
struct Student *p;
p = malloc(sizeof(struct Student));
p->roll = 101;
p->marks = 89.5;
```

The arrow (->) operator

`p->roll` is shorthand for `(*p).roll`. Almost everyone uses the arrow — including interviewers.

Interview Insight: If they ask you to implement a linked list, you'll be writing `p->next` a lot.

14.5 Nested Structures

C lets you build complex models by placing a structure inside another.

Example:

```
struct Date {
    int day, month, year;
};

struct Employee {
    int id;
    float salary;
    struct Date joining;
};
```

Access:

```
struct Employee e;
e.joining.year = 2024;
```

This is extremely common in real-world C code.

14.6 Arrays of Structures

When you want to store multiple records, you use an array of structs:

```
struct Student arr[3] = {
    {1, 89.3, 'A'},
    {2, 91.0, 'A'},
    {3, 76.5, 'B'}
};
```

This shows up in interviews for sorting, searching, and filtering questions.

14.7 Structure Initialization (Modern C Style)

C allows designated initializers:

```
struct Point p = {.x = 10, .y = 20};
```

This reduces mistakes and improves readability.

14.8 Unions — Shared Memory for Multiple Views

A **union** is like a structure, except all members share the same memory.

```
union Data {
    int i;
    float f;
    char c;
};
```

The size of a union is the size of its largest member.

Why use unions?

- For memory-efficient structures
- For variant data types
- For implementing tagged unions / polymorphism in C
- For low-level work (bit reinterpretation, network packets)

Can represent: int / float / char

Shared Memory Block

Figure 14.3: *All members of a union occupy the same memory.*

Example:

```
union Data d;
d.i = 65;
printf("%c", d.c);    // Input interpreted as char
```

Warning: Reading a field that wasn't most recently written is undefined behavior — but commonly exploited in systems programming.

14.9 Enums — Creating Meaningful Integral Types

Enums let you define your own symbolic integer constants.

```
enum Color { RED, GREEN, BLUE };
```

Internally, these are integers:

$$RED = 0, \; GREEN = 1, \; BLUE = 2$$

Why use enums?

- clearer code
- fewer mistakes

- safer parameters

Example:

```
enum Day { MON, TUE, WED, THU, FRI, SAT, SUN };

enum Day today = WED;
```

Interview Tip: Enums help when designing state machines — a favorite interview topic.

14.10 Typedef with Structures, Unions, and Enums

Typing `struct Student` repeatedly can be tedious.

Use `typedef`:

```
typedef struct {
    int x, y;
} Point;

Point p;
```

This is incredibly common in production C.

14.11 Building Real-World Data Models (Interview-Ready)

Let's build something interviewers love: a tiny geometric model.

```
typedef struct {
    int x, y;
} Point;

typedef struct {
```

```
    Point start;
    Point end;
} Line;

typedef struct {
    Line edges[4];
} Rectangle;
```

You can now manipulate rectangles using intuitive code:

```
rect.edges[0].start.x = 10;
```

This demonstrates your ability to use structs in a layered, readable way.

14.12 Common Interview Questions

Conceptual

1. Difference between `struct` and `union`.
2. Why does padding exist? How do you reduce it?
3. What is the size of a structure with mixed types?
4. Can you assign one structure variable to another?

Code Tracing

```
struct S { char c; int x; };
struct S s = {'A', 100};
printf("%d", sizeof(s));    // ?
```

Expected answer: usually 8 due to padding.

Find the Bug

```
union U { int x; char c[4]; };
union U u;
strcpy(u.c, "Hi!"); // potential UB
```

14.13 Quick Recap Before You Move On

- **Structures** let you group related variables into a single logical unit. They are the backbone of real-world data modeling in C.
- **Structure memory layout** follows member order, but padding is added for alignment. This is why structure size often surprises beginners—and why interviewers ask about it.
- **Accessing structure members** uses the dot operator (`p.x`), while pointers to structures use the arrow (p->x) for convenience.
- **Nested structures** help you build complex, layered models (like a Rectangle containing Lines containing Points).
- **Arrays of structures** are essential for real interview problems such as sorting records, filtering data, and modeling tables.
- **Unions** store multiple representations of the same memory. They are powerful—but must be used carefully, because only the most recent member

written is valid.

- **Enums** give names to integer constants, making code safer and more meaningful (especially with state machines and switch statements).
- **typedef** can dramatically improve readability when working with structures, unions, and enums—especially in data-structure-heavy code.
- **Padding, alignment, and size calculations** are frequent interview questions. Always think in terms of boundaries, word-size alignment, and member ordering.
- These three features—**structures, unions, and enums**—are the tools that let you model real data cleanly and naturally. Master them, and you'll be ready to build linked lists, trees, hash tables, and many of the most common interview data structures.

Do-It-Yourself: Practice Zone

Part A — Structure Fundamentals

1. Define a structure `Book` with fields `title`, `author`, and `price`. Write a function that prints a single `Book` in clean, readable format.
2. Create an array of `Book` structures and write a function to print all books priced above a user-defined threshold.
3. Implement a function `swapPoints(struct Point *a, struct Point *b)` that swaps two points using structure pointers.
4. Write a structure `Student` with fields for name, three test marks, and an average. Write a function to compute and update the average.

Part B — Structure Memory and Layout

1. Given a structure with mixed data types (char, int, double), write code to print its size. Rearrange members to minimize padding. Compare the size before and after.
2. Create a structure containing another structure (nested). Initialize all members and print them cleanly.
3. Build a structure containing a fixed-size char array and write a safe function (using `strncpy`) to set the

name field without risking overflow.

Part C — Unions and Type Reinterpretation

1. Define a union `Number` that can store an `int`, `float`, or `char[4]`. Write a demo that stores each type and prints the result.
2. Use the same union to show how storing one field and reading another can reveal the underlying byte representation.
3. Implement a simple tagged union:

```
        enum Type { INT, FLOAT };
        struct Value { enum Type t; union { int i;
    float f; } u; };
```

   Write a function that prints the value based on the active tag.

Part D — Enums in Action

1. Create an enum `Day` with seven values. Write a function `isWeekend(enum Day d)` that returns true or false.
2. Define an enum `State` with values `IDLE`, `RUNNING`, `ERROR`. Write a `switch`-based function that prints behavior based on state.
3. Build a small state machine using enums to model a traffic signal (`RED → GREEN → YELLOW → RED`).

Your Challenge — "Mini Database Manager"

Design a small program that uses structures, unions, and enums together:

- Each record should store an ID, a name, and a type tag.
- The tagged union should store either an integer score or a floating rating.
- Support operations: add record, update record, print all records.
- Use enums to represent the record type (e.g., `SCORE` or `RATING`).
- Focus on clean structure design, safe string handling, and readable output.

Pro Tip: Try writing the entire program without using any global variables. This forces you to design better structure-based APIs — exactly the kind of thinking that impresses interviewers.

Chapter 15

DYNAMIC MEMORY ALLOCATION

If you've made it this far, take a moment to appreciate the progress you've achieved. You now understand pointers, arrays, pointer arithmetic, memory layout, and even function pointers — topics that many learners struggle with for years.

You're ready for the next level.

Up to this point, most memory you've worked with has been either:

- defined at compile-time (global variables, static variables), or
- automatically managed by the stack (local variables inside functions).

But real programs — especially those you will face in interviews — rarely rely only on fixed-size memory. Whether you're building:

- dynamic arrays,

- variable-sized input systems,
- linked structures,
- trees, graphs, or hash tables,
- buffers that grow based on user input,

...you need memory that can grow, shrink, and adapt.

This is where **dynamic memory allocation** becomes essential.

Dynamic memory allocation gives your program the power to request memory at runtime.

In C, this power comes with incredible flexibility—and equally dangerous pitfalls. You get:

- full control over how much memory you allocate,
- full control over when you free it,
- full responsibility if something goes wrong.

This is why interviewers LOVE dynamic memory questions. They reveal instantly whether you understand:

- how the heap works,
- how to manage memory safely,
- how to avoid leaks and corruption,
- how data structures behave internally.

In this chapter, you will learn:

- what the heap really is and how it differs from the stack,
- how `malloc()`, `calloc()`, `realloc()`, and `free()` work,
- how dynamic arrays and linked structures use runtime allocation,
- what memory fragmentation is (and why it matters),
- tools and techniques to debug runtime memory errors,
- common interview traps — and how to avoid them confidently.

This topic is long, deep, and incredibly rewarding. By the end of this chapter, you'll understand memory the way professional C programmers do.

Ready? Let's begin.

15.1 Stack vs Heap: What Really Happens Behind the Scenes

Before we start allocating dynamic memory, we need to understand *where* this memory comes from. C uses two major regions for storing variables during program execution:

- the **stack** — managed automatically,
- the **heap** — managed manually (by *you*).

Both are crucial, but they behave very differently. Interviewers expect you to know the difference with real clarity.

The Stack — Fast, Structured, Automatic

The stack stores:

- function call frames,
- local variables,
- return addresses,
- function parameters.

Every time you call a function, a new "stack frame" is pushed.

```
void fun() {
    int x = 10;     // stored on stack
}
```

When the function returns:

- The frame is popped.
- All local variables disappear automatically.

Key Characteristics:

- very fast allocation and deallocation
- fixed size (a few MB)
- consecutive layout (great cache friendliness)
- memory lifetime tied to function scope

Interviewer Tip: If asked, "Why can't the stack store large arrays?" — answer: *because stack size is limited, and large objects risk stack overflow.*

The Heap — Flexible, Manual, and Powerful

The heap stores memory that:

- lives beyond function calls,
- can grow or shrink at runtime,
- must be requested manually using `malloc`, `calloc`, or `realloc`,
- must be released manually using `free`.

```
int *p = malloc(sizeof(int));
// allocated from heap
```

Heap allocation is:

- slower (because it uses system calls or allocators),
- more flexible (size determined at runtime),
- more dangerous (memory leaks, corruption, double free).

The Big Difference (Explained Simply)

Stack = automatic memory vs **Heap = manual memory**

Or even simpler:

Stack memory cleans itself. Heap memory does not.

This is why forgetfulness in heap management leads to:

- memory leaks (forgot to free),
- use-after-free errors,
- dangling pointers,
- fragmentation,
- heap corruption (writing out of bounds).

Memory Lifetime Comparison

- Stack variables exist **only inside their function.**
- Heap variables exist **until you explicitly free them.**

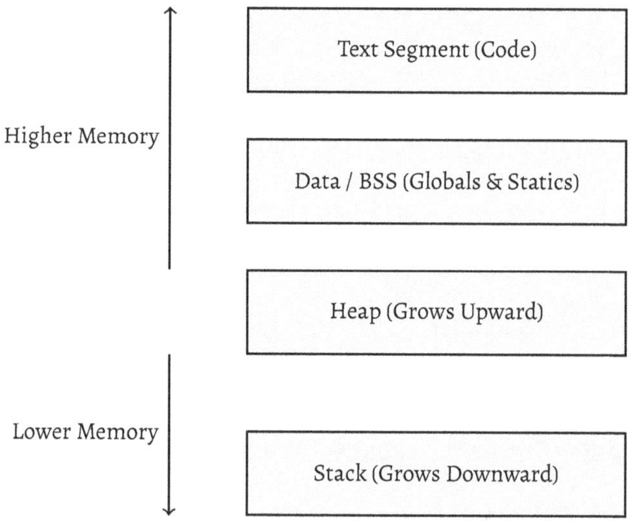

Figure 15.1: *Memory layout showing where stack and heap live.*

Example:

```
int* fun() {
    int x = 10;
    // on stack
    return &x;
    // BAD: returning address of dead variable
}
```

But:

```
int* fun() {
    int *p = malloc(sizeof(int));
    // on heap
    *p = 10;
    return p;
    // valid: memory persists after function ends
}
```

Interviewer Insight: A common interview question is: "Why is returning the address of a local variable wrong, but returning malloc'ed memory fine?" You now know the exact reason.

Why Interviewers Ask About Stack vs Heap

Because your answer tells them instantly:

- whether you understand variable lifetime,
- whether you can avoid classic pointer bugs,
- whether you can design safe structures,
- whether you can explain memory clearly (crucial for system-level roles).

Before we start using `malloc`, let's explore the rules and patterns that make dynamic allocation predictable and safe.

15.2 malloc(): The Foundation of Dynamic Memory Allocation

Now that you understand the difference between stack and heap, it's time to work with the function that unlocks the entire idea of dynamic memory in C:

malloc() → allocate memory from the heap

If you truly master `malloc()`, the rest of dynamic memory will feel natural.

What malloc() Actually Does

- It asks the operating system for a block of memory.
- It reserves that memory in the heap.
- It returns a `void *` pointer to the beginning of that block.

But here is the part interviewers really expect you to understand:

malloc does not initialize the memory. The memory you get contains garbage (whatever bits were there before).

Basic Usage

```
int *p = malloc(sizeof(int));
```

This allocates enough bytes to store one `int` and

returns its address.

But wait—there is one more crucial rule:

Always check if malloc() returned NULL.

If the system fails to allocate memory:

```
int *p = malloc(sizeof(int));
if (p == NULL) {
    // allocation failed
}
```

Failure is rare on desktops, but common in embedded systems — interviewers ask this because they want to see disciplined thinking.

Allocating Arrays Dynamically

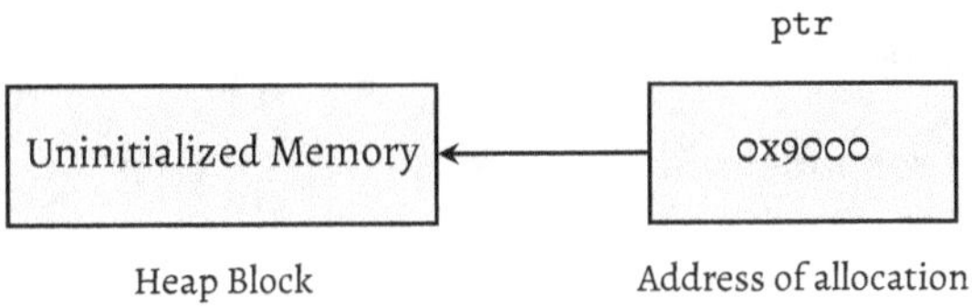

Figure 15.2: *malloc() returns a pointer to a block of uninitialized heap memory.*

Static version:

```
int arr[100];
```

Dynamic version:

```
int *arr = malloc(100 * sizeof(int));
```

This is your first true "dynamic array": The size can now come from user input, program logic, or runtime conditions.

malloc() Does Not Know Your Data Types

This is an insight that instantly improves your C-thinking.

`malloc()` only knows:

- the number of bytes you asked for,
- where the block begins.

It does **not** know:

- how many integers you meant to store,
- how many elements your array has,
- what type of data it is for.

That responsibility is entirely yours.

The Best Practice: Always Use sizeof(type)

Instead of writing:

```
int *p = malloc(20);        // risky!
```

Write this:

```
int *p = malloc(5 * sizeof(int));
```

This is:

- portable,

- readable,
- correct on systems where types grow/shrink,
- and the version interviewers expect you to write.

What Happens If You Forget sizeof?

Suppose you accidentally do this:

```
int *arr = malloc(5);
```

On a 4-byte int system, this gives you only 5 bytes — **not enough for even 2 integers!**

Accessing `arr[1]` or `arr[2]` becomes a heap corruption bug — extremely hard to debug and a classic interview trap.

Common malloc() Mistake in Interviews

Mistake:

```
int *p = malloc(sizeof p);      // WRONG!
```

`sizeof p` = size of pointer (8 bytes), **not** size of int.

Correct:

```
int *p = malloc(sizeof *p);    // RIGHT
```

This works even if you later change p to another type:

- readable
- safe
- beginner-friendly

- interview-friendly

malloc() and Memory Lifetime

malloc'ed memory lives until you call free().

It survives:

- function returns,
- loops,
- recursion,
- going out of scope.

This is why dynamic memory is powerful: you control the lifetime.

The Mental Model: You Get a "Bag of Bytes"

When you write:

```
int *p = malloc(4 * sizeof(int));
```

Think of it as:

> "You got 16 raw bytes. You are promising to use them as 4 integers. C trusts you. Do not break that trust."

This mindset makes you safer and gets you closer to how systems programmers think.

Interview Questions You Can Now Answer

- What does malloc return?
- Why should you use sizeof?
- Why can malloc fail?
- What does uninitialized memory contain?
- Does malloc know how many elements you allocated?
- Does malloc initialize memory?

If you can explain these clearly, your interviewer will know you're solid.

Next, we look at the safer cousin of malloc: `calloc()`, which zero-initializes memory and is extremely useful for real-world systems and interview tasks.

15.3 calloc(): Zero-Initialized Memory (The "Safer" malloc)

If `malloc()` gives you a raw block of uninitialized bytes, `calloc()` **gives you a clean, zero-filled block of memory.**

That one difference makes `calloc()` extremely useful in many real-world programs — and interviewers love asking when you should prefer it over `malloc()`.

calloc() Syntax

```
void *calloc(size_t count, size_t size);
```

Meaning:

`calloc(count, size)` = **count elements** × **size bytes each**

`malloc()` takes a single total byte count. `calloc()` takes two numbers — and multiplies them for you.

Basic Usage

```
int *arr = calloc(5, sizeof(int));
```

This allocates memory for 5 integers **and sets all bytes to zero**.

Why Zero Initialization Matters

With `malloc()`, memory contains garbage:

```
int *p = malloc(5 * sizeof(int));
printf("%d", p[0]);    // unpredictable!
```

With `calloc()`, everything starts at zero:

```
int *p = calloc(5, sizeof(int));
printf("%d", p[0]);    // prints 0
```

This is especially useful when you need:

- counters initialized to 0,
- arrays that assume zero-based defaults,
- buffers that should not contain leftover memory,
- structs where all fields must start clean.

calloc() and Struct Initialization

A powerful use of `calloc()` is initializing structs:

```
struct Point {
    int x, y;
};

struct Point *p = calloc(1, sizeof(struct Point));
```

Both x and y become 0 automatically.

Interviewers love this case because it shows you understand memory layout.

calloc() vs malloc() + memset

These two lines are equivalent:

```
int *p = calloc(5, sizeof(int));
```

and

```
int *p = malloc(5 * sizeof(int));
memset(p, 0, 5 * sizeof(int));
```

Which is better? Use `calloc()` — it's cleaner, safer, and optimized on many systems.

Diagram: calloc() vs malloc()

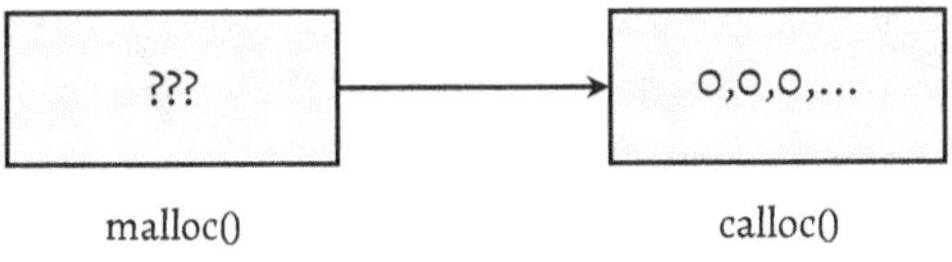

Figure 15.3: *malloc() gives garbage; calloc() gives zeroed memory.*

Performance Notes (Interview Level)

Interviewers sometimes ask:

> *"Is calloc slower than malloc?"*

You can impress them with this answer:

- On modern OSes, `calloc()` is often **not slower**.
- Many allocators use **zeroed pages** provided directly by the kernel.
- Some implementations use **lazy allocation**, making zeroing cheap.

So **calloc can be extremely fast**, depending on the OS and allocator.

Common Mistake: Using calloc() Incorrectly

This is wrong:

```
int *p = calloc(sizeof(int), 5);    // swapped arguments!
```

Arguments must be:

```
calloc(count, size)
```

Correct version:

```
int *p = calloc(5, sizeof(int));
```

Interviewer Trick: They will swap arguments and ask if it's valid — it is valid, but confusing.

Best practice: Always write the element count first, size second.

When Should You Use calloc()?

Use calloc when:

- You need everything initialized to zero.
- You are allocating arrays of integers, floats, structs.
- Your code expects a clean starting state.
- You want to avoid undefined values.

Use malloc when:

- You will immediately overwrite all memory.
- You want maximum control over initialization.

Interview Questions You Can Answer Now

- What is the difference between malloc and calloc?
- Which one is safer?
- Does calloc always zero memory?
- Is calloc slower?
- Why does calloc take two arguments?

Having a clear explanation for these will make you stand out.

15.4 realloc(): Resizing Dynamic Memory Safely

By now you know how to allocate memory using `malloc()` and `calloc()`. But real programs don't always know the required size in advance.

That's where **`realloc()`** comes in — the function that lets you **grow or shrink an existing memory block** without losing data.

Interviewers love `realloc()` because it tests:

- your understanding of dynamic memory,
- pointer safety,
- what happens behind the scenes,
- and your ability to write bug-free C code.

The realloc() Function Signature

```
void *realloc(void *ptr, size_t new_size);
```

Meaning:

- `ptr` — an existing allocation (from malloc/calloc/realloc),
- `new_size` — the new total size you want.

Behavior:

- It tries to resize the existing block.
- If possible, it expands/shrinks in place.

- If not, it allocates a new block, copies old data, frees the old block.

This makes `realloc()` extremely powerful — but also dangerous if used incorrectly.

Example: Growing an Array

```
int *p = malloc(3 * sizeof(int));
p = realloc(p, 6 * sizeof(int));    // grow to 6 ints
```

But There's a Big Catch

This is one of the most common interview traps in C:

```
p = realloc(p, new_size);
```

If `realloc()` fails, it returns NULL — but your original pointer is **lost forever** (memory leak!).

A safer version:

```
int *temp = realloc(p, new_size);
if (temp != NULL) {
    p = temp;    // success
} else {
    // handle allocation failure
}
```

This demonstrates clean thinking, and interviewers appreciate it.

Visualization of realloc() Behavior

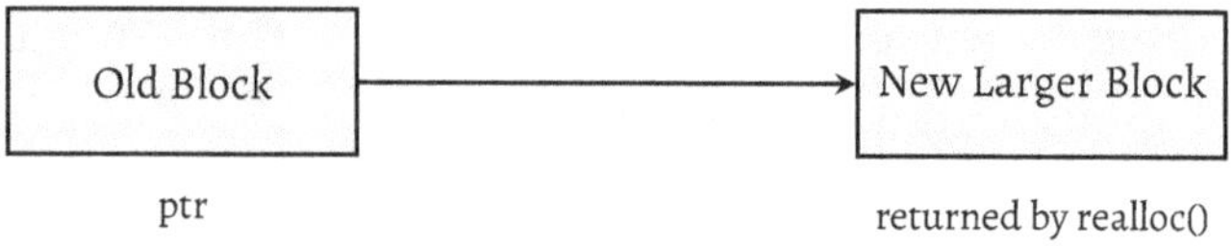

Figure 15.4: *If needed,* `realloc()` *moves data to a new memory block.*

Shrinking with realloc()

```
p = realloc(p, 2 * sizeof(int));  // shrink
```

Shrinking usually does not move the block — but it can.

Important: Never use memory beyond the resized region.

What Happens When realloc(ptr, 0) Is Called?

This is a surprisingly common interview question.

$$\textbf{realloc(ptr, 0)} \Longrightarrow \text{behaves like } free(ptr)$$

It frees the memory and returns either:

- `NULL`, or
- a unique pointer that must not be dereferenced.

So always assume it returns `NULL`.

What Happens When realloc(NULL, new_size)?

This behaves like `malloc(new_size)`.

This means you can write flexible code:

```
int *arr = NULL;
for (int i = 0; i < 10; i++) {
    arr = realloc(arr, (i+1) * sizeof(int));
}
```

Interview Trick: realloc() May Move Memory

Many beginners assume that the memory always grows "in-place."

But the truth is:

> `realloc()` **may move the block to a completely different address.**

So after calling realloc, **never use the old pointer again.** Always use the returned pointer.

Practical Example — Dynamic Array Growth

This pattern appears frequently in interviews:

```
size_t capacity = 2;
int *arr = malloc(capacity * sizeof(int));
size_t size = 0;

for (int x; scanf("%d", &x) == 1; ) {
    if (size == capacity) {
        size_t newcap = capacity * 2;
        int *temp = realloc(arr, newcap * sizeof(int));
        if (!temp) {
            printf("Error: out of memory\n");
```

```
            free(arr);
            exit(1);
        }
        arr = temp;
        capacity = newcap;
    }
    arr[size++] = x;
}
```

This demonstrates:

- dynamic growth,
- safe realloc usage,
- error handling — something interviewers deeply value.

When Should You Avoid realloc()?

Avoid `realloc()` when:

- You have multiple pointers referencing the same block.
- You need guaranteed stability of the address.
- You are storing pointers into the memory you're resizing.

Because if realloc moves memory, all old pointers become invalid.

Summary — realloc() in One Sentence

realloc() lets you resize memory flexibly, but you must always use a temporary pointer to avoid losing the original allocation.

15.5 free(): Releasing Memory Correctly (and Avoiding Hidden Bugs)

Dynamic memory is powerful — but it also comes with responsibility.

Every `malloc()`, `calloc()`, or `realloc()` must eventually be matched with a `free()`.

This is one of the simplest rules in C programming, yet it's also one of the most commonly violated during interviews (and even in production code).

The Basic Rule

```
free(ptr);
```

After freeing:

- the memory is returned to the heap,
- the pointer becomes invalid,
- dereferencing it causes undefined behavior.

This leads us straight to our first major concept.

A Freed Pointer Is Dangerous

- The pointer still *contains* the old address.
- But the memory at that address is no longer yours.
- So using it again is a classic **dangling pointer** bug.

```
int *p = malloc(sizeof(int));
free(p);
*p = 10;    //  undefined behavior (dangling pointer)
```

Interview Insight: Always set the pointer to NULL after freeing it:

```
free(p);
p = NULL;    //  safe
```

Visualizing free()

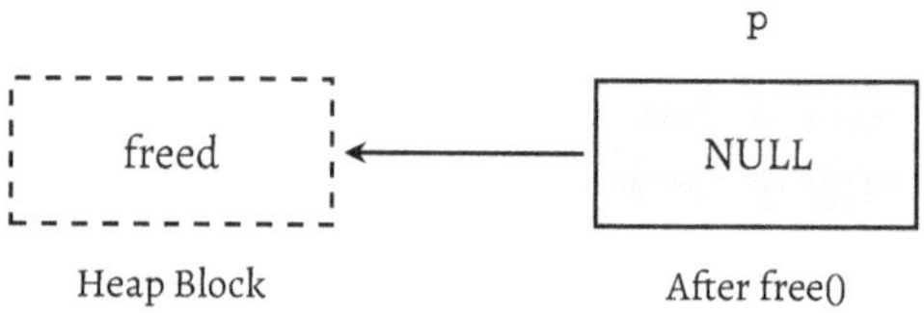

Figure 15.5: *After calling* `free(p)`*, always set* `p = NULL`*.*

Common Interview Question: Can You Free NULL?

Yes!

```
int *p = NULL;
free(p);    //  perfectly safe
```

The C standard guarantees that `free(NULL)` does nothing. This makes cleanup code safer and simpler.

What Does free() NOT Do?

It does NOT set your pointer to NULL. That is your job.

It does NOT zero the memory. Other processes may see old data (important in security-sensitive systems).

It does NOT free nested memory. You must free inner allocations manually:

```
int **m = malloc(3 * sizeof(int*));
for (int i = 0; i < 3; i++)
    m[i] = malloc(5 * sizeof(int));

free(m);  //  leaks 3 inner arrays
```

Correct version:

```
for (int i=0; i<3; i++)
    free(m[i]);         // free each row
free(m);                // free row pointers
```

This example appears in interviews very frequently.

Double Free — A Silent Killer

A "double free" happens when you free the same pointer twice:

```
int *p = malloc(10);
free(p);
free(p);      //  undefined behavior
```

Why is it dangerous?

- Heap metadata gets corrupted.
- Memory allocators may crash your program.
- Attackers can exploit it (security risk).

Interview Tip: Setting the pointer to `NULL` after freeing prevents most double frees:

```
free(p);
p = NULL;
free(p);    //  safe (no effect)
```

Freeing Stack Memory — NEVER Allowed

This is a common beginner mistake:

```
int x;
free(&x);    //  never free stack memory
```

Only memory allocated by:

- malloc()
- calloc()
- realloc()

may be freed.

Freeing Part of an Allocation — Also Wrong

```
int *p = malloc(10 * sizeof(int));
free(p + 5);    //  undefined behavior
```

Only
the exact pointer returned from malloc/calloc/realloc may be freed.

Memory Leak — The Most Common Real Bug

A memory leak occurs when you lose all references to allocated memory:

```
int *p = malloc(100);
p = NULL;        //  leak: original block lost forever
```

Interview Insight: This is why you free memory **before** overwriting a pointer:

```
free(p);
p = NULL;
```

15.6 Debugging Dynamic Memory Errors (Valgrind, ASan, and Interview-Level Bug Tracing)

No matter how carefully you write code, memory bugs eventually happen. In fact, most candidates fail pointer and dynamic memory questions *not because they don't understand the concept,* but because they don't recognize the bugs fast enough.

This section turns you into someone who can debug memory issues confidently — whether during an interview, in a coding round, or in real production systems.

Why Debugging Memory Bugs Is Hard

Memory errors are sneaky because:

- the crash happens **far away** from the actual bug,
- bugs often appear only for certain inputs,
- undefined behavior sometimes silently "works,"

- pointers don't come with safety checks.

Good news: modern tools can catch most of these instantly.

The Four Most Dangerous Dynamic Memory Bugs

1. **Out-of-bounds reads/writes**
2. **Use-after-free** (UAF)
3. **Leaks** (memory not freed)
4. **Double free**

And guess what?

Every interview question about dynamic memory eventually touches one of these.

Let's walk through each one with examples.

1. Out-of-Bounds Write (Heap Corruption)

```
int *p = malloc(4 * sizeof(int));
for (int i = 0; i <= 4; i++)    //  runs 5 times
    p[i] = i;
```

The write beyond the last index corrupts heap metadata — leading to unpredictable behavior much later.

Interview tip: This is the number one bug interviewers check when evaluating dynamic arrays.

2. Use-After-Free

```
int *p = malloc(sizeof(int));
```

```
free(p);
*p = 10;            //  UAF
```

The pointer still looks valid... until it explodes.

3. Memory Leaks

```
int *p = malloc(100);
// lost forever:
p = malloc(200);     //  100 bytes leaked
```

You replaced the pointer before freeing the original.

4. Double Free

```
int *p = malloc(10);
free(p);
free(p);             //  double free
```

This destroys heap internal structures and triggers a crash.

Tools That Save You (Valgrind & ASan)

These tools can detect almost every memory bug you'll ever make.

Valgrind (Linux)

Valgrind is slower, but incredibly thorough. It emulates your program and flags every invalid memory operation.

Run your program like this:

```
valgrind --leak-check=full ./a.out
```

It tells you:

- leakage amount,
- exact location of leaks,
- invalid reads/writes,
- use-after-free,
- double free.

AddressSanitizer (ASan)

ASan is a compiler feature — much faster than Valgrind.

Compile with:

```
gcc -fsanitize=address -g file.c -o a.out
```

Run normally:

```
./a.out
```

ASan prints:

- invalid heap reads/writes,
- buffer overflows,
- stack overflows,
- use-after-free,
- use-after-return,
- memory leaks (if combined with LSAN).

Which Should You Use?

- Use **Valgrind** for complete reports and leak summaries.
- Use **ASan** during development for fast crash detection.

Interviewers love when candidates mention both.

Example: ASan Detects an Out-of-Bounds Write

```
int *p = malloc(3*sizeof(int));
for (int i = 0; i <= 3; i++)  // bug: writes 4 times
    p[i] = i;
free(p);
```

ASan immediately prints something like:

```
== ERROR: AddressSanitizer: heap-buffer-overflow on address
    0x...
WRITE of size 4 at ...
```

This is an interviewer's dream answer: you didn't just say "bug exists," you demonstrated how to diagnose it.

Example: Catching a Leak with Valgrind

```
int *p = malloc(50);
return 0;
```

Valgrind finds it:

```
LEAK SUMMARY:
```

```
definitely lost: 50 bytes in 1 blocks
```

Interviewer smile level: HIGH.

15.7 Debugging Mindset (What Interviewers Look For)

Interviewers care less about syntax and more about thinking clearly around memory.

Here's what they expect:

- trace pointer changes,
- identify who "owns" which allocation,
- ensure every allocation is freed exactly once,
- avoid dereferencing freed pointers,
- avoid losing references (leaks),
- think about safety and predictability.

If you explain your reasoning like this, you immediately sound like an experienced C programmer.

Memory Debugging Checklist (Interview Gold)

- Did I match every allocation with a free?
- Did I free exactly once?
- Did I nullify the pointer after free?
- Did I avoid pointer arithmetic across different allocations?

- Did I check the result of malloc/calloc/realloc?
- Did I use Valgrind/ASan to verify correctness?

If you consciously follow this mental checklist, memory errors drop dramatically.

15.8 Quick Recap Before You Move On

Before we dive into even more advanced memory concepts, take a moment to reinforce what you've learned in this chapter. Dynamic memory allocation is one of the most important interview topics in C, and understanding it deeply sets you apart from the crowd.

- The heap is where memory grows dynamically using `malloc`, `calloc`, `realloc`, and `free`.
- **malloc()** allocates uninitialized memory; **calloc()** allocates and zero-initializes memory.
- **realloc()** can resize a block while preserving its contents— but always assign it to a temporary pointer to avoid losing memory on failure.
- **free()** releases previously allocated memory; failing to free leads to leaks, and freeing twice leads to undefined behavior.
- Always set pointers to `NULL` after freeing them to prevent use-after-free bugs.
- Pointer arithmetic depends on the `sizeof(type)`

being pointed to, not on raw bytes.

- Out-of-bounds writes, use-after-free, leaks, and double frees are the four most common dynamic memory bugs.
- Tools like **Valgrind** and **AddressSanitizer (ASan)** are essential for catching subtle heap errors and proving memory correctness.
- Thinking clearly about "ownership" of memory blocks is a sign of a mature C programmer.

If these ideas feel natural to you now, congratulations—that means you're thinking like someone who truly understands how C works under the hood.

Do-It-Yourself: Practice Zone

The best way to master dynamic memory is by writing small programs that force you to think about allocation, ownership, resizing, and freeing. These exercises are not just practice—they mirror the exact style of tasks interviewers love to ask.

Part A — Fundamentals

1. Allocate an integer array using `malloc`, fill it with values, and print them using only pointer arithmetic (no indexing).
2. Implement your own version of `calloc` using `malloc` and `memset`.
3. Write a function `int count_zeros(int *p, size_t n)` that counts how many elements are zero.
4. Demonstrate a safe use of `realloc` using an intermediate pointer.
5. Create a dynamic float array and write a function to compute its average.

Part B — Memory Resizing and Ownership

1. Write a dynamic array that automatically doubles its capacity whenever it becomes full. Implement `push`, `pop`, and `free_all`.

2. Implement `resize_array(int **p, size_t *n)` that doubles the size of the array and returns 1 on success, 0 on failure.
3. Build a simple integer buffer with functions: `write(value)`, `read(index)`, and `clear()`. Manage all memory safely.
4. Show an example of a memory leak, then fix it.

Part C — Linked and Structured Data

1. Build a singly linked list using dynamic memory: implement insert-at-head, insert-at-tail, delete-value, and `free_list`.
2. Create a dynamic matrix using two methods:
    - array-of-pointers (`int **`)
    - contiguous-row layout using a base pointer plus row pointers

    Compare their performance and memory layout.
3. Implement a dynamic stack (push/pop/top) using `malloc` and `realloc`.
4. Build a dynamic queue with head/tail pointers and test with 1,000 operations.

Your Challenge — "Memory Explorer"

Design a tiny interactive program that:

- allocates a dynamic buffer using `malloc`,

- keeps a "cursor pointer" inside the buffer,
- exposes commands `left()`, `right()`, `get()`, `set(v)`,
- prevents out-of-bounds movement with clear error messages,
- expands the buffer using `realloc` when needed,
- runs cleanly under both Valgrind and ASan.

Pro Tip: Document your solutions. Show where memory is allocated, how ownership moves, and where it is freed. Interviewers love candidates who can explain memory flow as clearly as they write code.

Chapter 16

FILE HANDLING IN C

C gives you a powerful set of tools to read from files, write to files, and even jump around inside them. But here's the part many students don't realize:

File handling is one of the most practical, interview-relevant, real-world skills in C.

You may write dozens of programs using arrays and pointers during college, but when you work with real systems—log tools, configuration parsers, transaction processors, compilers, game engines—*file handling is everywhere*.

This chapter is designed to make file I/O feel simple, intuitive, and reliable. Just like in the earlier chapters, we will take a friendly but in-depth approach, so you understand what's happening behind the scenes—not just the syntax.

By the end of this chapter, you'll confidently understand:

- What a file really is (OS perspective vs C perspective)
- What `FILE *` actually represents
- How buffered I/O works internally
- How to read and write text and binary files safely
- How `fseek`, `ftell`, and random access behave
- How to avoid all common file-related bugs
- How to handle large files (2GB+)

And most importantly: **you'll understand these topics deeply enough to answer interview questions with ease.**

16.1 What Exactly Is a File? (Human View vs System View)

Before writing any code, let's clear something up: a "file" is not just a '.txt' floating in your folder.

A file is, at the OS level, simply a **sequence of bytes stored somewhere**—on disk, SSD, network storage, virtual file system, or even inside memory.

C does not care whether the file contains:

- text
- numbers
- images
- binary data
- compiled programs

From C's point of view, every file is just a long sequence of bytes.

The OS View: File Descriptors

Operating systems expose files using small integers called **file descriptors**:

- `0` → `stdin`
- `1` → `stdout`
- `2` → `stderr`

When you open a file using the OS directly (via system calls), it gives you one of these descriptors.

The C View: FILE* Streams

C takes the OS file descriptor and wraps it in a higher-level structure called:

```
FILE *
```

A `FILE *` represents:

- an internal buffer
- a cursor position (read/write pointer)
- associated mode (read, write, append, etc.)
- whether an error or EOF has occurred

This is why C file handling functions expect a `FILE *` instead of a simple integer.

Diagram: How FILE* Connects to the OS

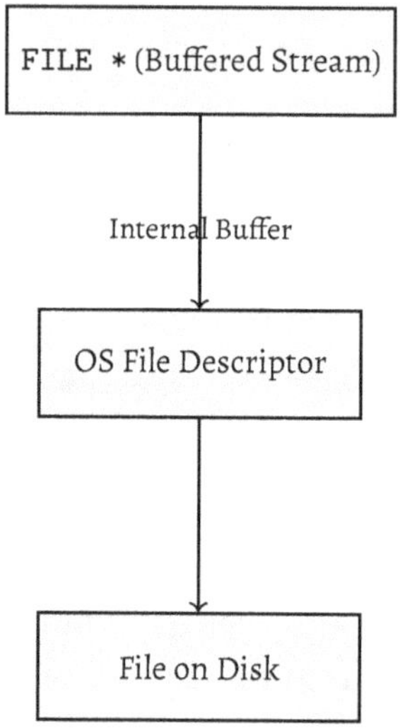

Figure 16.1: *FILE *is a buffered, high-level wrapper around OS file descriptors.*

Key Insight: Most interview mistakes happen because students don't know what a `FILE *` truly represents. Now you do.

16.2 Why Buffered I/O Exists

Reading from disk is slow. Really slow. Even SSDs cannot match memory access speed.

So C uses a **buffer** in RAM to improve efficiency:

- When reading: fill buffer once, serve many `getc()` calls quickly.

- When writing: accumulate output in buffer, flush in large blocks.

This is why:

```
fgetc(fp);
```

does NOT perform a disk access each time. It just reads from the in-memory buffer.

And this is why forgetting to call `fclose()` may result in:

- missing output
- incomplete writes
- corrupted files

We'll dive deeper into buffering later in the chapter.

16.3 Opening Files: fopen()

You open a file using `fopen()`:

```
FILE *fp = fopen("data.txt", "r");
```

Parameters:

- filename (string)
- mode (string)

Common modes:

`"r"`	read (file must exist)
`"w"`	write (creates/truncates)
`"a"`	append (creates if needed)
`"r+"`	read + write
`"w+"`	read + write (truncate)
`"a+"`	read + append

Always Check for NULL

If `fopen()` fails:

```
FILE *fp = fopen("missing.txt", "r");
if (fp == NULL) {
    printf("Could not open file.\n");
}
```

Common reasons:

- file doesn't exist
- permission denied
- directory missing
- disk full

16.4 Closing Files: fclose()

Every open file must be closed:

```
fclose(fp);
```

This:

- flushes buffers
- releases OS file descriptors
- prevents resource leaks

In interviews, a classic mistake is forgetting to close files inside loops.

16.5 Reading and Writing Characters

Now that you can open and close files, let's learn how to actually *read* and *write* data.

C provides simple, efficient character-level I/O functions:

- `fgetc()` — read a single character
- `fputc()` — write a single character
- `getc()` / `putc()` — often faster macros

Reading Characters: `fgetc()`

```
int ch = fgetc(fp);
```

Important notes:

- returns an `int`, not `char`
- returns `EOF` (-1) when the file ends or an error occurs

Typical pattern:

```
int ch;
while ((ch = fgetc(fp)) != EOF) {
    putchar(ch);
```

```
}
```

Interview Tip: Always store the result of `fgetc()` in an `int`. If you use `char`, you cannot distinguish between valid data and `EOF`.

Writing Characters: `fputc()`

```
fputc('A', fp);
```

The function returns the written character, or `EOF` on failure.

16.6 Reading and Writing Strings

Character I/O is great for low-level work, but most real programs read text one line at a time.

C provides:

- `fgets()` — safe line input
- `fputs()` — write a string

`fgets()` — Safe Line Reading

Syntax:

```
char *fgets(char *buffer, int size, FILE *fp);
\end{lstlistinglstlisting}

Usage:

\begin{lstlisting}
char line[100];
while (fgets(line, sizeof(line), fp)) {
```

```
    printf("%s", line);
}
```

Key behaviors:

- reads at most `size - 1` characters
- stops at newline or EOF
- includes the newline character if present
- null-terminates the string

Why interviewers love `fgets()`: It's safe, predictable, and avoids buffer overflow issues common with `gets()` (which was removed from C11 due to safety concerns).

`fputs()` — Writing Strings

```
fputs("Hello\n", fp);
```

Compare with `printf`:

- `fputs()` is simpler and faster
- does not add its own newline

16.7 Formatted I/O: `fprintf()` and `fscanf()`

These are the file versions of `printf` and `scanf`.

Formatted Output: `fprintf()`

```
fprintf(fp, "Name: %s Age: %d\n", name, age);
```

It behaves exactly like `printf()`, but writes to a file.

Formatted Input: `fscanf()`

```
fscanf(fp, "%d %f", &x, &y);
```

Warning (important!): `fscanf()` is powerful but risky:

- whitespace behavior is tricky
- badly formatted files cause failed reads
- missing & leads to crashes

Because of these issues, many production systems avoid `fscanf()`, preferring:

- `fgets()` + `sscanf()`
- manual parsing

Interview Advice

If an interviewer asks whether `fscanf()` is a good idea, say:

"It works, but it's brittle. For robust parsing, I prefer `fgets()` followed by `sscanf()` or custom tokenization."

This shows practical engineering judgment.

16.8 Detecting End-of-File Properly

A common error is:

```
while (!feof(fp)) { ... }    // Wrong!
```

Correct approach: Use the return value of the read function itself.

Examples:

- `fgetc()`: loop until it returns EOF
- `fgets()`: loop while the return value is non-NULL
- `fread()`: loop based on count of items read

Why `feof()` Cannot Be Used Alone

`feof()` only returns true *after* you attempt to read past the end, not before.

Interviewers love asking this.

16.9 Putting It All Together: Text Copy Program

Here is a classic example combining everything so far:

```
FILE *in = fopen("input.txt", "r");
FILE *out = fopen("output.txt", "w");

if (!in || !out) {
    printf("Error opening file.\n");
    return 1;
}

int ch;
while ((ch = fgetc(in)) != EOF) {
    fputc(ch, out);
}
```

```
fclose(in);
fclose(out);
```

This tiny program handles:

- reading
- writing
- buffering
- EOF logic

Understanding this example means you've mastered the basics of text file I/O.

16.10 Working with Binary Files

Text files are great for human readability, but binary files are the norm in:

- image processing
- audio/video tools
- serialization and persistence
- networking
- embedded systems

Binary I/O treats file data as raw bytes with *no formatting rules*. This gives you speed, precision, and full control over memory layout.

C provides two main functions:

- `fread()` — read binary data
- `fwrite()` — write binary data

Writing Binary Data

```
int x = 100;
FILE *fp = fopen("data.bin", "wb");
fwrite(&x, sizeof(int), 1, fp);
fclose(fp);
```

Meaning:

- Write 1 item
- Each item is `sizeof(int)` bytes
- Get data from &x

Reading Binary Data

```
int x;
FILE *fp = fopen("data.bin", "rb");
fread(&x, sizeof(int), 1, fp);
fclose(fp);
```

Just like that — you have restored the integer *exactly* as it was in memory.

16.11 Binary I/O with Arrays

Binary I/O becomes extremely efficient when dealing with arrays.

Writing an Array

```
int arr[5] = {1,2,3,4,5};

FILE *fp = fopen("arr.bin", "wb");
fwrite(arr, sizeof(int), 5, fp);
fclose(fp);
```

Reading It Back

```
int arr2[5];

FILE *fp = fopen("arr.bin", "rb");
fread(arr2, sizeof(int), 5, fp);
fclose(fp);
```

No loops. No formatting issues. Just raw data in, raw data out.

Interview Tip: Binary I/O is a major performance feature. Senior engineers often use it to build fast storage systems.

16.12 Structs in Binary Files

Binary I/O truly shines with `struct` data — perfect for storing records like:

- student details
- employee databases
- game save files
- sensor logs

Example structure:

```
struct Student {
    int roll;
    float marks;
    char name[30];
};
```

Writing a Struct

```
struct Student s = {1, 92.5, "Alice"};

FILE *fp = fopen("student.bin", "wb");
fwrite(&s, sizeof(s), 1, fp);
fclose(fp);
```

Reading a Struct

```
struct Student s;

FILE *fp = fopen("student.bin", "rb");
fread(&s, sizeof(s), 1, fp);
fclose(fp);
```

Everything — integers, floats, and arrays — is restored exactly as it was.

But here's the catch (and interviewers love this): Structs contain **padding**.

16.13 Understanding Padding and Alignment

C compilers insert extra bytes in structs to ensure data members are aligned properly for the CPU.

Example:

```
struct A {
    char c;    // 1 byte
    int x;     // 4 bytes (alignment may add padding)
};
```

This usually becomes:

c | padding (3 bytes) | x

Meaning the struct takes 8 bytes, not 5.

Why padding exists

Because CPUs read data efficiently when it's aligned to boundaries:

- `int` → usually 4-byte aligned
- `double` → usually 8-byte aligned

Interview Tip: If asked why your struct takes more memory than expected, mention **alignment** and **padding**.

16.14 Padding and Binary Files

Padding is harmless inside RAM, but becomes a problem in files.

If you write a struct with padding to disk:

- a different compiler
- a different CPU

- or even different optimization flags

may produce a completely different padding layout — making your file unreadable on that system.

This is a classic interview question.

Ways to avoid padding issues

- Reorder struct members (largest first)
- Use fixed-width types (`int32_t`, `uint16_t`)
- Manually serialize data (recommended)
- Use `__attribute__((packed))` on GCC (but with caution)

16.15 Endianness — The Hidden Detail Behind Binary Files

Even if padding is handled, binary data still depends on:

Endianness — how a system stores multi-byte values.

- **Little-endian** (Intel): least significant byte first
- **Big-endian** (some network/embedded CPUs): most significant byte first

Example integer:

$$0x12345678$$

Little-endian in memory:

78 56 34 12

Big-endian:

12 34 56 78

Why this matters: Binary files created on a little-endian machine may decode incorrectly on a big-endian system.

Interview Insight: If asked how to fix this — say:

"Always store multi-byte values in a fixed byte order. I prefer writing data byte-by-byte or converting to network byte order using `htonl` and `htons`."

16.16 Detecting Endianness at Runtime

A simple trick:

```
int x = 1;
char *p = (char*)&x;

if (*p == 1)
    printf("Little-endian\n");
else
    printf("Big-endian\n");
```

16.17 lstlistingBinary vs Text I/O — When to Use Which?

Use text files when:

- data must be human-readable
- version control diffs matter
- portability is important

Use binary files when:

- speed is important
- data is numeric or structured
- you want exact memory representation

Interview Summary: Text = readable and portable Binary = fast and precise Pick what the problem requires.

16.18 Random Access in Files: Moving Around Like a Pro

So far, you've been reading files from the beginning to end. But real programs often need to:

- jump to a specific location in the file,
- edit a portion without rewriting everything,
- skip headers or metadata,
- update a specific record in a binary database.

This style of operation is called **random access**, and the three heroes behind it are:

- `fseek()` — move the file pointer
- `ftell()` — tell you where you currently are
- `rewind()` — jump back to the start

Mastering these makes you look like someone who truly understands how low-level file systems work — interviewers immediately notice.

16.19 fseek(): Jump to Any Position

The syntax:

```
int fseek(FILE *fp, long offset, int origin);
```

Arguments:

- `offset` → how many bytes to move
- `origin` → reference point

Allowed origins

- SEEK_SET — beginning of file
- SEEK_CUR — current position
- SEEK_END — end of file

Example: Jump 10 bytes from start

```
fseek(fp, 10, SEEK_SET);
```

Example: Move 4 bytes forward

```
fseek(fp, 4, SEEK_CUR);
```

Example: Move 5 bytes before end

```
fseek(fp, -5, SEEK_END);
```

Note: Negative offsets are allowed for SEEK_CUR and SEEK_END.

16.20 ftell(): Where Are You Right Now?

```
long pos = ftell(fp);
```

This gives the file pointer position (in bytes) from the beginning.

```
printf("Currently at: %ld\n", pos);
```

Interview Tip: If someone asks how to compute file size quickly:

```
fseek(fp, 0, SEEK_END);
long size = ftell(fp);
rewind(fp);
```

This is one of the fastest and simplest methods.

16.21 rewind(): Instantly Reset to Start

```
rewind(fp);
```

Equivalent to:

```
fseek(fp, 0, SEEK_SET);
```

But also clears errors and EOF flags.

16.22 Random Access with Binary Files (The Real Power)

Random access becomes extremely useful when working with fixed-size binary records, like:

- Student databases
- Employee files
- Game save data
- Sensor logs

Consider:

```
struct Student {
    int roll;
    float marks;
    char name[30];
};
```

Each record has size:

```
sizeof(struct Student)
```

Jump to the Nth Record

```
int n = 5; // read the 5th record (0-index or 1-index
     depending on logic)
long offset = (n - 1) * sizeof(struct Student);
```

```
fseek(fp, offset, SEEK_SET);
fread(&s, sizeof(s), 1, fp);
```

Interview Insight: This is EXACTLY how databases, file systems, and index-based storage (like old-school ISAM) work.

16.23 Updating a Record at a Specific Position

You can even modify a record "in place."

```
long offset = (n - 1) * sizeof(struct Student);
fseek(fp, offset, SEEK_SET);

struct Student updated = {...};
fwrite(&updated, sizeof(updated), 1, fp);
```

No need to rewrite the entire file.

This is a huge performance advantage and why binary random access still matters in system programming.

16.24 Iterating Through Records Using fseek()

```
for (int i = 0; i < total; i++) {
    fseek(fp, i * sizeof(struct Student), SEEK_SET);
    fread(&s, sizeof(s), 1, fp);

    printf("%d %s %f\n", s.roll, s.name, s.marks);
}
```

16.25 Random Access in Text Files (Limited but Useful)

Text files do NOT have fixed record sizes. But random access still works for:

- skipping headers
- jumping to known offsets (e.g., CSV with fixed formatting)
- scanning for footers or metadata

Just remember: **Newline characters (\n) count as bytes too.**

16.26 Common Interview Traps Involving fseek()

1. "Can you fseek() on stdin?"

No — only on seekable streams (like disk files).

2. "Does fseek() work on text files the same way?"

Not guaranteed on all platforms; text mode can translate \n to \r\n on Windows. Binary mode is safer.

3. "What happens if you seek past EOF?"

The next write extends the file.

4. "Can you fseek() to a negative position?"

Only relative to SEEK_CUR or SEEK_END, and the final position must remain valid (>= 0).

16.27 Practical Example: Simple File-Based Indexing

Imagine a file with 100 student records. To access roll number 72:

```
index = 72 - 1;
offset = index * sizeof(struct Student);

fseek(fp, offset, SEEK_SET);
fread(&s, sizeof(s), 1, fp);
```

This is the foundation for:

- databases
- key-value stores
- data blocks in filesystems
- memory-mapped structures

Interviewers love when you demonstrate this level of thinking.

16.28 Checking End-of-File and Errors Properly

EOF Check

```
while (fread(&s, sizeof s, 1, fp) == 1) {
```

```
    ...
}
```

Never use:

```
while (!feof(fp))   // Wrong
```

16.29 Summary of Random File I/O

- `fseek()` moves the file pointer with precision.
- `ftell()` tells where you are.
- `rewind()` resets to start.
- Binary random access = powerful, fast, widely used.
- Record-based access is the backbone of many storage systems.
- Interviewers expect you to know fixed-size record navigation.

16.30 Real-World Text File Processing

Most files you work with during college projects, coding tests, or actual software development are plain text files:

- configuration files,
- logs,
- CSV spreadsheets,
- JSON-like structured data,

- program output,
- simple data dumps.

Interviewers often test whether you can:

- read a text file line-by-line,
- parse its contents,
- extract tokens (words, numbers, fields),
- handle unpredictable whitespace safely.

This section will turn you into someone who handles text files confidently.

16.31 Reading a File Line-by-Line Using fgets()

`fgets()` is the safest and most practical way to read a line from a text file.

```
char line[200];

while (fgets(line, sizeof(line), fp) != NULL) {
    printf("Read: %s", line);
}
```

Why `fgets()` and not `scanf()`?

- `fgets()` reads a full line including spaces.
- It prevents buffer overflows (limit is known).
- It stops at newline — convenient for processing.

Common Mistake

Forgetting that `fgets()` retains the \n at the end. Trim it manually if needed.

```
line[strcspn(line, "\n")] = '\0';
```

Interview Tip: If they ask "How do you safely read lines?", always say `fgets()`.

16.32 Splitting a Line Into Tokens

Use `strtok()` to split a string on delimiters.

Example: a CSV-like line

```
char line[] = "Alice,23,Engineer";
char *token = strtok(line, ",");

while (token != NULL) {
    printf("%s\n", token);
    token = strtok(NULL, ",");
}
```

Output:

```
Alice
23
Engineer
```

Important Behavior: `strtok()` modifies the original buffer by inserting \0 characters.

When NOT to use strtok()

When you need:

- thread-safety,
- to tokenize multiple strings in parallel,
- to keep the original string intact.

Then use:

```
strtok_r() // POSIX
strtok_s() // Microsoft
```

16.33 Reading Numbers From a Line

A common interview question is:

"Given a line containing numbers, extract them into an array."

Approach 1 — using `sscanf()`:

```
int a, b, c;
sscanf(line, "%d %d %d", &a, &b, &c);
```

Approach 2 — tokenizing first:

```
char *t = strtok(line, " ");
int arr[20], idx = 0;

while (t != NULL) {
    arr[idx++] = atoi(t);
    t = strtok(NULL, " ");
}
```

Interview Tip: Explain the trade-off:

- `sscanf()` is simple but rigid,
- tokenizing is flexible and robust.

16.34 Counting Words, Lines, and Characters

A practical exercise interviewers LOVE:

"Write a program to count words, lines, and characters in a file."

Pattern:

```
long chars = 0, words = 0, lines = 0;
int in_word = 0;

while (fgets(line, sizeof(line), fp)) {
    for (int i = 0; line[i] != '\0'; i++) {
        chars++;

        if (line[i] == '\n')
            lines++;

        if (isspace(line[i]))
            in_word = 0;
        else if (!in_word) {
            in_word = 1;
            words++;
        }
    }
}
```

This demonstrates:

- state management,
- string parsing,
- text understanding,
- use of `isspace()`.

16.35 Skipping Blank Lines and Comments

Common pattern when parsing configuration files:

```
if (line[0] == '\n' || line[0] == '#') {
    continue; // skip blank or commented line
}
```

This appears in 100s of C projects, including compilers and shells.

16.36 Reading Until a Specific Keyword

Useful in:

- log parsing,
- configuration reading,
- simple interpreters.

```
while (fgets(line, sizeof(line), fp)) {
    if (strstr(line, "ERROR") != NULL) {
        printf("Found error: %s", line);
    }
}
```

16.37 Text File Case Study: Parsing a Student Records File

Suppose the file contains:

```
101,Alice,90
102,Bob,85
```

```
103,Charlie,92
```

Task: read and print structured records.

```
struct Student {
    int roll;
    char name[50];
    int marks;
};

struct Student s;

while (fgets(line, sizeof(line), fp)) {
    char *t = strtok(line, ",");
    s.roll = atoi(t);

    t = strtok(NULL, ",");
    strcpy(s.name, t);

    t = strtok(NULL, ",");
    s.marks = atoi(t);

    printf("%d %s %d\n", s.roll, s.name, s.marks);
}
```

Why interviewers ask this: It demonstrates:

- reading a file safely,
- breaking input into tokens,
- using `structs`,
- combining multiple skills.

16.38 Common Text Parsing Pitfalls

- Forgetting to trim \n

- Assuming fixed number of fields in every line
- Using `atoi()` without validation
- Using `strtok()` on string literals (undefined behavior)
- Not handling empty lines or malformed input

A senior engineer avoids these mistakes instinctively — this section gets you there.

16.39 Quick Recap Before You Move On

Before you turn the page, pause for a moment. File handling is one of those topics that looks simple at first, but it quietly powers everything from operating systems to databases to log parsers to real-world C applications.

Here's what you should feel confident about by now:

- **Opening files safely** using `fopen()` with the correct mode (text vs binary, read vs write vs append).
- **Checking for failures** — every good C programmer tests whether a file pointer is `NULL` before going further.
- **Reading text files** using:
  - `fgetc()` — character-level control
  - `fgets()` — safest way to read full lines
  - `fscanf()` — formatted reading (with caution)

- **Writing to files** with:
  - `fputc()`
  - `fputs()`
  - `fprintf()`
- **Buffering concepts** — how C decides when to flush output, why line-buffered vs fully-buffered matters, and what `fflush()` does.
- **Text parsing fundamentals**: reading line-by-line, trimming newline characters, splitting lines using `strtok()`, and converting tokens to numbers.
- **Binary file operations**: using `fread()` and `fwrite()` to store complete `structs` efficiently and without text conversion overhead.
- **Random file access** via:
  - `fseek()`
  - `ftell()`
  - `rewind()`

  letting you jump anywhere inside a file — essential for building fast lookup tables, indexing systems, or databases.
- **File closing and cleanup**: always finishing with `fclose(fp)` and checking for errors.
- **Real-world parsing techniques**: counting words and lines, skipping blank or commented lines, scanning

logs, processing CSV-style input, and extracting structured data.

If you understand these ideas clearly, you're already ahead of most students — and more importantly, you're thinking in the way real C developers do.

The next chapter will take these skills even further as we explore how file handling connects with data structures, binary storage formats, and building simple data systems.

Take a short break, stretch your hands, and get ready for the next step.

Do-It-Yourself: Practice Zone

This is where the real learning happens. Practice these exercises slowly and intentionally. Every challenge below mirrors the type of questions interviewers ask — because file handling is as much about correctness and safety as it is about understanding how data flows through a program.

Part A — Text File Basics

1. Write a program that opens a text file and prints its contents character-by-character using fgetc(). Try adding line numbers as you print.
2. Write a function `count_lines(const char *filename)` that returns the number of lines in a text file. Handle empty files and missing newline at EOF.
3. Create a program that copies one text file to another using `fgets()` and `fputs()`. Make sure the formatting is preserved exactly.
4. Modify a text file by appending a user-provided message using `"a"` mode. Verify the message was written correctly.

Part B — Parsing and Processing Text

1. Write a function `count_words(const char *filename)` that counts all words in a text file. Consider sequences of whitespace as separators.

2. Given a file of comma-separated integers (e.g., `12,5,40,7,3`), read them into an integer array using `strtok()` and print their sum.
3. Write a log scanner that counts:
   - lines starting with "INFO"
   - lines starting with "WARN"
   - lines starting with "ERROR"

   Useful in many interviews.
4. Create a function `remove_blank_lines(const char *in, const char *out)` that copies only non-empty lines from one file to another.

Part C — Binary Files

1. Define a `struct Student { int roll; float cgpa; }`. Write 10 students to a binary file using `fwrite()`, then read them back using `fread()`.
2. Write a program that appends a single new struct to an existing binary file of students without corrupting earlier entries.
3. Implement random access: create a function `read_student(const char *file, int index)` that seeks to the correct record using:
   - `fseek()`

   - `index * sizeof(struct Student)`

4. Write a program that:
   - stores 100 integers in a binary file
   - seeks to the 50th integer
   - updates only that integer
   - leaves all others untouched

Part D — Robust File Handling

1. Write a "safe open" function:

   ```
   FILE* safe_fopen(const char *name, const char *
    mode);
   ```

   which prints a clear error message and exits if opening fails.

2. Simulate file corruption: write random garbage into a binary file and then write code that detects whether the file contains a valid sequence of integers.

3. Implement a function that reads a file safely into a dynamically allocated buffer, growing the buffer as needed (like `getline()` does on Linux).

4. Create a function `tail(filename, n)` that prints the last `n` lines of a text file — a classic interview question.

Your Challenge — "Mini File Inspector"

Design a small tool that takes a filename and performs:

- count lines
- count words
- detect empty or missing files
- detect binary vs text files
- optionally print the first 5 lines

Add a menu-driven interface and keep it clean, safe, and error-proof. Run it on multiple files — logs, code, CSVs — and observe how your tool behaves.

Pro Tip: Interviewers love candidates who show careful file handling, proper error checks, and clean resource management. These exercises will get you there.

Chapter 17

PREPROCESSORS AND MACROS

Before your C program ever reaches the compiler, something interesting happens behind the scenes. Your code goes through a special "mini-compiler" that prepares it, rewrites it, expands it, cleans it up, and only *then* hands it to the actual compiler.

This hidden step is powered by the **C Preprocessor** — a tool most beginners overlook, but almost every interviewer cares about.

Why? Because preprocessors are where:

- header files get included,
- macros get expanded,
- constants get defined,
- conditional compilation happens,
- and code becomes more flexible, readable, and maintainable.

If pointers show how C thinks about memory, **preprocessors show how C thinks about code itself.**

And here's the good news: Preprocessor concepts look complicated from the outside, but once someone explains them clearly (which is what we'll do here), they become surprisingly logical — even enjoyable.

By the end of this chapter, you'll understand:

- what the preprocessor actually does,
- how macros, constants, and inline snippets work,
- why macros can be both powerful and dangerous,
- how header files are processed internally,
- how conditional compilation helps in real projects,
- and which preprocessor tricks show up repeatedly in interviews.

This chapter aims to make preprocessors feel less like "compiler magic" and more like a practical tool you can use with confidence — whether you're debugging, optimizing, or answering questions in a technical interview.

Let's start by demystifying the preprocessor itself.

17.1 What Exactly Is the Preprocessor?

Before the compiler even looks at your code, the C Preprocessor (often called the cpp stage) performs a series of text transformations. Think of it as a "smart text editor" that prepares your code for compilation.

A simple way to understand it:

Your Code

↓

(Preprocessor edits it)

↓

Compiler gets the final expanded version

The preprocessor does not understand C variables, functions, loops, or data types. It does not check errors in logic. It only works with **plain text**, following commands that begin with #.

What the Preprocessor Actually Does

Here are the four most important responsibilities:

1. **File Inclusion** It pulls in header files using `#include`. This is how your code learns about `printf()`, `malloc()`, and other library functions.

2. **Macro Expansion** It replaces macro names with their

definitions (like a search-and-replace, but smarter).

3. **Conditional Compilation** It allows you to include or exclude sections of code using conditions like `#if`, `#ifdef`, etc.
4. **Symbol Definition** Using `#define`, you can define symbolic constants or short code snippets to reuse.

In short: **The preprocessor prepares your code — the compiler understands it.**

A Helpful Mental Model

Imagine writing an assignment in college. Before submitting it:

- you attach pages from your notebook (like `#include`),
- you replace abbreviations with full forms (like `#define`),
- you strike out parts meant only for you (like `#ifdef DEBUG`),
- and finally you give a clean, ready-to-read version to your professor (like the compiler).

This is exactly how the preprocessor works.

Why Interviewers Love This Topic

Because preprocessors are:

- easy to misuse,

- powerful when used properly,
- something many candidates overlook,
- essential for debugging large projects,
- and the foundation of how headers, macros, and conditional builds work.

Interviewers often ask:

- "What happens during preprocessing?"
- "Explain the difference between a macro and a function."
- "How does `#include` actually work?"
- "Why do we use header guards?"

This chapter prepares you for all of it.

17.2 The `#include` Mechanism — How Header Files Really Work

You've used `#include` since your very first C program:

```
#include <stdio.h>
```

But what really happens when you write this line?

Most students say something like "It includes the file," but interviewers expect a deeper understanding. So here is the full story — clean, simple, and accurate.

What `#include` Actually Does

When the preprocessor sees:

```
#include <stdio.h>
```

it literally **copies the entire contents** of `stdio.h` into your file — before compilation.

Not a function call. Not a library import. Just raw text insertion.

If `stdio.h` is 1000 lines long, all 1000 lines are injected into your file.

This is why preprocessing output becomes huge.

Two Types of Includes

1. Angle Bracket Include

```
#include <stdio.h>
```

This tells the compiler:

- Look for the file in system include directories (like `/usr/include`, compiler-specific folders, etc.)
- Use standard library search paths

This is used for system headers and compiler-provided libraries.

2. Quote Include

```
#include "myheader.h"
```

This tells the compiler:

- Look in the current directory first
- If not found, search in system directories

This is used for your own project headers.

Interview Tip:

If an interviewer asks:

> *“What’s the difference between < > and " " in #include?”*

A clean answer:

> *Angle brackets search system directories only. Quotes search the current directory first, then system directories.*

Short, accurate, and confident.

Why Do We Even Need Header Files?

Headers provide:

- function prototypes (so the compiler knows about available functions)
- type definitions (`typedef`, `struct`, enum)
- macros and constants
- external variable declarations

They help separate:

- **interface** — what your code exposes

- **implementation** — the actual logic in `.c` files

This separation is essential for large projects.

Header Guards — Preventing Multiple Inclusion

What happens if you include the same header file twice?

```
#include "file.h"
#include "file.h"
```

You'll get redefinition errors.

To prevent this, we wrap every header with an "include guard":

```
#ifndef FILE_H
#define FILE_H

// declarations go here

#endif
```

This ensures the content is included only once.

Interview Tip: If asked why we need header guards:

> *"To prevent multiple definition errors during preprocessing."*

Modern Alternative: `#pragma once`

Many compilers support:

```
#pragma once
```

This is shorter and less error-prone, but not part of the C standard.

Mini Example — How #include Expands

If your code is:

```
#include "mathutils.h"

int main() {
    return add(2,3);
}
```

And `mathutils.h` contains:

```
int add(int, int);
```

Then the preprocessor produces:

```
int add(int, int);

int main() {
    return add(2,3);
}
```

The preprocessor literally pastes the header content in place.

Why This Matters for Interviews

Because understanding `#include` helps you explain:

- how the compiler knows about functions
- why forward declarations exist
- how large projects are organized
- why linking errors happen
- how circular includes can break builds

Preprocessors are simple, but their impact is huge.

17.3 Object-Like Macros with `#define` (Constant Substitution)

Now that you understand how `#include` works, let's explore the second most common preprocessor tool you'll see everywhere in C programs:

`#define`

This is the feature that lets you "teach" the preprocessor to replace text before the code even reaches the compiler.

And once again, the preprocessor does not understand C syntax — it performs **pure text substitution**.

What is an Object-Like Macro?

An object-like macro is simply a name that the preprocessor replaces with a value.

Example:

```
#define PI 3.14159
```

Every time the preprocessor sees `PI`, it replaces it with `3.14159` before compilation.

That's it. No variables. No memory. Just substitution.

Macro Expansion Example

Code:

```
#define MAX 100

int arr[MAX];
```

Preprocessor output becomes:

```
int arr[100];
```

This is why macros are sometimes called "compile-time constants."

Why Use `#define` Instead of a Constant Variable?

Interviewers love this question.

A clean answer:

> *#define is handled by the preprocessor — the compiler never sees the macro name. A constant variable uses memory and has a type. A macro is just compile-time text substitution.*

This distinction is important in embedded systems and old C codebases.

Parentheses Matter: Avoid Macro Bugs

Macros do not respect operator precedence. You **must** use parentheses.

```
#define SQUARE(x) x * x    // buggy
```

Watch what happens:

```
int y = SQUARE(3+2);
```

Expands to:

```
int y = 3+2 * 3+2;    // wrong!
```

Correct version:

```
#define SQUARE(x) ((x) * (x))    // safe
```

Interview Tip: If they ask why macros are error-prone, mention the need for parentheses and the fact that macros do not obey C syntax.

Defining Symbolic Flags

Macros are often used for compile-time switches:

```
#define DEBUG
```

Then:

```
#ifdef DEBUG
    printf("Debug mode on\n");
#endif
```

This lets you compile different versions of the same program without modifying source code.

Using `#define` for Constants (The Good and Bad)

Good:

- avoids magic numbers

- easy to change in one place
- compile-time replacement

Bad:

- no type checking
- hard to debug (errors show expanded code)
- overuse leads to unreadability

Modern C code often prefers:

```
const int MAX = 100;
```

But macros still remain essential for:

- conditional compilation
- cross-platform code
- header guards
- performance-critical embedded systems

Predefined Macros You Should Know

The C preprocessor provides several built-in macros:

- `__FILE__` — current filename
- `__LINE__` — current line number
- `__DATE__` — compilation date
- `__TIME__` — compilation time

Example:

```
printf("Error at %s:%d\n", __FILE__, __LINE__);
```

Useful for logging and debugging.

Mini Example: Debugging Macro

```
#define LOG(x)  printf(
"[LOG %s:%d] %s\n",
__FILE__, __LINE__,
x
)

LOG("Program started");
```

This becomes:

```
printf("[LOG main.c:12] Program started\n");
```

Very popular in large codebases.

Interview Insight

If asked:

"Why do programmers still use #define when const variables exist?"

Your short answer:

> *#define works at compile time, has no type, and is required for conditional compilation, header guards, and many low-level patterns.*

Clean. Confident. Professional.

17.4 Function-Like Macros (Powerful but Dangerous)

So far, you've used `#define` to create constant-like values. But the preprocessor can do something even more surprising:

It can create "functions" that run before the compiler runs.

These are called **function-like macros**, and you'll definitely see them in old C codebases, embedded systems, and system-level projects.

They look like real functions — but they are actually just text substitutions with arguments.

Basic Syntax

```
#define ADD(a, b)  ( (a) + (b) )
```

Using it:

```
int x = ADD(10, 20);    // expands to: ( (10) + (20) )
```

There is **no actual function call** here. The compiler sees only the expanded expression.

Why Use Function-Like Macros?

Before inline functions existed, this was the only way to avoid function call overhead in performance-critical code.

Even today, macros are used when:

- You want to write platform-independent code
- You need conditional compilation inside "function-like" logic
- You write code that must work in pre-C99 environments
- You want to create simple wrappers around repeated expressions

Interviewers love asking about macros because you must understand the risks.

The Biggest Danger: No Type Checking

A macro doesn't know what types you pass:

```
#define MUL(a, b)  ((a) * (b))
```

This works:

```
MUL(3, 4)
```

But this also works:

```
MUL("hello", 5)   //  compiles, but meaningless
```

The compiler complains only after expansion, not at the macro itself.

Interview Insight: If asked "Why are macros unsafe?" mention **lack of type checking** first.

Parentheses Are Mandatory

This is the #1 source of macro bugs.

Consider the classic broken example:

```
#define SQUARE(x) x * x     //  wrong
```

Test it:

```
int y = SQUARE(3 + 2);
```

It expands to:

```
int y = 3 + 2 * 3 + 2;    //  wrong math
```

Correct version:

```
#define SQUARE(x)   ((x) * (x))   //  safe
```

Rule of macros:

> **Wrap everything in parentheses. Always.**

Another Subtle Bug: Arguments May Be Evaluated Multiple Times

Example:

```
#define INC_AND_GET(x)   (++(x))
```

This is fine.

But consider:

```
#define DOUBLE(x)   ((x) + (x))
```

What happens here?

```
int i = 5;
int y = DOUBLE(i++);    // Uh oh
```

Expands to:

```
int y = ((i++) + (i++));    //  double increment!
```

Interview Tip: If asked "Why shouldn't you pass expressions with side effects to macros?" —this is the exact reason.

Safer Alternative: Inline Functions

Modern C allows you to write efficient, type-safe replacements:

```
inline int add(int a, int b) {
    return a + b;
}
```

Many macros can (and should) be replaced with inline functions.

But macros still matter for:

- Debug logging
- Compile-time checks
- Platform-specific blocks
- Expression wrappers
- Code that must run before type-checking

Function-Like Macros in Real Code

Logging:

```
#define LOG(msg) \
    printf("[LOG %s:%d] %s\n", __FILE__, __LINE__, msg)
```

Min/max operations:

```
#define MAX(a,b)    ((a) > (b) ? (a) : (b))
#define MIN(a,b)    ((a) < (b) ? (a) : (b))
```

Compile-time assertions:

```
#define STATIC_ASSERT(cond, msg) \
    typedef char static_assertion_##msg[(cond)?1:-1]
```

(Very common in low-level system code!)

Interview Insight

If an interviewer asks:

> *"When should you avoid function-like macros?"*

Your safe, strong answer:

> *Avoid macros when a normal function or inline function can do the job. Macros have no type checking, poor debuggability, and can evaluate arguments multiple times.*

Perfect answer. Reliable. Memorably short.

17.5 The `do {...} while(0)` Macro Pattern (Professional-Grade Macros)

If you ever look at real-world C libraries — Linux kernel, BSD code, embedded firmware, or even popular open-source projects — you will eventually see this:

```
#define SAFE_RUN(x)     \
    do {                \
        x;              \
    } while (0)
```

Students often ask:

> **"Why on earth would anyone wrap a macro in a do-while loop?"**

The answer is: *to make multi-statement macros behave like a single safe statement.*

And interviewers love this question because not many people know the **real** reason behind it.

Let's break it down in the cleanest possible way.

The Problem With Multi-Statement Macros

Consider this macro:

```
#define SWAP(a, b)  temp = a; a = b; b = temp;
```

Looks innocent.

But what if you use it in an `if` statement?

```
if (x > y)
```

```
    SWAP(x, y);
else
    printf("Not swapped\n");
```

It expands to:

```
if (x > y)
    temp = x; x = y; y = temp;;
else
    printf("Not swapped\n");
```

This breaks the control flow — the compiler thinks your `else` belongs to `x = y`, not the original `if`.

This is a classic macro bug.

The Solution: Force the Macro Into a Single Controlled Block

The famous pattern fixes everything:

```
#define SWAP(a, b)                  \
    do {                            \
        temp = a;                   \
        a = b;                      \
        b = temp;                   \
    } while(0)
```

Now the macro ALWAYS expands into a single statement:

```
do {
    temp = a;
    a = b;
    b = temp;
} while (0);
```

This behaves exactly like a normal function call.

No dangling else. No syntactic surprises.

Why `while(0)`? Why not `while(1)`?

Because:

- `while(0)` executes the block exactly once.
- The semicolon after the macro expands becomes the semicolon after the loop.
- It behaves just like a single function call with a trailing semicolon.

This is the safest structure that survives all tricky usage patterns.

Real-World Example: Linux Kernel

The kernel uses this pattern everywhere, often in error-handling macros:

```
#define WARN_IF(cond, msg)                  \
    do {                                    \
        if (cond)                           \
            printk("Warning: %s\n", msg);\
    } while (0)
```

Why?

Because people will call this macro inside `if`, `for`, loops, and nested logic. The pattern ensures it will **never** break code structure.

What Makes This an Interview Favorite?

Because it tests real, practical knowledge.

A typical interview question:

"Why do macros often use `do{...}while(0)`?"

Your answer should be:

"It forces the macro to behave like a single statement. It prevents bugs when using the macro inside if/else structures, and allows a safe trailing semicolon after the macro call."

Perfect. Concise. Confident.

One More Benefit: Local Scope

The block gives temporary variables a clean scope:

```
#define WITH_TEMP(a, b)        \
    do {                       \
        int temp = a;          \
        a = b;                 \
        b = temp;              \
    } while(0)
```

Outside the macro, `temp` does not pollute your namespace.

This makes macro-based operations safer and cleaner.

When Should YOU Use This Pattern?

Use it when writing macros that contain:

- more than one statement

- control-flow logic (if/else)
- temporary variables
- early exits

Avoid using it for single-expression macros like:

```
#define MAX(a,b) ((a) > (b) ? (a) : (b))
```

Those do not need the wrapper.

Your Takeaway

The moment you start writing multi-line macros, this pattern becomes your shield.

It turns fragile macros into safe, professional-grade tools.

And understanding it is one of the clearest signals that you're no longer writing "beginner C." You're writing *real-world C* — the kind interviewers respect.

17.6 Macro Operators: # and ## (Stringizing & Token-Pasting)

The C preprocessor isn't just about replacing text — it can also *transform* your code in surprisingly powerful ways.

Two special operators, # and ##, turn macros into a miniature code-generation engine. These appear everywhere in production C code, and interviewers love them because they test whether you understand what happens *before* compilation.

Let's explore both operators with clean examples and an intuitive explanation.

The # Operator — "Stringizing"

The # operator converts a macro argument into a string literal.

```
#define STR(x)    #x

printf("%s", STR(Hello));
```

Expands into:

```
printf("%s", "Hello");
```

Yes — the macro literally wraps the token `Hello` in quotes.

This is incredibly useful for:

- debugging
- logging
- generating readable messages
- printing variable names along with their values

Real-World Debug Example

```
#define DEBUG_VAR(v)  printf(#v " = %d\n", v);
```

If you write:

```
DEBUG_VAR(score);
```

It becomes:

```
printf("score = %d\n", score);
```

Super clean, and incredibly useful when debugging complex logic.

The ## Operator — "Token Pasting"

If # is about converting things into strings, ## is about gluing tokens together to create new identifiers.

```
#define MAKE_VAR(name, num)   name##num
```

Usage:

```
int MAKE_VAR(value, 1) = 10;
```

Expands to:

```
int value1 = 10;
```

This allows macros to generate variable names, function names, or struct field names dynamically.

When is token-pasting used?

- implementing generic containers
- auto-generating getters/setters
- building test frameworks

- building domain-specific languages (DSLs)
- combining names based on parameters

Putting Them Together: Powerful Patterns

You can combine both operators inside a single macro:

```
#define LOG_VALUE(name, value) \
    printf(#name ": %d\n", value)
```

Or even use ## to build identifiers and # to print them:

```
#define MAKE_AND_PRINT(base, id)        \
    int base##id = id * 100;            \
    printf(#base #id " = %d\n", base##id);
```

Calling:

```
MAKE_AND_PRINT(x, 7);
```

Becomes:

```
int x7 = 700;
printf("x7 = %d\n", x7);
```

This is the level of macro usage found in system libraries.

Building a Tiny Generic Function Using

Let's create a function that prints arrays of integers or floats using the same macro:

```
#define MAKE_PRINTER(type)                          \
    void print_##type(type *arr, int n) {           \
        for (int i = 0; i < n; ++i)                 \
            printf("%f ", (double)arr[i]);          \
```

```
        printf("\n");                            \
    }
```

Usage:

```
MAKE_PRINTER(int)
MAKE_PRINTER(float)
```

Expands to two functions:

`print_int()` and `print_float()`.

A lot of C libraries do exactly this to simulate generics.

Interview Tip: What Should You Say?

If asked:

"What do the # and ## operators do?"

Your answer:

> **"The # operator converts a macro argument into a string literal. The ## operator concatenates two tokens to form a new identifier. These features allow macros to generate readable logs and dynamic function or variable names."**

That answer covers both purpose and real-world use — interviewers love it.

Common Pitfalls (Interview Favorite)

- Stringizing happens **before** macro expansion of arguments.

- Token-pasting only works with valid identifiers — you cannot paste tokens that result in invalid C syntax.
- Overuse of token-pasting creates unreadable code; use it wisely.

Most candidates either don't know these or explain them incorrectly. Your job is simply to be clear and calm — the interviewer will spot that immediately.

Your Takeaway

Both operators extend the C preprocessor from a text-replacement tool into a flexible code-generation system.

> **The moment you understand # and ##, you unlock a whole new level of expressive power in C.**

They are fun, powerful, and surprisingly elegant — once you get used to thinking like the preprocessor.

17.7 Variadic Macros, Debug Macros, and Error-Handling Macros

By now, you've seen how macros can mimic functions, generate code, and even build identifiers dynamically. But the C preprocessor has one more superpower: **it can accept a variable number of arguments** — just like `printf()`.

These are called **variadic macros**, and they're essential for writing clean, debuggable, production-quality C.

Let's explore them step by step.

Variadic Macros — Macros That Behave Like printf

A variadic macro uses `...` to accept any number of extra arguments.

```
#define LOG(fmt, ...)   printf(fmt, __VA_ARGS__)
```

Usage:

```
LOG("Sum = %d\n", a + b);
```

Expands to:

```
printf("Sum = %d\n", a + b);
```

This lets you write wrapper macros around `printf`, `fprintf`, or any function that accepts a flexible argument list.

Safer Version

```
#define LOG(fmt, ...)    \
    do { printf("[LOG] " fmt, __VA_ARGS__); } while (0)
```

Why use the `do    while(0)` trick? It ensures the macro behaves like a single statement even inside `if-else` blocks.

This is one of the most commonly used macro patterns in the C ecosystem.

Debug Macros — Enable or Disable Prints Automatically

Every real C project needs debug prints. But nobody wants to manually comment/uncomment them everywhere.

Enter debug macros.

```
#ifdef DEBUG
  #define DEBUG_PRINT(fmt, ...) \
      printf("[DEBUG] " fmt, __VA_ARGS__)
#else
  #define DEBUG_PRINT(fmt, ...) \
      do {} while (0)
#endif
```

Usage:

```
DEBUG_PRINT("x = %d\n", x);
```

If you compile with:

```
gcc -DDEBUG file.c
```

You get debug logs.

If you compile normally:

```
gcc file.c
```

All debug messages disappear — zero cost, zero overhead.

Interview Insight: This is how logging works in embedded systems and performance-critical applications.

Debug Macro with File and Line Info

Many debugging macros include file name and line number automatically:

```
#define DEBUG_PRINT(fmt, ...) \
    printf("[%s:%d] " fmt, __FILE__,
    __LINE__, __VA_ARGS__)
```

This prints:

```
[main.c:42] x = 10
```

The interview-level takeaway:

> **__FILE__, __LINE__ and variadic macros give you powerful debugging tools for free.**

Error-Handling Macros — Cleaner, Faster, Safer Code

Variadic macros help centralize error handling.

Here's a simple example:

```
#define DIE(fmt, ...) \
    do { \
        fprintf(stderr, "[FATAL] " fmt, __VA_ARGS__); \
        exit(1); \
    } while (0)
```

Usage:

```
if (!ptr)
    DIE("Allocation failed for size %zu\n", size);
```

This is extremely common in production C — especially system utilities or CLI tools.

Professional Tip: Centralizing all fatal error handling in one macro improves readability and guarantees a consistent format across your project.

Automatic Cleanup: Validate and Jump

Many C programmers also create "validate" macros that reduce boilerplate:

```
#define CHECK(ptr) \
    do { \
        if (!(ptr)) { \
            fprintf(stderr, "Null pointer: %s:%d\n", \
                    __FILE__, __LINE__); \
            goto cleanup; \
        } \
    } while (0)
```

Usage:

```
CHECK(buffer);
CHECK(file);
CHECK(result);
```

Suddenly 10 lines of error-checking shrink to one line each.

Interview Tip: If asked about error handling in C, mention:

- centralized error macros
- __FILE__ and __LINE__
- cleanup labels with `goto`

This demonstrates maturity in writing real-world C.

Silent Consumption of Empty Variadic Arguments

C99 introduced a special GNU extension: `__VA_OPT__`.

It allows macros to handle "no extra arguments" cleanly.

```
#define LOG(fmt, ...) \
    printf(fmt __VA_OPT__(,) __VA_ARGS__)
```

This avoids trailing commas when no extra args are passed.

Example:

```
LOG("hello");
LOG("x = %d", x);
```

Expands cleanly in both cases.

Note: Supported by GCC/Clang, not by strict old C99 compilers.

Real-World Pattern: ASSERT Macros

Assertions are extremely common in C projects.

```
#define ASSERT(expr) \
    do { \
        if (!(expr)) { \
            fprintf(stderr, "Assertion failed:
                    %s (%s:%d)\n", \
                    #expr, __FILE__, __LINE__); \
            abort(); \
        } \
    } while (0)
```

Usage:

```
ASSERT(ptr != NULL);
```

The key detail?

The expression itself is stringized using #expr.

This directly connects to the macro operators learned earlier — perfect interview synergy.

Interview Summary: What to Say

If an interviewer asks:

"Why do we use variadic macros?"

Your response should be:

> **"They let us build printf-like logging, debugging, and error-handling tools without writing repetitive code. They make C projects more maintainable and keep error handling consistent."**

If they ask:

"How do debugging macros work?"

You say:

> **"By wrapping logs inside #ifdef DEBUG, we can enable or disable them at compile time with zero runtime cost."**

These are interview-winning answers.

Your Takeaway

Variadic macros are one of the most practical features of the C preprocessor.

They help you write:

- clean logging systems
- structured error handlers
- debug tools with file + line numbers
- consistent assert frameworks
- maintainable codebases with fewer repetitive patterns

Once you master them, macros stop being “weird syntax” and become a real power tool in your C programming toolbox.

17.8 Conditional Compilation — Controlling What Gets Compiled

The C preprocessor can do more than replace text or generate code. It can also decide *which parts of your program will even be compiled.*

This is called **conditional compilation**, and it is one of the most powerful features in C.

Programmers use it to:

- enable or disable debugging features
- compile different code on Linux, Windows, or macOS
- switch between optimized and safe versions of a function
- include experimental features only when needed
- avoid multiple inclusion of header files

Interviews LOVE this topic, especially system-level and embedded interviews.

Let's break it down.

#ifdef — "Compile this block only if defined"

```
#ifdef DEBUG
    printf("Debug mode ON\n");
#endif
```

If you compile with:

```
gcc -DDEBUG file.c
```

The code inside the block becomes active.

If not, it disappears completely — it's as if it never existed.

Use case: Debugging, logging, optional features.

#ifndef — "Compile if NOT defined"

Commonly used in header guards:

```
#ifndef MY_HEADER_H
#define MY_HEADER_H

// declarations here

#endif
```

Meaning: - If macro is **not** defined → compile the block. - If already defined → skip it.

This prevents duplicate declarations when a header is included multiple times.

Interview Tip: If asked, say:

> "Header guards prevent multiple inclusion by ensuring the header is compiled only once."

#if — Compile only if the condition is true

#if allows numeric expressions.

```
#define VERSION 2

#if VERSION >= 2
    printf("New feature enabled\n");
#endif
```

You can do comparisons, arithmetic, even nested conditions.

This is extremely useful in cross-platform code.

#elif — "Else if" for conditional compilation

```
#if VERSION == 1
    printf("Legacy mode\n");
```

```
#elif VERSION == 2
    printf("Modern mode\n");
#else
    printf("Unknown version\n");
#endif
```

This lets you build multi-branch compile-time logic.

#else — the default case

If all previous conditions fail:

```
#if LEVEL == 0
    ...
#else
    ...
#endif
```

Simple, predictable, and widely used.

Practical Example: Cross-Platform Code

Real production C code often looks like this:

```
#if defined(_WIN32)
    printf("Running on Windows\n");
#elif defined(__linux__)
    printf("Running on Linux\n");
#elif defined(__APPLE__)
    printf("Running on macOS\n");
#else
    printf("Unknown OS\n");
#endif
```

This is how libraries and system tools adapt to different operating systems.

Interview Gold: Understanding platform macros

shows that you're comfortable writing portable, real-world C.

Practical Example: Enable Debug + Verbose Modes

```
#ifdef DEBUG
    #define LOG(...) printf(__VA_ARGS__)
#else
    #define LOG(...) do{}while(0)
#endif

#ifdef VERBOSE
    #define TRACE(...) printf("[TRACE] " __VA_ARGS__)
#else
    #define TRACE(...) do{}while(0)
#endif
```

Compiled with:

```
gcc -DDEBUG -DVERBOSE file.c
```

It activates both debug levels.

Takeaway: You decide at compile time what parts of the program exist.

Feature Flags — Provide Optional Functionality

```
#define FEATURE_X

#ifdef FEATURE_X
void run_feature_x() { printf("Feature X active\n"); }
#endif
```

This is how large C programs keep experimental or optional modules without removing them.

Compile-Time Error Triggers

You can force errors using #error:

```
#ifndef CONFIG_OK
#error "Configuration missing!"
#endif
```

This stops compilation immediately.

Use case: Prevent building the program incorrectly.

Conditional Includes

Even #include can be conditional:

```
#if defined(USE_FAST_MATH)
    #include "fast_math.h"
#else
    #include "safe_math.h"
#endif
```

This helps you:

- switch libraries at compile time
- support multiple backends
- reduce code duplication

Interview Answers You Should Give

If asked:

"Why do we use conditional compilation?"

Say:

"It lets us enable/disable features, debug

> **modes, or platform-specific code at compile time. It keeps the final binary lean and avoids unnecessary runtime checks."**

If they ask:

"What's the difference between #if and #ifdef?"

Say:

> **"#ifdef checks if a name is defined. #if evaluates a numeric expression."**

Short, clear, precise — exactly what interviewers want.

Your Takeaway

Conditional compilation turns the C preprocessor into a **feature switchboard**. It gives you:

- platform-specific builds
- debug and verbose modes
- experimental feature flags
- safe header guards
- compile-time validation
- zero-cost configuration

Once you master it, you'll write cleaner, safer, more flexible C than most beginners ever will.

17.9 The Full Power of `#include`, Header Guards, and Modular Project Structure

By now, you've seen how macros and conditional compilation can shape your code at compile time. But there's another superpower of the preprocessor that every serious C programmer must master:

Organizing code across multiple files using `#include`.

If pointers are the "brain" of C, then modular structure is its "architecture." Without it, large programs become messy, duplicated, or unmaintainable. Interviewers frequently test this topic because it reveals whether you can write clean, scalable C beyond a single file.

Let's explore this in a friendly, practical way.

Why Do We Even Need Multiple Files?

Small programs fit in a single file. But real projects use multiple modules:

- one file for math utilities
- one for file handling
- one for network logic
- one for linked lists, etc.

Separating code improves:

- readability
- debugging
- reusability
- collaboration in teams

This is where headers and `#include` come in.

What `#include` Actually Does

Many students think `#include` "links files together." Not true.

It literally performs a *copy–paste* of the contents of the included file into the source file.

Example:

```
#include "mathutils.h"
```

This tells the preprocessor:

- open mathutils.h
- copy its contents
- paste them right here

That's it. No magic — just text insertion before compilation begins.

Header Files: Your Project's "Interface" Layer

A header file typically contains:

- function declarations
- struct and enum definitions
- macros and constants
- typedefs

Example:

```
// mathutils.h
int add(int a, int b);
int subtract(int a, int b);
```

And the corresponding implementation:

```
// mathutils.c
#include "mathutils.h"

int add(int a, int b) { return a + b; }
int subtract(int a, int b) { return a - b; }
```

Your main file:

```
// main.c
#include <stdio.h>
#include "mathutils.h"

int main() {
    printf("%d\n", add(5,3));
}
```

This structure is used in almost every professional C program.

Why Header Guards Are Essential

Since `#include` just copies and pastes content, accidentally including a file twice is very easy —

and dangerous.

- Struct redefinitions → compilation error
- Function declarations repeated → harmless but messy
- Macro collisions → subtle bugs

To prevent this, we wrap headers in guards:

```
// mathutils.h
#ifndef MATHUTILS_H
#define MATHUTILS_H

int add(int a, int b);
int subtract(int a, int b);

#endif
```

Now even if included multiple times, the content is compiled once.

Interview Tip: If asked, answer like this:

> "Header guards prevent multiple inclusion by ensuring the header is processed only once during preprocessing."

Short. Sharp. Perfect.

Common Variations: `#pragma once`

Some compilers allow:

```
#pragma once
```

This also prevents re-inclusion. It's cleaner, but not

standard C — interviewers may ask this!

Best answer:

> "#pragma once is simpler but not part of the C standard. Header guards are portable and recommended."

Where to Put What? (Beginner-Friendly Rules)

Headers (.h) should contain:

- function declarations
- typedefs, enums, structs
- macros and constants
- documentation on how to use the module

Source files (.c) should contain:

- function **definitions**
- static helper functions
- internal logic not exposed publicly

Think of .h as the interface and .c as the implementation.

Practical Example: A Modular String Library

```
// strutils.h
#ifndef STRUTILS_H
#define STRUTILS_H

int count_words(const char *s);
```

```
int is_palindrome(const char *s);

#endif
```

```
// strutils.c
#include "strutils.h"
#include <ctype.h>
#include <string.h>

int count_words(const char *s) { ... }
int is_palindrome(const char *s) { ... }
```

```
// main.c
#include <stdio.h>
#include "strutils.h"

int main() {
    printf("%d\n", count_words("hello world"));
}
```

This structure mirrors how real libraries like OpenSSL, SQLite, and GTK are organized.

Conditional Includes: The Professional Touch

Using conditions with includes gives maximum flexibility:

```
#if defined(_WIN32)
  #include "windows_network.h"
#else
  #include "posix_network.h"
#endif
```

This is how:

- cross-platform networking libraries
- database systems

- embedded firmware

stay portable.

Static vs. Extern: Keeping Symbols Clean

Headers often include:

```
extern int global_counter;
```

Definition goes in exactly one .c:

```
int global_counter = 0;
```

Why? To avoid "multiple definition" errors during linking.

Similarly, "private" functions in a module should be:

```
static int helper() { ... }
```

Static restricts their visibility to that file only.

How to Structure a Real Project

A clean project looks like this:

```
project/
  include/
    mathutils.h
    strutils.h
  src/
    mathutils.c
    strutils.c
    main.c
  Makefile
```

Compile with:

```
gcc src/*.c -I include -o app
```

Neat. Modular. Professional.

Interview Question Patterns You MUST Nail

Q. Why use header files? A. To separate declarations from definitions, improve modularity, and support multi-file programs.

Q. What are header guards? Why required? A. To prevent multiple inclusion errors and redefinition conflicts.

Q. Difference between `#include <...>` and `#include "..."` ? A. Angle brackets search system paths; quotes search locally first.

Q. Why is `#pragma once` not fully reliable? A. It's non-standard; header guards are portable.

Q. What is the role of `extern`? A. Declares a variable defined elsewhere.

These appear constantly in interview MCQs and oral rounds.

Your Takeaway

After mastering this section, you can:

- organize programs cleanly across multiple files
- write reusable interfaces in headers

- protect headers using guards
- use conditional includes for cross-platform code
- avoid linking errors by proper declaration/definition separation

This is one of the biggest "level-up" jumps in C — you are now writing code the way real software engineers do.

17.10 Quick Recap Before You Move On

Before you step into the next chapter, here's a friendly, high-impact summary of everything you learned about preprocessors and macros. If you understand these points well, you're already ahead of most candidates in interviews.

- The C preprocessor runs **before compilation**, performing text substitution, conditional inclusion, macro expansion, and file inclusion.
- **#include** literally pastes external file contents into your code — knowing the difference between angle brackets < > and quotes " " helps you manage project structure cleanly.
- **#define** creates constants or expression-like macros. Parentheses matter. A lot. *Always wrap parameters and the full macro body.*
- Macros are not functions — they don't do type-checking, argument evaluation rules differ, and

debugging can be messy. This is why parentheses and careful design matter.

- Use **do { ... } while(0)** for multi-statement macros. It prevents if/else bugs and turns the macro into a single clean statement.
- Macros can evaluate arguments multiple times — this is a common source of tricky bugs. Inline functions are often safer and cleaner.
- The preprocessor offers powerful tools:
  - **#** for stringizing
  - **##** for token pasting
  - __FILE__, __LINE__, __DATE__, __TIME__ for metadata

  These
  let you build debugging tools, logging mechanisms, and even code generators.
- Conditional compilation with **#if**, **#ifdef**, **#ifndef**, and friends allows you to create platform-specific, version-specific, or debug-mode-specific builds with minimal effort.
- Macro pitfalls every good programmer knows:
  - missing parentheses
  - multiple evaluation
  - variable shadowing

  - unsafe expansion in if/else blocks
  - harder debugging due to text substitution

- Best practices:
  - Prefer ALL_CAPS names for macros
  - Use inline functions when possible
  - Wrap macro bodies safely
  - Avoid creating new variables inside macros unless absolutely necessary
  - Keep macros simple, clear, and predictable

You've just completed one of the most "interview-dense" topics in the C language. Most candidates fear macros; you now understand not just how to use them, but how to avoid their traps and write them like a professional.

Take a breath — you earned it.

Do-It-Yourself: Practice Zone

This is where you turn understanding into confidence. Try these exercises on your own — each one is intentionally designed to build the exact skills interviewers look for when they ask about macros, conditional compilation, and preprocessor behavior.

Part A — Preprocessor Fundamentals

1. Write a program that prints the values of `__FILE__`, `__LINE__`, `__DATE__`, and `__TIME__`. Now modify the file and observe which macros change.
2. Create a header file `config.h` with:

   ```
   #define VERSION 3
   #define FEATURE_X 1
   ```

   Include it in a C file and print both macros. Then try removing them and see how the compiler behaves.
3. Use `#ifndef` to write an include guard for a header file named `mylib.h`. Verify it prevents multiple inclusion.

Part B — Macro Writing Skills

1. Create a macro `SQR(x)` that safely computes `(x)*(x)` without double-evaluating `x`. Test it with:

   ```
   SQR(3+2)
   SQR(i++)
   ```

2. Write a macro MAX(a,b) with full parentheses. Then purposely remove parentheses and demonstrate the bug it produces.

3. Implement a multi-statement macro SWAP(a,b) for integers using the do ... while(0) pattern. Explain why this wrapper is necessary.

4. Use the # operator to turn:

   ```
   LOG(x)
   ```

   into: printf("x = %d
   textbackslash n", x);

Part C — Token Pasting, Conditional Compilation, Debug Modes

1. Write a macro that uses ## to generate variable names:

   ```
   #define MAKE_VAR(id) var_##id
   ```

   Use it to create variables var_a, var_b, and assign values.

2. Create a debug logging system:

   ```
   #ifdef DEBUG
       #define LOG(x)  printf("DEBUG: %s:%d --> %s\n", \
                               __FILE__, __LINE__, x)
   #else
       #define LOG(x)
   #endif
   ```

   Write a program that compiles differently with and

without `-DDEBUG`.

3. Write code that uses:
    - `#if VERSION >= 3`
    - `#elif VERSION == 2`
    - `#else`

    to conditionally enable different feature messages.

Part D — Mini Project: "Build Your Own Configurable Logger"

Create a file `logger.h` that contains:

- a `LOG(msg)` macro with file/line metadata
- a `WARN(msg)` macro that prints only when `ENABLE_WARN` is defined
- an `ERROR(msg)` macro that always prints

Then:

1. Compile the program normally — only `ERROR` messages show.
2. Compile with `-DENABLE_WARN` — now warnings appear.
3. Compile with `-DDEBUG` — add debug-level logs too.

Pro Tip: This mini-project teaches you exactly what real projects use: flexible builds, debug flags, and environment-driven behaviors.

Final Challenge — "Macro Analyzer"

Write a small program that prints out:

- whether the build is debug or release
- the version number
- the compiler used (`__GNUC__`, `__clang__`, etc.)
- the file name and line number

Use conditional compilation to adapt behavior based on these macros.

This tiny tool helps you understand exactly how large C projects use preprocessors to manage platform differences and debug modes.

Chapter 18

ADVANCED C CONCEPTS

If you've reached this chapter, take a moment and appreciate how far you've come.

You've already mastered pointers, memory management, dynamic allocation, file handling, preprocessors, and macros. That alone puts you ahead of most learners.

But there's still one more category of ideas that interviewers love asking about — the "miscellaneous advanced topics" of C. These don't belong inside a single theme like memory or structs, but together they reveal a programmer's *true* depth of understanding.

This chapter brings together those powerful concepts.

Why this chapter matters for interviews:

When interviewers want to go beyond syntax-level knowledge, they test whether you understand:

- how programs receive data from the command line
- how C interacts with the machine through bits and flags
- how compilers optimize code — and how to prevent unsafe optimizations
- how memory alignment and padding affect performance
- how storage classes change the lifetime and visibility of variables

These topics are small individually, but together they form the backbone of systems-level C. Understanding them makes you sound sharp, confident, and comfortable with low-level ideas — exactly the impression you want to make in interviews.

What you'll learn in this chapter:

- Command-line arguments: `argc`, `argv`, and real interview examples
- Bitwise
  operators and how to use them to manipulate flags and registers
- The `volatile` keyword — why compilers "optimize too much"
- Memory alignment and padding inside structures
- Storage classes like `extern`, `static`, and `register`

- Common pitfalls, undefined behaviors, and tricky interview questions

This chapter stays true to the spirit of the book: **friendly, deep, and deliberately paced** — always focusing on understanding, not memorizing.

You'll find diagrams, real-world explanations, and interview insights throughout. By the time you finish, topics that once looked intimidating will feel logical and approachable.

Let's begin.

18.1 Command-Line Arguments: `argc` and `argv`

Most beginners meet `main()` only in its simplest form:

```
int main() {
    ...
}
```

But real-world C programs almost always use a more powerful version:

```
int main(int argc, char *argv[])
```

This version allows your program to receive inputs directly from the command line — a skill that shows up frequently in interviews because it demonstrates that you can work with "real" C programs rather than classroom-style examples.

What Are argc and argv?

- **argc** (argument count) The number of arguments passed to the program, including the program name.
- **argv** (argument vector) An array of char*, where each element points to one argument string.

If you run:

```
./a.out hello world
```

Then:

- argc == 3
- argv[0] == "./a.out"
- argv[1] == "hello"
- argv[2] == "world"

A Simple Example

```
#include <stdio.h>

int main(int argc, char *argv[]) {
    printf("Number of arguments: %d\n", argc);

    for (int i = 0; i < argc; i++) {
        printf("argv[%d] = %s\n", i, argv[i]);
    }

    return 0;
}
```

Try running:

```
./a.out apple banana cherry
```

You will see all three printed.

Why Do Interviewers Ask About This?

Because it demonstrates that you understand:

- how C handles arrays of strings
- how pointers to pointers work (`char **argv`)
- how real-world software accepts user input

It also naturally leads into discussions about:

- dynamic memory (parsing long argument lists)
- file handling (passing filenames as arguments)
- validation (checking whether input exists)

A More Practical Example: Summing Numbers

```
#include <stdio.h>
#include <stdlib.h>

int main(int argc, char *argv[]) {
    if (argc < 2) {
        printf("Usage: %s <numbers>\n", argv[0]);
        return 1;
    }

    int sum = 0;

    for (int i = 1; i < argc; i++) {
        sum += atoi(argv[i]);    // convert string to int
    }

    printf("Sum = %d\n", sum);
    return 0;
}
```

Run:

```
./a.out 5 10 15
```

Output:

```
Sum = 30
```

Common Interview Questions

1. Why does argv have type char **?
2. What is argv[argc] guaranteed to contain? (A null pointer.)
3. Can you modify argv inside the program?
4. Why is argv[0] not always the actual file name?

Interview Tip: If asked to explain argv, don't just say "array of strings." Say: *"argv is an array of character pointers, where each pointer refers to a null-terminated string passed from the command line."*

18.2 Bitwise Operations — Working Directly with Bits

Up to now, most of the data processing you've done in C has been at the level of integers, characters, or arrays. But behind every variable, every value, and every operation is a pattern of bits — 0s and 1s moving through memory and registers.

Bitwise operators give you **direct control** over those

bits.

This is the level of control system programmers, embedded engineers, and interviewers expect you to be comfortable with. And the good news? Bitwise operations are far less mysterious than students fear. Once you understand them, they feel surprisingly elegant.

C provides six bitwise operators:

- & — bitwise AND
- | — bitwise OR
- ^ — bitwise XOR
- ~ — bitwise NOT
- << — left shift
- >> — right shift

Let's walk through them one by one, with simple, interview-friendly examples.

Bitwise AND (&)

This operator compares each bit of two numbers: a bit is 1 only if **both** corresponding bits are 1.

```
int a = 6;    // 110
int b = 5;    // 101

int c = a & b;    // 100  (decimal 4)
```

Uses:

- masking bits (turning unwanted bits off)

- checking if certain flags are set

Bitwise OR (|)

A bit becomes 1 if **either** operand has a 1.

```
int a = 6;    // 110
int b = 5;    // 101

int c = a | b;    // 111  (decimal 7)
```

Uses:

- turning flags ON
- combining bitfields

Bitwise XOR (^)

A bit becomes 1 only if the bits are different.

```
int a = 6;    // 110
int b = 5;    // 101

int c = a ^ b;    // 011  (decimal 3)
```

Uses:

- toggling bits
- detecting changes
- a classic interview trick: swap two numbers without a temp

Try this:

```
a = a ^ b;
b = a ^ b;
```

```
a = a ^ b;
```

Bitwise NOT (~)

This flips all bits: 0 becomes 1, 1 becomes 0.

```
int a = 6;    // 000...0110
int b = ~a;   // 111...1001  (depends on integer size)
```

Note: Because C uses two's complement representation for negatives, ~a equals `-a - 1`.

Left Shift (<<)

Shifts bits to the left — each shift multiplies the number by 2.

```
int a = 3;       // 011
int b = a << 2;     // 1100  (decimal 12)
```

Use cases:

- fast multiplication by powers of two
- creating bitmasks
- embedded programming

Right Shift (>>)

Shifts bits to the right — divides the number by 2 per shift.

```
int a = 12;       // 1100
int b = a >> 2; // 0011  (decimal 3)
```

Arithmetic vs Logical shift depends on compiler for signed values. Unsigned values always perform a logical shift.

Bit Masks — Reading and Writing Individual Bits

If you want to set, clear, or toggle a specific bit, you use masks.

Setting a bit:

```
x = x | (1 << k);
```

Clearing a bit:

```
x = x & ~(1 << k);
```

Toggling a bit:

```
x = x ^ (1 << k);
```

Checking a bit:

```
if (x & (1 << k)) { ... }
```

Practical Example — File Permission Flags

```
#define READ   (1 << 0)
#define WRITE  (1 << 1)
#define EXEC   (1 << 2)

int perm = 0;

perm |= READ;          // enable read
perm |= WRITE;         // enable write
perm &= ~WRITE;        // disable write
perm ^= EXEC;          // toggle execute
```

Interviewers love this because it tests:

- bit manipulation
- masking
- symbolic constants

Why Interviewers Care

Because bitwise thinking shows that you understand:

- low-level data representation
- memory-efficient coding
- control over hardware and protocols
- embedded-systems style problem-solving

If you're interviewing for systems, embedded, or OS-level work, you will almost certainly be asked a question involving:

- setting bits
- toggling flags
- checking bits
- decoding a single byte

18.3 The `volatile` Keyword — When the Compiler Must Not Optimize

The C compiler is extremely smart. It tries to remove unnecessary work by caching variables in registers, eliminating repeated reads, and reordering instructions for performance. Most of the time, this is great.

But sometimes, a variable may change *outside* the program's normal flow:

- hardware updates it
- an interrupt handler modifies it
- another thread changes it
- a signal handler writes to it

In such cases, the compiler *must not* assume the variable is stable. This is what the `volatile` keyword enforces:

"Always read this variable from memory. Never optimize it away."

A volatile variable is declared like this:

```
volatile int flag;
```

Where `volatile` is Required

1. Hardware and Memory-Mapped I/O

When interacting with hardware registers, the value may change at any moment:

```
volatile int *STATUS = (int*)0x80000000;

while (!(*STATUS & 1)) {
    // wait for hardware event
}
```

Without `volatile`, the compiler may optimize the loop into an infinite loop because it thinks STATUS never changes.

2. Variables Modified by Interrupts

```
volatile int ready = 0;

void ISR() {
    ready = 1;     // interrupt sets flag
}

int main() {
    while (!ready) {
        // wait here
    }
}
```

Without `volatile`, the compiler may remove the repeated reads of `ready`.

3. Shared Variables in Multithreading

```
volatile int stop = 0;

void* worker(void *arg) {
    while (!stop) {
        // do work
    }
}
```

Note: `volatile` does *not* make this thread-safe. It only ensures visibility, not atomicity or ordering.

What `volatile` Does NOT Do

A common interview trap is believing that `volatile` provides threading guarantees.

It DOES NOT:

- make operations atomic
- prevent race conditions
- act as a lock or mutex
- prevent instruction reordering across threads

A great interview answer:

> ***volatile*** ensures *visibility* of memory changes, but not *synchronization*.

Combining `const` and `volatile`

This appears often in embedded systems:

```
const volatile int timerValue;
```

Meaning:

- `const` → the program cannot modify it
- `volatile` → the value may change unexpectedly (hardware writes)

Classic Interview Traps

1. Busy-wait without `volatile`

```
int flag = 0;
```

```
while (!flag) {}
// compiler may optimize away the loop condition
```

Fix:

```
volatile int flag = 0;
```

2. Thinking `volatile` fixes multithreading

It does not. Thread safety needs `mutex`, `atomic`, or memory barriers.

3. Forgetting that I/O registers MUST be volatile

Without `volatile`, the compiler may skip reading hardware values entirely.

Simple Demonstration

```
volatile int x = 10;

int main() {
    int y = x;     // must read x from memory
    x = y + 1;     // must write x back to memory
}
```

The compiler is forbidden from optimizing these accesses.

18.4 Quick Recap Before You Move On

Before you head into the next chapter, pause for a moment and make sure the big ideas from this chapter are clear.

Storage classes and variable lifetime are core concepts in C, and interviewers love testing whether you truly understand how memory, scope, and linkage work behind the scenes.

- **auto** is the default storage class for local variables. They live on the stack and disappear when the function returns.
- **static (local)** variables retain their value across function calls and live for the entire program duration, even though their scope is local.
- **static (global)** restricts visibility to a single file and provides *internal linkage*.
- **extern** tells the compiler "this variable exists somewhere else." It does not allocate memory — it only declares.
- **register** was once a hint to store variables in CPU registers. Modern compilers ignore it, but it may still appear in older code.
- **Scope vs. Lifetime vs. Linkage:** They are completely different concepts —
  - **Scope**: where the variable can be accessed
  - **Lifetime**: how long the variable exists in memory
  - **Linkage**: whether the name is visible across files
- **Global variables** have static lifetime automatically

(they exist for the entire run of the program).

- **File-scope static** limits a variable to one translation unit. If you hear an interviewer say "internal linkage," this is what they mean.
- **extern** is essential for multi-file projects. This is how you share variables or function prototypes across files.
- **Shadowing** can hide outer variables. While legal, it can cause bugs and confusion — interviewers may ask about it.
- **Best rule of thumb:** If a variable should keep its value across function calls → use `static`. If it needs to be visible across files → use `extern`. If it's temporary → plain local variable is enough.

You've now covered one of the most fundamental pieces of how C organizes and manages memory. With this foundation, you're ready for the next chapters, where memory, modularity, and system behavior start coming together in powerful ways.

Do-It-Yourself: Practice Zone

This is where you strengthen your intuition about scope, lifetime, and linkage. Each exercise is designed to mimic exactly the kind of corner-cases and reasoning interviewers love to test.

Part A — Storage Classes Basics

1. Write a program that shows the lifetime of a local variable vs. a local `static` variable by calling the same function multiple times.

```
void demo() {
    int a = 0;
    static int b = 0;

    a++;
    b++;

    printf("a = %d, b = %d\n", a, b);
}

int main() {
    demo();
    demo();
    demo();
}
```

   Observe the difference in behavior.

2. Declare a global variable in one file and use `extern` to access it from another file. Create two programs: one that compiles, and one that breaks because the definition was removed.

```
// file1.c
```

```
int count = 10;

// file2.c
extern int count;
int main() { printf("%d\n", count); }
```

3. Write a function using `register` and verify that modern compilers no longer guarantee register allocation.

Part B — Linkage, Visibility, and Shadowing

1. Demonstrate the difference between:
   - a global variable
   - a file-scope `static` variable

```
// file1.c
int x = 10;
static int y = 20;

// file2.c
extern int x;    // works
extern int y;    // causes linker error! (internal
      linkage)
```

   Explain why the second `extern` fails.

2. Write code that causes variable shadowing, then fix it by renaming variables.

```
int x = 5;

void test() {
    int x = 20;    // shadows the global x
    printf("%d\n", x);
}
```

3. Create a function where a block-scope variable shadows a function-scope variable.

Part C — Lifetime Experiments

1. Show that a pointer can safely refer to:

    - static storage
    - global storage

    but **not** to a function's local variables after the function ends.

```
int *danger() {
    int x = 10;         // local
    return &x;          // unsafe!
}

int *safe() {
    static int y = 10;
    return &y;          // valid for entire program
}
```

2. Show an example where a function returns a pointer to a global variable.

```
int g = 42;

int* get_g() {
    return &g;    // safe
}
```

3. Write a program where a static local variable retains state between calls.

Part D — Mini Project: "Multi-File Statistics Counter"

Create a tiny project with three files:

- `counter.c` — contains a global counter and functions to modify it
- `counter.h` — declares the functions and uses `extern` for the counter
- `main.c` — calls the functions repeatedly

Your tasks:

1. Use a global variable for the main counter.
2. Add a **file-scope static** variable inside `counter.c` that tracks how many times the counter was incremented.
3. Print both values from `main.c`.

Example skeleton:

```
// counter.h
extern int counter;
void inc();
void dec();
```

```
// counter.c
#include "counter.h"

int counter = 0;          // global
static int calls = 0;     // internal linkage

void inc() { counter++; calls++; }
void dec() { counter--; calls++; }
```

```
// main.c
#include "counter.h"
#include <stdio.h>

int main() {
    inc(); inc(); dec();
    printf("counter = %d\n", counter);
}
```

Final Challenge — "Lifetime Detective"

Write a program that prints the addresses of:

- a global variable
- a static local variable
- a plain local variable
- a dynamically allocated variable

and compare their memory regions.

Interpreting these addresses correctly is a powerful interview skill — it proves you really understand stack, heap, and static storage duration.

Phase 3

Cracking the C Interview

"It's not about knowing everything — it's about knowing how to think."

Turning your understanding into real interview performance

Chapter 19

OUTPUT-BASED PRACTICE

Welcome to the hands-on section of your C journey. This chapter is about testing what you've learned — the kind of short, sharp questions that real interviews use to judge how deeply you understand C's behavior. Don't rush. Read each question carefully, predict the output, and only then verify it by running the code yourself.

19.1 Basic Variables and Operators

These questions test your understanding of expression evaluation, operator precedence, and increment behavior. Keep a pencil handy — trace values on paper before assuming the answer!

1. What will be printed?

```
#include <stdio.h>
int main() {
    int a = 5, b = 10;
    printf("%d", a++ * ++b);
}
```

2. Predict the output:

```
#include <stdio.h>
int main() {
    int x = 2;
    x = x++ + ++x;
    printf("%d", x);
}
```

3. Observe carefully:

```
#include <stdio.h>
int main() {
    int i = 5;
    printf("%d %d %d", i, i++, ++i);
}
```

4. Evaluate this arithmetic:

```
#include <stdio.h>
int main() {
    int a = 10, b = 4;
    printf("%d", a++ + ++b * 2);
}
```

5. Identify what's printed and why:

```
#include <stdio.h>
int main() {
    int x = 7;
    printf("%d", (x > 5) ? x++ : ++x);
    printf(" %d", x);
}
```

6. Slight twist:

```
#include <stdio.h>
int main() {
    int a = 5;
    float b = 2;
    printf("%d", a / b * 2);
```

```
}
```

19.2 Conditional Statements and Loops

Focus on control flow — subtle details in ‘if‘, ‘else‘, and loops often change everything.

7. What happens here?

```
#include <stdio.h>
int main() {
    int x = 0;
    if (x = 5)
        printf("Inside if");
    else
        printf("Inside else");
}
```

8. Count the number of iterations:

```
#include <stdio.h>
int main() {
    int i;
    for (i = 0; i < 3; i++)
        printf("%d", i);
    printf("%d", i);
}
```

9. Can you spot the missing braces effect?

```
#include <stdio.h>
int main() {
    int i = 0;
    while (i < 3)
        printf("%d", i++);
        printf("End");
}
```

10. Think carefully about the condition:

```
#include <stdio.h>
int main() {
    int i = 5;
    while (i-- > 0)
        printf("%d", i);
}
```

11. What will this print?

```
#include <stdio.h>
int main() {
    int i, j;
    for (i = 1; i <= 2; i++) {
        for (j = 1; j <= 2; j++) {
            if (i == j)
                continue;
            printf("%d%d ", i, j);
        }
    }
}
```

12. A logic puzzle:

```
#include <stdio.h>
int main() {
    int n = 3;
    do {
        printf("%d", n);
    } while (n-- > 0);
}
```

13. Predict carefully:

```
#include <stdio.h>
int main() {
    int i = 0;
    for (; i < 3; i++);
    printf("%d", i);
}
```

Pro Tip: These questions train your brain to trace execution step by step — a crucial interview habit. When you feel confident, cover the next sections without using a compiler first!

19.3 Functions and Parameter Passing

Now we test your understanding of how variables behave when passed into functions. Remember: C uses **pass-by-value**, meaning functions receive a copy unless pointers are involved. Static variables and recursion can make things interesting — think before predicting!

14. What will this print?

```
#include <stdio.h>
void fun(int a) {
    a = a + 5;
    printf("%d ", a);
}
int main() {
    int a = 10;
    fun(a);
    printf("%d", a);
}
```

15. Can you trace the variable changes?

```
#include <stdio.h>
void change(int *p) {
    *p = *p + 10;
}
int main() {
    int x = 5;
    change(&x);
    printf("%d", x);
```

```
}
```

16. Notice the static keyword effect:

```
#include <stdio.h>
void count() {
    static int x = 0;
    printf("%d ", ++x);
}
int main() {
    count(); count(); count();
}
```

17. How does recursion behave here?

```
#include <stdio.h>
int fun(int n) {
    if (n == 0)
        return 1;
    else
        return n * fun(n - 1);
}
int main() {
    printf("%d", fun(4));
}
```

18. Think carefully about return value vs. print order:

```
#include <stdio.h>
int fun(int n) {
    printf("%d ", n);
    if (n == 0) return 0;
    return fun(n - 1);
}
int main() {
    fun(3);
}
```

19. What's happening here?

```
#include <stdio.h>
```

```
int fun() {
    static int x = 10;
    return x--;
}
int main() {
    printf("%d ", fun());
    printf("%d ", fun());
}
```

19.4 Pointers and Arrays

You've already met pointers earlier, but now they'll appear in fast-paced output puzzles. Each question checks whether you really understand how arrays and pointers relate in memory.

20. Predict the output:

```
#include <stdio.h>
int main() {
    int arr[] = {10, 20, 30};
    int *p = arr;
    printf("%d %d", *p, *(p + 2));
}
```

21. Same code, but different twist:

```
#include <stdio.h>
int main() {
    int a[] = {1, 2, 3, 4};
    int *p = a + 1;
    printf("%d", *(p++));
    printf(" %d", *p);
}
```

22. Spot the pointer arithmetic trap:

```
#include <stdio.h>
```

```
int main() {
    int a[] = {5, 10, 15, 20};
    int *p = a;
    printf("%d ", *p++);
    printf("%d", *++p);
}
```

23. Understand the memory relation:

```
#include <stdio.h>
int main() {
    int a[3] = {1, 2, 3};
    printf("%p %p", a, &a[0]);
}
```

24. Observe how the pointer increments:

```
#include <stdio.h>
int main() {
    int arr[3] = {10, 20, 30};
    int *p = arr;
    p++;
    printf("%d", *p);
}
```

25. This one tests your mental model:

```
#include <stdio.h>
int main() {
    char str[] = "ABC";
    char *p = str;
    printf("%c", *++p);
}
```

26. Bonus: Array decay and sizeof difference:

```
#include <stdio.h>
int main() {
    int arr[5];
    printf("%lu %lu", sizeof(arr), sizeof(&arr));
}
```

Pro Tip: Don't rush pointer questions — even experienced programmers get them wrong the first time. If you can mentally trace these without errors, you're ready for the trickier pointer puzzles ahead.

19.5 Strings and Characters

Strings in C are character arrays ending with "\0". These questions train you to think about pointer movement, string literals, and hidden null terminators.

27. What will be printed?

```
#include <stdio.h>
int main() {
    char s[] = "C";
    char *p = "C";
    printf("%lu %lu", sizeof(s), sizeof(p));
}
```

28. Predict the result:

```
#include <stdio.h>
int main() {
    char str[] = "Hello";
    printf("%c", *(str + 1));
}
```

29. How many characters are stored?

```
#include <stdio.h>
int main() {
    char name[] = "ABC";
    printf("%lu", sizeof(name));
}
```

30. Watch the pointer increment carefully:

```
#include <stdio.h>
int main() {
    char s[] = "CODE";
    char *p = s;
    printf("%c ", *p++);
    printf("%c", *p);
}
```

31. Observe pointer vs. array behavior:

```
#include <stdio.h>
int main() {
    char a[] = "Hi";
    char *b = "Hi";
    a[0] = 'h';
    // b[0] = 'h';    // What happens if this is
     uncommented?
    printf("%s %s", a, b);
}
```

32. Find the output:

```
#include <stdio.h>
#include <string.h>
int main() {
    char s[] = "Interview";
    printf("%d", strlen(s));
}
```

33. Null terminator twist:

```
#include <stdio.h>
int main() {
    char str[5] = {'A','B','C','D'};
    printf("%s", str);
}
```

19.6 Storage Classes and Scope

Storage classes define ***where*** variables live, ***how long*** they live, and ***who*** can see them. Interviewers love static and extern puzzles — trace variable lifetimes carefully.

34. Static vs automatic:

```
#include <stdio.h>
void counter() {
    static int c = 0;
    printf("%d ", ++c);
}
int main() {
    counter(); counter(); counter();
}
```

35. Observe variable hiding:

```
#include <stdio.h>
int x = 5;
int main() {
    int x = 10;
    printf("%d", x);
}
```

36. Scope confusion:

```
#include <stdio.h>
int x = 1;
void f() {
    int x = 2;
    {
        int x = 3;
        printf("%d ", x);
    }
    printf("%d ", x);
}
int main() {
    f();
```

```
    printf("%d", x);
}
```

37. Static inside a function:

```
#include <stdio.h>
void f() {
    static int n = 5;
    printf("%d ", n--);
}
int main() {
    f(); f(); f();
}
```

38. The extern declaration puzzle:

```
#include <stdio.h>
int x = 10;
void fun();
int main() {
    printf("%d ", x);
    fun();
}
void fun() {
    extern int x;
    x++;
    printf("%d", x);
}
```

39. What does this print?

```
#include <stdio.h>
void f() {
    auto int x = 5;
    printf("%d ", x);
}
int main() {
    f(); f();
}
```

Pro Tip: Static variables are interview goldmines. If you can trace how their values persist across calls, you're already thinking like a systems programmer.

19.7 Macros and Preprocessors

Preprocessor questions reveal whether you understand what happens *before* compilation. Watch for parenthesis errors, multiple evaluations, and hidden bugs that only macros can cause.

40. What's printed?

```
#include <stdio.h>
#define SQR(x) (x * x)
int main() {
    printf("%d", SQR(3+2));
}
```

41. Spot the issue:

```
#include <stdio.h>
#define SQR(x) ((x) * (x))
int main() {
    int i = 3;
    printf("%d", SQR(i++));
}
```

42. Conditional compilation puzzle:

```
#include <stdio.h>
#define DEBUG 1
int main() {
#ifdef DEBUG
    printf("Debug Mode");
#else
    printf("Release Mode");
#endif
```

```
}
```

43. Nested macros in action:

```
#include <stdio.h>
#define MAX(a,b) ((a) > (b) ? (a) : (b))
#define DOUBLE(x) (2 * (x))
int main() {
    printf("%d", MAX(5, DOUBLE(3)));
}
```

44. Using predefined macros:

```
#include <stdio.h>
int main() {
    printf("%s - %d\n", __FILE__, __LINE__);
    printf("%s\n", __DATE__);
    printf("%s\n", __TIME__);
}
```

45. Observe what expands:

```
#include <stdio.h>
#define LOG(x) printf("Value of " #x " = %d\n", x)
int main() {
    int n = 10;
    LOG(n);
}
```

46. The token-pasting operator:

```
#include <stdio.h>
#define JOIN(a,b) a##b
int main() {
    int num12 = 100;
    printf("%d", JOIN(num,12));
}
```

47. Controlled compilation:

```
#include <stdio.h>
#define VERSION 2
int main() {
#if VERSION >= 3
    printf("Advanced Features");
#elif VERSION == 2
    printf("Standard Features");
#else
    printf("Legacy Mode");
#endif
}
```

48. Macro vs. inline function:

```
#include <stdio.h>
#define INC(x) ++x
inline int inc(int x) { return ++x; }

int main() {
    int a = 1, b = 1;
    printf("%d ", INC(a));
    printf("%d", inc(b));
}
```

49. Which prints first?

```
#include <stdio.h>
#define MSG printf("Macro\n");
int main() {
    MSG
    printf("Main\n");
}
```

Pro Tip: Macros are easy to misuse — always expand them mentally before answering. Interviewers love to see if you understand evaluation order and operator safety.

19.8 Challenge Zone (Mixed Concepts)

This is the real interview zone. Each question mixes multiple ideas — pointers, macros, arrays, recursion, and memory. If you can trace these without guessing, you've mastered C's foundations.

50. Predict the output (pointers + arrays):

```
#include <stdio.h>
int main() {
    int a[] = {1, 2, 3};
    int *p = a;
    printf("%d", *p + *(p + 1) + *(p + 2));
}
```

51. String and pointer:

```
#include <stdio.h>
int main() {
    char *p = "Hello";
    printf("%c", *++p);
}
```

52. Function + static + recursion:

```
#include <stdio.h>
int f() {
    static int x = 1;
    if (x > 5) return x;
    x++;
    return f();
}
int main() {
    printf("%d", f());
}
```

53. Multi-dimensional array pointer:

```
#include <stdio.h>
int main() {
    int a[2][2] = {{1,2},{3,4}};
    printf("%d", *(*(a+1)+1));
}
```

54. Macro + increment confusion:

```
#include <stdio.h>
#define ADD(x,y) x + y
int main() {
    printf("%d", 5 * ADD(2,3));
}
```

55. Pointer to function:

```
#include <stdio.h>
int add(int a, int b) { return a + b; }
int main() {
    int (*p)(int, int) = add;
    printf("%d", p(2,3));
}
```

56. String literal vs. char array:

```
#include <stdio.h>
int main() {
    char *s = "Hi";
    char t[] = "Hi";
    s[0] = 'h';    // ?
    printf("%s %s", s, t);
}
```

57. Pointer to pointer:

```
#include <stdio.h>
int main() {
    int x = 5;
    int *p = &x;
```

```
    int **q = &p;
    printf("%d", **q);
}
```

58. sizeof with pointers:

```
#include <stdio.h>
int main() {
    int *p = NULL;
    printf("%lu %lu", sizeof(p), sizeof(*p));
}
```

59. Bonus challenge:

```
#include <stdio.h>
#define INC(x) ++x
int main() {
    int i = 5;
    printf("%d ", INC(i));
    printf("%d", i);
}
```

Final Tip: Every question here is a mini-interview. When you can explain why the output occurs — not just what it is — you've achieved true mastery of C's behavior. Run each one, trace line by line, and make your own notes right beside the code.

Chapter 20

DEBUGGING AND ERROR ANALYSIS

This is your hands-on debugging workbook. Each exercise is designed to help you identify, reason about, and fix bugs — exactly the skill set interviewers expect from a strong C developer.

Part A — Syntax and Logical Basics

1. Missing semicolon:

```
#include <stdio.h>
int main() {
    int x = 10
    printf("%d", x);
    return 0;
}
```

Hint: Check statement endings.

2. Parenthesis mismatch:

```
printf("Sum = %d\n", (a + b);
```

Hint: Every opening has a closing.

3. Assignment vs comparison:

```
int i = 0;
while (i = 5) {
    printf("%d ", i);
    i++;
}
```

Hint: Did you mean ==?

4. Infinite loop logic:

```
for (int i = 0; i < 10; i--)
    printf("%d ", i);
```

Hint: Direction of iteration matters.

5. Missing initialization:

```
int sum;
for (int i = 1; i <= 5; i++)
    sum += i;
printf("%d", sum);
```

Hint: What is the starting value of `sum`?

6. Wrong format specifier:

```
float f = 3.14;
printf("%d", f);
```

Hint: Always match variable type with format code.

7. Integer division issue:

```
int a = 5, b = 2;
printf("%f", a / b);
```

Hint: One of them should be float.

8. Missing return type:

```
main() {
    printf("Hello");
}
```

Hint: Modern C needs explicit `int main(void)`.

9. Variable declared inside for-loop:

```
for (int i = 0; i < 3; i++);
printf("%d", i);
```

Hint: Scope of `i`.

10. Extra semicolon:

```
if (x > 0);
    printf("Positive");
```

Hint: The semicolon ends the `if` early.

Part B — Pointers and Memory Bugs

11. Uninitialized pointer:

```
#include <stdio.h>
int main() {
    int *p;
    *p = 10;
    printf("%d", *p);
}
```

Hint: A pointer must point somewhere before dereferencing.

12. Dangling pointer after free:

```
#include <stdlib.h>
int main() {
    int *p = malloc(sizeof(int));
    *p = 42;
    free(p);
    printf("%d", *p);
}
```

Hint: Accessing freed memory is undefined behavior.

13. Double free:

```
#include <stdlib.h>
int main() {
    int *p = malloc(sizeof(int));
    free(p);
    free(p);
}
```

Hint: Free once. Reset pointer to NULL after freeing.

14. Memory leak:

```
int *p = malloc(10 * sizeof(int));
p = malloc(5 * sizeof(int)); // old block lost
```

Hint: Free before overwriting the pointer.

Part C — Functions and Recursion

15. Missing function declaration:

```
#include <stdio.h>
int main() {
    hello();
}
void hello() {
    printf("Hi");
}
```

Hint: Declare or prototype before using.

16. Recursive function missing base case:

```
void recurse() {
    printf("Run ");
    recurse();
}
int main() { recurse(); }
```

Hint: Infinite recursion causes stack overflow.

Part D — Arrays and Strings

17. Out-of-bounds access:

```
int a[3] = {1, 2, 3};
for (int i = 0; i <= 3; i++)
    printf("%d ", a[i]);
```

Hint: Check loop condition.

18. Missing null terminator:

```
char s[5] = {'H','e','l','l','o'};
printf("%s", s);
```

Hint: Strings need a '\0' at the end.

Part E — Memory Management and Dynamic Arrays

19. Freeing part of an array:

```
int *a = malloc(5 * sizeof(int));
int *b = a + 2;
free(b);
```

Hint: Only free the original pointer.

Part F — Preprocessor, Macros, and Conditional Compilation

20. Missing parentheses in macro:

```
#define SQR(x) x * x
int main() {
    printf("%d", SQR(3+2));
}
```

Hint: Without parentheses, expands incorrectly.

Part G — Mixed Concepts & Tricky Debug Scenarios

21. Function returning local variable:

```
int* f() {
    int x = 10;
    return &x;
}
int main() {
    int *p = f();
    printf("%d", *p);
}
```

Hint: Returning address of a local variable is unsafe.

Do-It-Yourself: Practice Zone

Part A — Syntax and Logical Basics

1. Missing semicolon:

```
#include <stdio.h>
int main() {
    int x = 10
    printf("%d", x);
    return 0;
}
```

Hint: Every statement in C must end with a semicolon.

2. Parenthesis mismatch:

```
printf("Sum = %d\n", (a + b);
```

Hint: Check that every opening bracket has a matching closing one.

3. Assignment vs. comparison:

```
int i = 0;
while (i = 5) {
    printf("%d ", i);
    i++;
}
```

Hint: Use == for comparison, not =.

4. Infinite loop direction:

```
for (int i = 0; i < 10; i--)
    printf("%d ", i);
```

Hint: Verify increment/decrement direction matches the condition.

5. Uninitialized variable:

```
int sum;
for (int i = 1; i <= 5; i++)
    sum += i;
printf("%d", sum);
```

Hint: Always initialize variables before using them.

6. Wrong format specifier:

```
float f = 3.14;
printf("%d", f);
```

Hint: Use %f for floating-point numbers.

7. Integer division issue:

```
int a = 5, b = 2;
printf("%f", a / b);
```

Hint: Cast at least one operand to `float`.

8. Missing return type in `main`:

```
main() {
    printf("Hello");
}
```

Hint: Modern C requires `int main(void)`.

9. Scope error after for-loop:

```
for (int i = 0; i < 3; i++);
printf("%d", i);
```

Hint: The variable `i` exists only inside the loop.

10. Extra semicolon after `if`:

```
if (x > 0);
```

```
    printf("Positive");
```

Hint: The semicolon ends the condition prematurely.

11. Operator precedence confusion:

```
int x = 2, y = 3;
printf("%d", x + y << 1);
```

Hint: Shift operators have lower precedence than arithmetic ones.

12. Chained assignment surprise:

```
int a, b, c;
a = b == c = 5;
printf("%d %d %d", a, b, c);
```

Hint: Equality and assignment associate differently—use parentheses.

13. Implicit narrowing conversion:

```
char c = 300;
printf("%d", c);
```

Hint: `char` *range overflow wraps the value.*

14. Unused variable warning:

```
int temp;
printf("Done\n");
```

Hint: Either use the variable or remove it.

15. Mismatched braces:

```
int main() {
    int x = 5;
```

```c
    if (x > 0) {
        printf("OK");
    // missing closing brace here
```

Hint: Count every opening { and closing }.

16. Nested comment error:

```c
/* start /* nested comment */ end */
```

Hint: C does not support nested block comments.

17. Using uninitialized array index:

```c
int a[3];
int i;
printf("%d", a[i]);
```

Hint: Index variable must have a defined value.

18. Forgetting header inclusion:

```c
printf("Hello world\n");
```

Hint: Add #include <stdio.h> at the top.

19. Extra comma in initializer:

```c
int nums[] = {1, 2, 3, };
```

Hint: The trailing comma is invalid in older C standards.

20. Using undeclared variable:

```c
int main() {
    x = 10;
    printf("%d", x);
}
```

Hint: Declare before use—C does not auto-create variables.

Part B — Pointers and Memory Bugs

21. Uninitialized pointer:

```
#include <stdio.h>
int main() {
    int *p;
    *p = 10;
    printf("%d", *p);
}
```

Hint: You must assign a valid address to p before dereferencing it.

22. Dangling pointer after free:

```
#include <stdlib.h>
int main() {
    int *p = malloc(sizeof(int));
    *p = 42;
    free(p);
    printf("%d", *p);
}
```

Hint: Accessing freed memory causes undefined behavior.

23. Double free:

```
#include <stdlib.h>
int main() {
    int *p = malloc(sizeof(int));
    free(p);
    free(p);
}
```

Hint: Freeing the same pointer twice is dangerous. Set it to NULL after freeing.

24. Memory leak:

```
int *p = malloc(10 * sizeof(int));
p = malloc(5 * sizeof(int)); // old block lost
```

Hint: Free the first allocation before reassigning p.

25. Invalid pointer arithmetic:

```
int a[3] = {1, 2, 3};
int *p = a + 5;
printf("%d", *p);
```

Hint: You stepped outside the array bounds.

26. Returning address of local variable:

```
int* foo() {
    int x = 10;
    return &x;
}
```

Hint: Local variables vanish after the function returns.

27. Use-after-free:

```
#include <stdlib.h>
int main() {
    int *p = malloc(sizeof(int));
    free(p);
    *p = 9;
}
```

Hint: Never write to memory that has been freed.

28. Modifying string literal:

```
char *s = "Hello";
s[0] = 'h';
```

Hint: String literals are stored in read-only memory.

29. Forgetting to check `malloc()`:

```
int *p = malloc(1000000000 * sizeof(int));
p[0] = 1;
```

Hint: Always verify that `malloc()` succeeded.

30. Using pointer after scope ends:

```
int* ptr;
{
    int x = 5;
    ptr = &x;
}
printf("%d", *ptr);
```

Hint: The variable x no longer exists outside the block.

31. Misaligned pointer cast:

```
double d = 3.14;
int *p = (int*)&d;
printf("%d", *p);
```

Hint: Type punning violates strict aliasing rules.

32. Pointer-to-pointer confusion:

```
int x = 5;
int *p = &x;
int **q;
*q = p;
printf("%d", **q);
```

Hint: q itself was never initialized.

33. Wrong level of dereference:

```
int a = 10;
int *p = &a;
printf("%d", **p);
```

*Hint: Only one * is valid here.*

34. Stack memory used after return:

```
char* greet() {
    char msg[] = "Hi";
    return msg;
}
```

Hint: The array msg is destroyed when the function ends.

35. Not freeing heap allocation:

```
#include <stdlib.h>
int main() {
    int *arr = malloc(100 * sizeof(int));
    // forgot free()
    return 0;
}
```

Hint: Always release dynamically allocated memory.

36. Dereferencing NULL:

```
int *p = NULL;
*p = 10;
```

Hint: Always check pointer validity before dereferencing.

37. Writing beyond allocated size:

```
int *p = malloc(3 * sizeof(int));
for (int i = 0; i <= 3; i++)
    p[i] = i;
```

Hint: Valid indices are 0–2.

38. Freeing stack memory:

```
int x = 5;
int *p = &x;
```

```
free(p);
```

Hint: Only dynamically allocated memory should be freed.

39. Incorrect size in allocation:

```
int *p = malloc(sizeof(p));
```

Hint: `sizeof(p)` is pointer size, not `sizeof(int)`.

40. Mixing memory spaces:

```
int *p = malloc(sizeof(int));
int *q = &p;
free(q);
```

Hint: Never free an address that wasn't allocated by `malloc()`.

Part C — Functions and Recursion

41. Missing function declaration:

```
#include <stdio.h>
int main() {
    hello();
}
void hello() {
    printf("Hi");
}
```

Hint: Either declare `hello()` before `main()` or add a prototype.

42. Function declared `int` but returns nothing:

```
int greet() {
    printf("Hello");
}
```

Hint: A non-void function must explicitly return a value.

43. Passing wrong parameter type:

```
void show(int x) { printf("%d", x); }
int main() {
    char *s = "Hi";
    show(s);
}
```

Hint: Mismatched types cause undefined behavior.

44. Recursive call without base case:

```
void recurse() {
    printf("Run ");
    recurse();
}
int main() { recurse(); }
```

Hint: Always include a termination condition.

45. Returning local variable address:

```
int* fun() {
    int x = 10;
    return &x;
}
```

Hint: Locals disappear once the function ends.

46. Missing return statement:

```
int add(int a, int b) {
    int c = a + b;
}
```

Hint: Must return c.

47. Infinite recursion:

```
int fact(int n) {
    if (n == 0) return 1;
    return n * fact(n);
}
```

Hint: Decrement n before recursive call.

48. Order of evaluation surprise:

```
int f(int x) {
    printf("%d ", x);
    return x;
}
int main() {
    int y = f(1) + f(2) * f(3);
}
```

Hint: The order of function calls is compiler-dependent.

49. Missing argument in function call:

```
int add(int a, int b) { return a + b; }
int main() {
    printf("%d", add(5));
}
```

Hint: Too few arguments; both must be supplied.

50. Using recursion where iteration suffices:

```
void print(int n) {
    if (n == 0) return;
    print(n - 1);
    printf("%d ", n);
}
```

Hint: Consider loops for efficiency on large inputs.

51. Static variable in recursion:

```
int countDown() {
    static int x = 3;
    if (x-- == 0) return 0;
    printf("%d ", x);
    countDown();
}
```

Hint: `static` *variables retain values between calls.*

52. Variable shadowing:

```
int n = 5;
void print(int n) { printf("%d", n); }
int main() {
    print(n);
}
```

Hint: Parameter `n` *hides the global one.*

53. Premature return:

```
int sum(int n) {
    if (n == 0) return 0;
    return n;
    sum(n - 1);
}
```

Hint: Code after `return` *never executes.*

54. Call-by-value misunderstanding:

```
void inc(int x) { x++; }
int main() {
    int a = 5;
    inc(a);
    printf("%d", a);
}
```

Hint: Arguments are copied; original unchanged.

55. Missing function prototype with implicit int:

```
int main() {
    test();
}
test() { printf("Hi"); }
```

Hint: Modern C forbids implicit declarations. Add a prototype.

Part C — Functions and Recursion

56. Missing function declaration:

```
#include <stdio.h>
int main() {
    hello();
}
void hello() {
    printf("Hi");
}
```

Hint: Either declare `hello()` before `main()` or add a prototype.

57. Function declared `int` but returns nothing:

```
int greet() {
    printf("Hello");
}
```

Hint: A non-void function must explicitly return a value.

58. Passing wrong parameter type:

```
void show(int x) { printf("%d", x); }
int main() {
    char *s = "Hi";
    show(s);
```

```
}
```

Hint: Mismatched types cause undefined behavior.

59. Recursive call without base case:

```
void recurse() {
    printf("Run ");
    recurse();
}
int main() { recurse(); }
```

Hint: Always include a termination condition.

60. Returning local variable address:

```
int* fun() {
    int x = 10;
    return &x;
}
```

Hint: Locals disappear once the function ends.

61. Missing return statement:

```
int add(int a, int b) {
    int c = a + b;
}
```

Hint: Must return `c`.

62. Infinite recursion:

```
int fact(int n) {
    if (n == 0) return 1;
    return n * fact(n);
}
```

Hint: Decrement n before recursive call.

63. Order of evaluation surprise:

```
int f(int x) {
    printf("%d ", x);
    return x;
}
int main() {
    int y = f(1) + f(2) * f(3);
}
```

Hint: The order of function calls is compiler-dependent.

64. Missing argument in function call:

```
int add(int a, int b) { return a + b; }
int main() {
    printf("%d", add(5));
}
```

Hint: Too few arguments; both must be supplied.

65. Using recursion where iteration suffices:

```
void print(int n) {
    if (n == 0) return;
    print(n - 1);
    printf("%d ", n);
}
```

Hint: Consider loops for efficiency on large inputs.

66. Static variable in recursion:

```
int countDown() {
    static int x = 3;
    if (x-- == 0) return 0;
    printf("%d ", x);
    countDown();
}
```

Hint: `static` variables retain values between calls.

67. Variable shadowing:

```
int n = 5;
void print(int n) { printf("%d", n); }
int main() {
    print(n);
}
```

Hint: Parameter `n` *hides the global one.*

68. Premature return:

```
int sum(int n) {
    if (n == 0) return 0;
    return n;
    sum(n - 1);
}
```

Hint: Code after `return` *never executes.*

69. Call-by-value misunderstanding:

```
void inc(int x) { x++; }
int main() {
    int a = 5;
    inc(a);
    printf("%d", a);
}
```

Hint: Arguments are copied; original unchanged.

70. Missing function prototype with implicit int:

```
int main() {
    test();
}
test() { printf("Hi"); }
```

Hint: Modern C forbids implicit declarations. Add a prototype.

Part E — Memory Management and Dynamic Arrays

71. Forgetting to free allocated memory:

```
#include <stdlib.h>
int main() {
    int *p = malloc(100 * sizeof(int));
    // forgot to free(p)
    return 0;
}
```

Hint: Always pair every `malloc()` with a `free()`.

72. Accessing memory after free:

```
#include <stdlib.h>
int main() {
    int *p = malloc(sizeof(int));
    *p = 42;
    free(p);
    printf("%d", *p);
}
```

Hint: This is a classic use-after-free bug.

73. Realloc mistake (losing original pointer):

```
int *p = malloc(5 * sizeof(int));
p = realloc(p, 10 * sizeof(int));
if (!p) free(p);    // bug
```

Hint: Always use a temporary pointer when calling `realloc()`.

74. Using malloc without checking return:

```
int *arr = malloc(10000000000 * sizeof(int));
arr[0] = 1;
```

Hint: Large allocations may fail; check for NULL.

75. calloc vs malloc difference:

```
#include <stdio.h>
#include <stdlib.h>
int main() {
    int *a = malloc(5 * sizeof(int));
    int *b = calloc(5, sizeof(int));
    for (int i = 0; i < 5; i++)
        printf("%d %d\n", a[i], b[i]);
}
```

Hint: `calloc()` zero-initializes; `malloc()` does not.

76. Writing beyond allocated memory:

```
int *p = malloc(3 * sizeof(int));
for (int i = 0; i <= 3; i++)
    p[i] = i;
```

Hint: Valid indices are 0–2 only.

77. Freeing pointer not from heap:

```
int x = 5;
int *p = &x;
free(p);
```

Hint: Only free heap-allocated memory.

78. Allocating wrong size:

```
int *p = malloc(sizeof(p));
```

Hint: Should be `sizeof(*p)` or `sizeof(int)`.

79. realloc with zero size:

```
int *p = malloc(4 * sizeof(int));
p = realloc(p, 0);
*p = 1;
```

Hint: `realloc(p, 0)` frees p — it becomes invalid.

80. Memory leak by reassignment:

```
char *s = malloc(10);
s = "Hello";
free(s);
```

Hint: Lost the original heap block; and string literals must not be freed.

81. Not allocating space for '\0':

```
char *s = malloc(5);
strcpy(s, "Hello");
```

Hint: Need 6 bytes including the null terminator.

82. Dynamic 2D array cleanup bug:

```
int **m = malloc(3 * sizeof(int*));
for (int i = 0; i < 3; i++)
    m[i] = malloc(3 * sizeof(int));
free(m);
```

Hint: Free each row first, then the outer pointer.

83. Shallow vs deep copy confusion:

```
char *a = malloc(5);
char *b = a;
strcpy(a, "Hi");
free(a);
printf("%s", b);
```

Hint: Both point to the same memory — now dangling.

84. Allocating struct incorrectly:

```
struct Point { int x, y; };
```

```
struct Point *p = malloc(sizeof(struct Point*));
p->x = 5; p->y = 10;
```

Hint: Allocate `sizeof(struct Point)`*, not pointer size.*

85. Using freed pointer in another variable:

```
int *p = malloc(sizeof(int));
int *q = p;
free(p);
*q = 5;
```

Hint: q becomes dangling too; set both to NULL.

Part F — Preprocessor, Macros, and Conditional Compilation

86. Missing parentheses in macro:

```
#include <stdio.h>
#define SQR(x) x * x
int main() {
    printf("%d", SQR(3+2));
}
```

*Hint: Expands to 3 + 2 * 3 + 2. Always wrap macros in parentheses!*

87. Double evaluation in macro:

```
#define INC(x) (++x)
int main() {
    int i = 3;
    printf("%d", INC(i) * INC(i));
}
```

Hint: Each call modifies `i` *— never use side effects in* *macros.*

88. Multi-statement macro error:

```
#define SWAP(a,b) { int t=a; a=b; b=t; }
int main() {
    int x=3,y=5;
    if (x>y) SWAP(x,y);
    else printf("ok");
}
```

Hint: Wrap multi-statement macros in do ... while(0).

89. Token-pasting confusion:

```
#define MAKE(name,num) name##num
int main() {
    int var1 = 10;
    printf("%d", MAKE(var, 1));
}
```

Hint: Works only if the pasted identifier already exists.

90. Stringizing operator misuse:

```
#define LOG(x) printf("x = %d\n", x)
int main() {
    int n = 5;
    LOG(n);
}
```

Hint: To print variable name, use #x not literal "x".

91. Conditional compilation skipped:

```
#define VERSION 2
#if VERSION >= 3
printf("New feature");
#endif
```

Hint: Nothing prints — block excluded by preprocessor.

92. Undefined macro in condition:

```
#if DEBUG
printf("Debug mode");
#endif
```

Hint: Undefined macros evaluate to 0.

93. Redefining macro without undef:

```
#define PI 3.14
#define PI 3.14159
```

Hint: Use `#undef PI` before redefining.

94. Missing backslash in multi-line macro:

```
#define MSG(x) printf("Hello %s\n", x)
               printf("Bye\n");
```

Hint: Each continued line needs a trailing backslash.

95. Header include guard missing:

```
/* mylib.h */
int add(int,int);
/* accidentally included twice */
```

Hint: Protect with `#ifndef ... #define ... #endif`.

Part G — Mixed Concepts & Tricky Debug Scenarios

96. Pointer vs. array size confusion:

```
#include <stdio.h>
int main() {
    int a[5];
```

```
    int *p = a;
    printf("%lu %lu", sizeof(a), sizeof(p));
}
```

Hint: Arrays know their total size; pointers only their own.

97. Undefined order of evaluation:

```
int i = 5;
printf("%d %d", i++, ++i);
```

Hint: Order between operands is undefined — never rely on it.

98. File not closed:

```
#include <stdio.h>
int main() {
    FILE *fp = fopen("data.txt", "w");
    fprintf(fp, "Hello");
}
```

Hint: Always call `fclose(fp);` to flush data.

99. Static variable retention:

```
void f() {
    static int x = 0;
    printf("%d ", ++x);
}
int main() {
    f(); f(); f();
}
```

Hint: Static retains its value across calls.

100. Integer overflow:

```
int x = 2147483647;
x++;
```

```
printf("%d", x);
```

Hint: Overflow of signed int is undefined. Use long long.

101. Uninitialized pointer in printf:

```
int *p;
printf("%p", p);
```

Hint: Garbage pointer — initialize before use.

102. Macro semicolon confusion:

```
#define PRINT(x) printf("%d\n", x);
int main() {
    if (1)
        PRINT(5)
    else
        PRINT(10)
}
```

Hint: Macro already ends with semicolon — breaks the else branch.

103. Type promotion surprise:

```
char c = 250;
printf("%d", c);
```

Hint: `char` may be signed; prints a negative number.

104. Returning local variable:

```
int* f() {
    int x = 10;
    return &x;
}
int main() {
    int *p = f();
    printf("%d", *p);
```

```
}
```

Hint: x disappears after return — undefined behavior.

105. Operator precedence (&& vs ||):

```
int a=1,b=0,c=1;
if (a || b && c) printf("yes");
else printf("no");
```

Hint: && binds tighter — evaluate that first.

106. Mixed signed/unsigned comparison:

```
int x = -1;
unsigned int y = 1;
if (x < y) printf("true");
else printf("false");
```

Hint: Signed x converts to unsigned — huge positive number!

107. Using variable before initialization:

```
int x;
if (x > 0)
    printf("Positive");
```

Hint: Undefined behavior — initialize all locals.

108. Logical vs bitwise operators:

```
int a = 2, b = 4;
printf("%d", a & b);
```

Hint: & is bitwise AND, not logical AND.

109. Mixing input formats:

```
int x; float y;
```

```
scanf("%d %f", &y, &x);
```

Hint: Argument order mismatch — undefined behavior.

110. Loop with off-by-one boundary:

```
int a[5];
for (int i = 0; i <= 5; i++)
    a[i] = i;
```

Hint: Valid indices are 0–4 only.

Do-It-Yourself: Practice Zone (Extended Challenge Set)

You've studied dozens of code snippets and debugging patterns — now it's time to test your instincts. Each of the following challenges represents a realistic C bug, logic flaw, or interview-style debugging puzzle. Treat this section like a personal coding lab: fix the issues, explain the cause, and verify the corrected output.

Part A — Syntax and Logic Warm-Ups

1. Find and fix the syntax error:

```
#include <stdio.h>
int main() {
    printf("Hello, world!"
    return 0;
}
```

2. Predict the output:

```
int x = 5, y = 10;
printf("%d", x+++y);
```

3. Identify the logical error:

```
int sum = 0;
for (int i = 1; i <= 5; i++);
    sum += i;
printf("%d", sum);
```

4. Fix the format specifier:

```
float f = 10.5;
printf("%d", f);
```

5. Spot the infinite loop:

```
for (int i = 10; i >= 0; i++)
    printf("%d ", i);
```

Part B — Pointers and Memory Safety

6. Correct the pointer initialization:

```
int *p;
*p = 10;
```

7. Detect and fix the dangling pointer:

```
int *p = malloc(sizeof(int));
free(p);
*p = 20;
```

8. Locate the memory leak:

```
int *a = malloc(10 * sizeof(int));
a = malloc(5 * sizeof(int));
```

9. Explain why this crashes:

```
char *msg = "Hi";
msg[0] = 'h';
```

10. Identify the correct usage of `realloc`:

```
p = realloc(p, 20);
if (!p) free(p);
```

Part C — Arrays, Strings, and Pointers Together

11. Find the off-by-one:

```
int a[5];
for (int i = 0; i <= 5; i++)
    a[i] = i;
```

12. Debug the missing null terminator:

```
char s[4] = {'C', 'o', 'd', 'e'};
printf("%s", s);
```

13. Explain what happens:

```
char str[] = "C";
printf("%lu %lu", sizeof(str), strlen(str));
```

14. Trace the output:

```
int a[] = {10,20,30};
int *p = a;
printf("%d", *p + *(p+1));
```

15. Fix the undefined behavior:

```
int a[3] = {1,2,3};
printf("%d", *(a+5));
```

Part D — Preprocessor and Macros

16. Correct the macro parentheses:

```
#define SQR(x) x * x
printf("%d", SQR(2+3));
```

17. Identify the redefinition warning:

```
#define SIZE 10
#define SIZE 20
```

18. Debug the missing backslash:

```
#define MSG(x) printf("Hello %s\n", x)
                printf("Bye\n");
```

19. Fix the token pasting:

```
#define VAR(n) var##n
int VAR(1) = 10;
printf("%d", VAR(1));
```

20. Debug conditional compilation:

```
#if VERSION >= 3
printf("New");
#else
printf("Old");
#endif
```

Part E — Mixed and Tricky Debug Challenges

21. Explain the undefined output:

```
int i = 5;
printf("%d %d", i++, ++i);
```

22. Analyze this recursion:

```
void f() { printf("Hi "); f(); }
int main() { f(); }
```

23. Diagnose the segmentation fault:

```
int *p;
printf("%d", *p);
```

24. Find and fix the shadowed variable:

```
int n = 10;
void show(int n) { printf("%d", n); }
int main() { show(n); }
```

25. Bonus: Predict and fix output order:

```
int f(int x) { printf("%d ", x); return x; }
int main() {
    int y = f(1) + f(2) * f(3);
}
```

Your mission: Go through each question, spot the bug, fix it, and write the corrected output. Every solved exercise brings you one step closer to thinking like a real debugger — the kind interviewers remember.

Pro Tip: Try running each snippet on your own compiler after fixing it. Note how small changes — like a missing brace, type mismatch, or wrong loop condition — can entirely alter program behavior.

The Debugger's Commandments

1. **Initialize everything.** Uninitialized variables and pointers cause chaos fast.
2. **Every `malloc()` needs a `free()`.** Memory leaks don't show—until they crash.
3. **Parentheses save macros.** Wrap parameters and expressions to avoid surprises.
4. **Trace the flow.** Track scope, lifetime, and recursion carefully.
5. **Undefined ≠ random.** It's dangerous, not mysterious.
6. **Read warnings.** They predict 90% of runtime errors.
7. **Think like memory.** Who owns it, how long it lives, and where it's stored.
8. **Test edge cases.** Bugs hide in zeros and empty strings.
9. **Instrument your code.** Use `printf()`, `assert()`, Valgrind, ASan.
10. **Slow down to debug faster.** Don't patch—understand the cause.

Debugging isn't about memorizing errors— it's about mastering how programs think. Every bug is a lesson in disguise.

Chapter 21

POINTER PUZZLES & MEMORY TRAPS

You've understood pointers. You've debugged them. Now, it's time to test whether you can *think like a pointer.*

This chapter is all about the real mind-benders — those short, innocent-looking pieces of code that make even experienced C programmers stop, stare, and ask, "Wait, what just happened here?"

Pointer puzzles are the ultimate test of whether you truly understand how memory works in C. They reveal how much you've internalized concepts like:

- pointer arithmetic and precedence,
- array decay and memory layout,
- stack vs. heap lifetimes,
- and the subtle difference between what's defined and what's merely allowed.

Memory traps, on the other hand, are the hidden dangers — the bugs that compile cleanly, run silently, and only fail when you least expect them to. If you can spot them here, you'll never fall for them again in an interview (or production code).

Think of this chapter as a *workbook of surprises*. Each puzzle challenges your understanding, not your typing speed. You'll predict the output, then uncover what's really happening — line by line.

How to Use This Chapter:

- First, read each code block carefully. Don't rush.
- Predict the output before you scroll to the explanation.
- Try running it later — some might behave differently on different compilers!
- Focus on "*why*" more than "*what*".

By the end of this chapter, you won't just remember pointer rules — you'll develop something far more powerful: **pointer intuition.**

Let's begin.

Part A — Pointer Expression Puzzles

These puzzles explore one of the most feared parts of C — the combination of operators ∗, &, and pointer increments.

Tip: In interviews, pointer arithmetic puzzles often test your order-of-evaluation reasoning, not your syntax memorization.

1. **Basic Pointer Increment**

```
#include <stdio.h>
int main() {
    int a[] = {10, 20, 30};
    int *p = a;
    printf("%d ", *p);
    printf("%d", *++p);
    return 0;
}
```

Predict the Output: What prints, and why?

Explanation: Initially, p points to a[0]. The first printf prints 10. Then ++p moves the pointer to a[1], so ∗p prints 20. Output: 10 20.

2. **Pointer Post-Increment Trick**

```
#include <stdio.h>
int main() {
    int a[] = {10, 20, 30};
    int *p = a;
    printf("%d ", *p++);
    printf("%d", *p);
}
```

Predict the Output: What happens when you use ∗p++ instead of ∗++p?

Explanation: *p++ means "use the value pointed by p, then move p." So, first prints 10, then p points to a[1], printing 20. Output: 10 20.

3. **Mixing Prefix and Postfix**

```
#include <stdio.h>
int main() {
    int a[] = {1, 2, 3, 4};
    int *p = a;
    printf("%d ", *++p + *p++);
    printf("%d", *p);
}
```

Predict the Output:

Explanation: *++p moves first (points to 2), then dereferences (2). *p++ dereferences (2) then moves (now points to 3). So, 2 + 2 = 4. Afterward, *p = 3. Output: 4 3.

4. **Pointer and Array Equivalence**

```
#include <stdio.h>
int main() {
    int arr[3] = {10, 20, 30};
    printf("%d %d", *(arr + 1), arr[1]);
}
```

Explanation: arr[i] × *(arr + i). Both print 20.

5. **Pointer to Pointer Puzzle**

```
#include <stdio.h>
int main() {
    int x = 10;
    int *p = &x;
    int **q = &p;
    printf("%d", **q);
```

```
}
```

Explanation: q points to p, which points to x. Dereferencing twice gives 10.

6. **Pointer Difference**

```
#include <stdio.h>
int main() {
    int a[] = {10, 20, 30, 40};
    int *p = &a[1];
    int *q = &a[3];
    printf("%ld", q - p);
}
```

Explanation: Pointer subtraction gives the number of elements apart. Here, `q - p = 2`.

7. **Array Decay Subtlety**

```
#include <stdio.h>
void show(int *p) {
    printf("%lu ", sizeof(p));
}
int main() {
    int a[10];
    printf("%lu ", sizeof(a));
    show(a);
}
```

Explanation: Inside `main`, `sizeof(a)` = size of array (40 if int=4). Inside `show()`, a decays to pointer, so `sizeof(p)` = size of pointer (typically 8).

8. **Misleading Dereference**

```
#include <stdio.h>
int main() {
    int x = 5;
```

```
    int *p = &x;
    printf("%d", *p++);
}
```

Explanation: *p++ increments p, not *p. Output: prints 5, but pointer moves (harmless here, but risky later).

9. **Order of Evaluation Surprise**

```
#include <stdio.h>
int main() {
    int a[] = {1,2,3};
    int *p = a;
    printf("%d", *p + *++p);
}
```

Explanation: *p is 1, then ++p moves to 2. 1 + 2 = 3. But technically, order of evaluation is undefined — compilers may differ!

10. **Pointer and Function Call Combo**

```
#include <stdio.h>
int fun(int *p) { return (*p)++; }
int main() {
    int x = 5;
    printf("%d ", fun(&x));
    printf("%d", x);
}
```

Explanation: fun() returns old value (5), increments x to 6. Output: 5 6.

Checkpoint: If you could predict at least 7 out of 10 correctly — congratulations! You've got the pointer arithmetic intuition most interviewers look for.

Part B — Memory Traps in Action

Welcome to the darker side of pointers — where everything *looks* fine but quietly breaks memory rules. Interviewers love these examples because they reveal whether you truly understand how C manages storage.

Each trap here shows a real bug that compiles cleanly yet misbehaves in unpredictable ways. Your job: spot it before it happens.

11. **Trap 1 — The Vanishing Local**

```
#include <stdio.h>
int* foo() {
    int x = 10;
    return &x;
}
int main() {
    int *p = foo();
    printf("%d", *p);
}
```

Explanation: x dies when `foo()` returns, leaving p dangling. The program compiles but prints garbage or crashes.

Interview Tip: Returning the address of a local variable is always undefined behavior.

12. **Trap 2 — Freed but Still Used**

```
#include <stdlib.h>
int main() {
```

```
    int *p = malloc(sizeof(int));
    *p = 42;
    free(p);
    printf("%d", *p);
}
```

Explanation: Memory was released, but p still points there — a *dangling pointer*. Always set it to NULL after free().

13. **Trap 3 — Memory Leak by Reassignment**

```
#include <stdlib.h>
int main() {
    int *p = malloc(5 * sizeof(int));
    p = malloc(10 * sizeof(int)); // leak
}
```

Explanation: The first allocation's address is lost before freeing. This creates a silent leak.

Fix: Always free(p) before overwriting it.

14. **Trap 4 — Stack Pointer Escaping Scope**

```
#include <stdio.h>
int* getPointer() {
    int a = 5;
    return &a;
}
int main() {
    int *ptr = getPointer();
    printf("%d", *ptr);
}
```

Explanation: Same problem as before — a is destroyed on return. Pointer now refers to invalid stack space.

15. **Trap 5 — Partial Free Disaster**

```
#include <stdlib.h>
int main() {
    int *arr = malloc(5 * sizeof(int));
    int *mid = arr + 2;
    free(mid); // wrong
}
```

Explanation: Only the original pointer returned by `malloc()` may be freed. Here, freeing `mid` corrupts the heap.

16. **Trap 6 — Misaligned Type Cast**

```
double d = 3.14;
int *p = (int*)&d;
printf("%d", *p);
```

Explanation: Casting between incompatible pointer types breaks the strict aliasing rule and may misalign access. This is undefined behavior — don't assume it "just works."

17. **Trap 7 — Off-by-One Heap Write**

```
#include <stdlib.h>
int main() {
    int *a = malloc(3 * sizeof(int));
    for (int i = 0; i <= 3; i++)
        a[i] = i; // writes 4 elements
}
```

Explanation: Valid indices are 0–2. a[3] overruns the heap — sometimes silently, sometimes catastrophically.

18. **Trap 8 — Wrong sizeof**

```
#include <stdlib.h>
int main() {
    int *p = malloc(sizeof(p)); // wrong
    *p = 10;
    printf("%d", *p);
}
```

Explanation: sizeof(p) gives pointer size (8 bytes), not sizeof(int). This allocates the wrong amount of memory — a subtle but common bug.

19. **Trap 9 — Double Free**

```
#include <stdlib.h>
int main() {
    int *p = malloc(sizeof(int));
    free(p);
    free(p);
}
```

Explanation: Freeing memory twice corrupts the allocator's internal structures. Some systems detect this and abort immediately.

20. **Trap 10 — Shallow Copy Pitfall**

```
#include <string.h>
#include <stdlib.h>
int main() {
    char *a = malloc(5);
```

```
    char *b = a;
    strcpy(a, "Hi");
    free(a);
    printf("%s", b);
}
```

Explanation: Both pointers refer to the same block. After `free(a)`, b becomes dangling too.

21. **Trap 11 — Dynamic 2D Leak**

```
#include <stdlib.h>
int main() {
    int **m = malloc(3 * sizeof(int*));
    for (int i = 0; i < 3; i++)
        m[i] = malloc(3 * sizeof(int));
    free(m); // leak rows
}
```

Explanation: Each row must be freed individually before freeing `m`. Otherwise, nine integers leak silently.

22. **Trap 12 — Using Freed Pointer in Another Function**

```
#include <stdlib.h>
void release(int *p) { free(p); }
int main() {
    int *q = malloc(sizeof(int));
    *q = 100;
    release(q);
    printf("%d", *q);
}
```

Explanation: `release()` frees memory, but caller still uses the pointer. Always set freed pointers to

NULL in the calling scope.

23. **Trap 13 — Writing to String Literal**

```
char *s = "Hello";
s[0] = 'h';
```

Explanation:
String literals live in read-only memory. Modifying them is undefined behavior — and crashes on most systems.

24. **Trap 14 — Return of the Null Check**

```
#include <stdlib.h>
int main() {
    int *p = malloc(1000000000 * sizeof(int));
    p[0] = 1;
}
```

Explanation: If allocation fails, `malloc()` returns `NULL`. Accessing `p[0]` then segfaults instantly.

Rule: Always check `if (!p)` after allocation.

25. **Trap 15 — Realloc Without Temp Variable**

```
#include <stdlib.h>
int main() {
    int *p = malloc(5 * sizeof(int));
    p = realloc(p, 1000000000 * sizeof(int));
    if (!p) printf("realloc failed\n");
}
```

Explanation: If `realloc()` fails, the original block

is lost — leak + crash risk. Use a temporary pointer:

```
int *tmp = realloc(p, newsize);
if (tmp) p = tmp;
```

Checkpoint: If you can explain what each trap violates — congratulations! You're thinking like a systems programmer, not just a coder.

Interview Pro Tip: When asked "What happens here?" never just say "undefined behavior." Briefly explain why it's undefined — memory lifetime, aliasing, or allocation rule. That's how interviewers spot real understanding.

Part C — Spot the Bug Challenge

Now that you've seen how memory traps hide in plain sight, it's time to train your eyes to **spot the bug instantly** — the skill interviewers truly test.

Each of the following programs is short enough to fit on a single line, yet tricky enough to derail even an experienced coder.

26. **Pointer Arithmetic Gone Wrong**

```
int a[] = {1,2,3};
int *p = a;
printf("%d", *p + *++p);
```

Hint: Order of evaluation is not guaranteed. On one compiler it may print 3, on another 4 — both undefined.

27. **Wrong Operator Binding**

```
int x = 5, *p = &x;
printf("%d", *p+1);
```

Hint: `*p+1` means "value plus one," not "next address." If you meant the next element, you needed `*(p+1)`.

28. **Precedence Confusion**

```
int a = 10, b = 5;
int *p = &a, *q = &b;
printf("%d", *p + *q++);
```

Hint: Post-increment binds tighter — `*q++` increments pointer, not value. Always use parentheses to clarify intention.

29. **Double Dereference Error**

```
int x = 5, *p = &x;
printf("%d", **p);
```

Hint: Only one level of indirection here. `**p` tries to dereference an integer — invalid.

30. **Returning Local Address Again**

```
int* fun() { int x = 7; return &x; }
int main() { printf("%d", *fun()); }
```

Hint: You're returning the address of a dead variable. Every interviewer loves this trap.

31. **Lost in Translation**

```
int arr[3] = {1,2,3};
int *p = arr;
printf("%p", &arr + 1);
```

Hint: `&arr` has type `int (*)[3]`, so adding 1 jumps 3 ints ahead. Pointer types matter.

32. **Misused sizeof**

```
int *p = malloc(sizeof(p) * 5);
```

Hint: Allocates space for 5 pointers, not 5 integers. Use `sizeof(*p)` instead.

33. **Forgot to Null-Terminate**

```
char s[4] = {'C','o','d','e'};
printf("%s", s);
```

Hint: Strings must end with `'\0'`. Otherwise, printing runs off into random memory.

34. **Pointer Not Initialized**

```
int *p;
*p = 10;
```

Hint: Wild pointer! Always initialize before dereferencing.

35. **Post-Increment Illusion**

```
int x = 3, y = 4;
```

```
printf("%d", x++ + ++y);
```

Hint: Looks simple, but order of evaluation between operands is undefined in older C standards. Never rely on it.

36. **Array vs Pointer Confusion**

```
int a[5];
printf("%lu %lu", sizeof(a), sizeof(&a));
```

Hint: `sizeof(a)` = size of full array; `sizeof(&a)` = size of pointer. Two very different things.

37. **Wrong Free Target**

```
int a[3] = {1,2,3};
free(a);
```

Hint: Only memory from `malloc()` or friends can be freed.

38. **Dereferencing NULL**

```
int *p = NULL;
printf("%d", *p);
```

Hint: Classic crash — null dereference.

39. **Dangling After Free**

```
int *p = malloc(sizeof(int));
*p = 9;
free(p);
*p = 10;
```

Hint: Never touch memory after freeing. Set to `NULL` immediately.

40. **Wrong printf Format**

```
float f = 3.14;
printf("%d", f);
```

Hint: Always match format specifier to variable type.

41. **Operator Precedence Surprise**

```
int x=2, y=3;
printf("%d", x + y << 1);
```

Hint: Shifts have lower precedence — expression is `(x + y) << 1`.

42. **Nested Dereference Confusion**

```
int x = 10;
int *p = &x;
int **q = &p;
printf("%d", *q);
```

Hint: Prints the address of `x`, not its value. `**q` would print `10`.

43. **Modifying String Literal**

```
char *s = "Hi";
s[0] = 'h';
```

Hint: Read-only segment! Causes segmentation fault on most systems.

44. **Misused realloc**

```
int *p = NULL;
p = realloc(p, 10 * sizeof(int));
```

Hint: Works like malloc here, but always check the return for `NULL`. If you reallocate an existing block, use a temp pointer.

45. **Incorrect scanf Usage**

```
int n;
scanf("%d", n);
```

Hint: Missing `&`. Scanf needs the variable's address.

Checkpoint: If you spotted at least 15 bugs on first reading, your debugging instincts are strong. If not — great! Revisit the traps above until you can predict each failure.

Interview Pro Tip: When facing short C puzzles, think in three passes: (1) operator precedence, (2) pointer movement, (3) memory lifetime. If any of the three looks suspicious — that's the bug.

Part D — Do-It-Yourself: Pointer Puzzle Practice Zone

You've learned the rules. You've spotted the traps. Now it's time to test your reflexes.

Each of the following puzzles hides a subtle pointer or memory concept. Predict the output, identify the bug (if any), and write down the rule it tests. *Remember: these are not "run and guess" questions — they're "think and reason" ones.*

1. Basic pointer dereference:

```
int x = 5, *p = &x;
printf("%d", *p);
```

2. Postfix vs prefix increment:

```
int a[] = {10,20,30};
int *p = a;
printf("%d %d", *p++, *p);
```

3. Pointer subtraction:

```
int a[] = {1,2,3,4};
int *p = &a[1], *q = &a[3];
printf("%ld", q - p);
```

4. Double pointer dereference:

```
int x = 42;
int *p = &x;
int **q = &p;
printf("%d", **q);
```

5. Array decay in function:

```
void test(int *a) { printf("%lu", sizeof(a)); }
```

```
int main() {
    int arr[5];
    test(arr);
}
```

6. Wild pointer:

```
int *p;
*p = 10;
```

7. Pointer overflow:

```
int a[3] = {1,2,3};
int *p = a + 3;
printf("%d", *p);
```

8. Return address of local variable:

```
int* foo() { int x = 7; return &x; }
int main() { printf("%d", *foo()); }
```

9. String literal modification:

```
char *s = "Hi";
s[0] = 'h';
```

10. Difference between arrays and pointers:

```
int a[5];
int *p = a;
printf("%lu %lu", sizeof(a), sizeof(p));
```

11. Pointer increment with dereference:

```
int a[] = {1,2,3};
int *p = a;
printf("%d", *++p);
```

12. Dereference before increment:

```
int a[] = {1,2,3};
int *p = a;
printf("%d", *p++);
```

13. Pointer arithmetic with cast:

```
char *p = (char*)1000;
p += 5;
printf("%p", p);
```

14. Pointer difference in bytes:

```
int a[4];
printf("%ld", (char*)(&a[3]) - (char*)(&a[0]));
```

15. Function pointer basics:

```
int add(int a,int b){return a+b;}
int main() {
    int (*fptr)(int,int) = add;
    printf("%d", fptr(2,3));
}
```

16. Macro + pointer confusion:

```
#define INC(x) ++x
int main(){
    int *p = malloc(sizeof(int));
    *p = 10;
    printf("%d", INC(*p));
}
```

17. Pointer-to-array declaration:

```
int a[3] = {1,2,3};
int (*p)[3] = &a;
printf("%d", (*p)[1]);
```

18. Array of pointers:

```
int x=1,y=2,z=3;
int *arr[3] = {&x,&y,&z};
printf("%d", *arr[2]);
```

19. Function modifying pointer:

```
void f(int *p){ *p = 50; }
int main(){
    int x=10; f(&x);
    printf("%d", x);
}
```

20. Dynamic memory arithmetic:

```
int *p = malloc(3*sizeof(int));
for(int i=0;i<3;i++) p[i]=i+1;
printf("%d", *(p+2));
free(p);
```

21. Dangling pointer:

```
int *p = malloc(sizeof(int));
free(p);
printf("%d", *p);
```

22. sizeof and dereference:

```
int x = 10;
int *p = &x;
printf("%lu %lu", sizeof(p), sizeof(*p));
```

23. Pointer aliasing:

```
int x=5;
int *p=&x, *q=&x;
(*p)++; (*q)++;
printf("%d", x);
```

24. Memory leak:

```
int *p = malloc(sizeof(int));
p = malloc(sizeof(int)); // leak
```

25. Struct with pointer:

```
struct S { int *ptr; };
int x = 100;
struct S s = { &x };
printf("%d", *s.ptr);
```

26. Pointer difference confusion:

```
int arr[5] = {10,20,30,40,50};
int *p = &arr[4];
printf("%d", p - arr);
```

27. Function returning pointer:

```
int* get(){ static int x=9; return &x; }
int main(){ printf("%d", *get()); }
```

28. Mixed operators:

```
int a[]={1,2,3};
int *p=a;
printf("%d", *p + *++p);
```

29. Postfix and precedence:

```
int a[]={10,20,30};
int *p=a;
printf("%d %d", *p++, *p);
```

30. Triple pointer (bonus challenge):

```
int x=5; int *p=&x; int **q=&p; int ***r=&q;
printf("%d", ***r);
```

Pro Tip: While solving, speak aloud what each operator

is doing — "increment pointer," "dereference result," "decay array," etc. If you can explain it clearly, you already think like a pointer.

Interview Pro Tip: Pointer puzzles aren't about luck — they test control flow, memory awareness, and precision. The more patterns you recognize here, the faster you'll debug real systems later.

POINTER PUZZLES & MEMORY TRAPS — CHEATSHEET

Pointer Basics

- A pointer holds the **address** of another variable.
- `*p` = value at address; `&x` = address of `x`.
- Arrays decay to pointers (except with `sizeof` & &).

Memory Safety Rules

- Always initialize pointers; uninitialized = wild.
- Every `malloc()` needs one `free()`.
- Free only what you allocate; then set to `NULL`.

Pointer Arithmetic

- `p+1` jumps by size of type, not bytes.
- Pointer subtraction gives element count.
- Don't mix types — misalignment breaks rules.

Strings & Arrays

- String literals are read-only — never modify them.
- Always end strings with `'\0'`.
- `sizeof(array)` ≠ `sizeof(pointer)`.

Debugging Mindset

- "Compiles" ≠ "safe." Undefined behavior is real.
- Trace lifetime and ownership of every variable.
- Use `printf("%p")` to print pointer addresses.

Mantra: Initialize → Allocate → Verify → Free → Nullify.

Chapter 22

CODE OPTIMIZATION & BEST PRACTICES

When you first start programming in C, your goal is simple — make the program work. But as you grow, you begin to realize that **"working" and "working well"** are two very different things.

That's where this chapter steps in.

Ask any experienced C developer or interviewer: They'll tell you that optimization isn't about writing fancy code — it's about writing **smart, efficient, and maintainable** code. The kind that runs fast, uses memory wisely, and can be understood a year later without headaches.

This chapter teaches you exactly that — how to think like an optimizer. Not the kind who memorizes compiler flags, but the kind who understands what happens under the hood.

By the end of this chapter, you'll know:

- When optimization actually matters (and when it doesn't)
- How compilers optimize your code automatically
- How to write faster loops and smarter memory code
- How to profile, measure, and reason about performance
- How to write clean, readable code that interviewers love

Let's start with a truth that every developer learns eventually.

22.1 Why Optimize?

Optimization isn't about making your code "look smart." It's about making it **behave smartly**.

Your computer doesn't care how many lines your code has — it cares how efficiently you use memory, how predictably your loops run, and how much unnecessary work you make it do.

Here's a quick example:

Listing 22.1: Unoptimized vs Optimized Code Example

```
/* Unoptimized */
for (int i = 0; i < n; i++) {
    result = pow(2, 3);
    sum += result;
}

/* Optimized */
```

```
int result = 8;
for (int i = 0; i < n; i++) {
    sum += result;
}
```

Both versions give the same output. But the first one recalculates something every single time that never changes. The second version does it once.

That's optimization — not magic, just mindfulness.

Interview Tip: Interviewers often ask "How would you make this code more efficient?" They don't expect you to micro-optimize — they want to see if you can reason logically about *where time is being wasted.*

22.2 The Philosophy of Optimization

Optimization in C is less about memorizing tricks and more about developing the right mindset.

Here are the three golden rules of optimization — the same ones used by professionals everywhere:

1. **Make it work.** Don't optimize code that doesn't even run correctly. Write it clearly, test it thoroughly.
2. **Make it right.** Once your program is correct, make sure it's logically sound — no redundant operations, no unnecessary memory usage.
3. **Make it fast.** Only then should you focus on speeding things up — but always based on evidence, not instinct.

Premature optimization is the root of all evil. It's one of the most quoted truths in software engineering (Donald Knuth). It simply means: *don't optimize code before you even know what's slow.*

Before optimizing, always ask:

- Is this code even a performance bottleneck?
- Can the compiler already optimize it for me?
- Am I sacrificing readability for a small gain?

Optimization Mindset: Don't think of optimization as "faster code." Think of it as "smarter effort." Let the compiler handle what it can — and fix what only humans can.

22.3 When to Optimize (and When Not To)

Optimization has a cost: your time and your code's clarity. The key is knowing when it's worth paying that cost.

Optimize when:

- A profiler identifies a real bottleneck
- The code runs in a tight loop or is performance-critical
- You're working on embedded or low-memory systems

Don't optimize when:

- The code runs once or rarely
- The improvement is microscopic or uncertain
- It makes the code unreadable

A good programmer makes code fast enough. A great programmer makes it maintainable and predictable.

In short: **Correctness first, clarity second, optimization third.**

Interview Insight: Many optimization questions in interviews aren't about math — they're about reasoning. They test whether you can identify inefficiency and fix it gracefully, without breaking logic.

22.4 Loop Optimization and Expression Simplification

Loops are the heartbeat of most programs — they're where time is spent, memory is touched, and performance lives or dies. If your program feels "slow," it's almost always because of a loop that's doing a little too much work.

Let's learn to make those loops lean and efficient.

1. Moving Invariants Out of Loops

A simple but powerful idea: If something doesn't change inside a loop, don't compute it inside the loop.

Listing 22.2: Removing Invariants from Loops

```
/* Inefficient */
```

```
for (int i = 0; i < n; i++) {
    total += i * MAX_SIZE;
}

/* Optimized */
int factor = MAX_SIZE;
for (int i = 0; i < n; i++) {
    total += i * factor;
}
```

Why it matters: Even small savings multiplied by thousands of iterations make a difference. Compilers can optimize some invariants automatically, but recognizing them yourself shows true understanding — exactly what interviewers look for.

Interview Tip: If asked how you'd optimize a loop, first look for *repeated computations* and move them out.

2. Minimizing Work per Iteration

Here's a subtle but common inefficiency:

```
for (int i = 0; i < strlen(s); i++)
    printf("%c", s[i]);
```

`strlen()` walks the whole string every time! That's $O(n^2)$ work hiding in plain sight.

```
int len = strlen(s);
for (int i = 0; i < len; i++)
    printf("%c", s[i]);
```

Now it's $O(n)$. Small fix — massive impact.

Pro Tip: When you see a function call inside a loop, ask yourself — "Does it really need to run every time?"

3. Using Efficient Loop Constructs

Sometimes, structure alone matters.

```
for (int i = 0; i < 1000000; i++) sum += arr[i];   // good
while (i++ < 1000000) sum += arr[i];               // less
    readable, same work
```

Modern compilers make them run at similar speeds, but clarity always wins. Readable loops are easier to analyze — for both compilers and humans.

4. Strength Reduction: Replacing Expensive Operations

Division, modulus, and power operations are slow compared to addition or bitwise shifts.

```
/* Before */
for (int i = 0; i < n; i++)
    arr[i] = i / 2;

/* After */
for (int i = 0; i < n; i++)
    arr[i] = i >> 1;    // divide by 2 faster
```

Concept: Replacing an expensive operation with a cheaper equivalent is called **strength reduction**. Compilers often handle this automatically, but being aware of it helps in low-level optimization or embedded systems.

Common Replacements:

- `x / 2` → `x >> 1`

- `x * 2` → `x << 1`
- `x % 2` → `x & 1`

5. Avoiding Unnecessary Function Calls

Every function call has overhead — parameters, return addresses, stack frames. In critical code, even small calls add up.

```
/* Frequent small calls */
for (int i = 0; i < 1000; i++)
    update_sum(i);

/* Inline approach */
int sum = 0;
for (int i = 0; i < 1000; i++)
    sum += i;
```

Use functions for clarity, not for tiny repeated tasks. If you must, mark small utility functions as `inline` — but only when profiling justifies it.

Interview Insight: When asked about optimization, say this: *"I prefer profiling before inlining functions, because readability is usually more valuable than a few cycles."*

6. Loop Fusion and Unrolling

Loop fusion means combining multiple loops that iterate over the same range.

```
/* Before */
for (int i = 0; i < n; i++) a[i] = i;
for (int i = 0; i < n; i++) b[i] = i * 2;

/* After */
```

```
for (int i = 0; i < n; i++) {
    a[i] = i;
    b[i] = i * 2;
}
```

Loop unrolling means manually repeating body operations to reduce iteration overhead.

```
for (int i = 0; i < n; i += 4) {
    sum += a[i];
    sum += a[i+1];
    sum += a[i+2];
    sum += a[i+3];
}
```

This can improve cache usage and reduce branch cost, but only when used carefully — too much unrolling increases code size.

Rule of Thumb: Unroll for data-heavy loops, not control-heavy ones.

Optimization Habit: Before touching code, understand what it actually does in each iteration. Optimization is 90% observation, 10% action.

7. The Bigger Picture

Modern compilers (like GCC and Clang) already perform:

- Constant folding
- Common sub-expression elimination
- Loop invariant motion

- Dead code removal

So your real job isn't to outsmart the compiler — it's to write code it can understand and optimize easily.

Readable, well-structured code gives compilers more room to help you.

In short: *Write code for humans first, compilers second — they'll both thank you.*

22.5 Memory Access Patterns and Cache Efficiency

Even the fastest CPU waits when memory can't keep up. Modern processors are lightning-fast, but memory access can still slow your program to a crawl if data isn't laid out efficiently.

That's why understanding **cache locality** is one of the most valuable — and most underrated — optimization skills in C.

1. Locality of Reference

When your program accesses memory, the CPU fetches data in **cache lines** (small fixed-size chunks, usually 64 bytes). If you access consecutive elements, they arrive together in one cache load. If you jump around randomly — the cache must fetch from main memory again and again.

Listing 22.3: Sequential vs Random Access

```
/* Sequential access - cache friendly */
for (int i = 0; i < n; i++)
    sum += arr[i];

/* Random access - cache misses galore */
for (int i = 0; i < n; i++)
    sum += arr[rand() % n];
```

Interview Insight: When asked why arrays are faster than linked lists, say this: *"Because arrays have contiguous memory and benefit from cache locality."*

2. Row-Major vs Column-Major Access

C stores multi-dimensional arrays in **row-major order**: elements of the same row are stored next to each other.

```
int a[3][3];
/* Memory layout:
   a[0][0] a[0][1] a[0][2]
   a[1][0] a[1][1] a[1][2]
   a[2][0] a[2][1] a[2][2] */
```

So this loop order is cache-friendly:

```
for (int i = 0; i < 3; i++)
    for (int j = 0; j < 3; j++)
        process(a[i][j]);
```

But swapping the loops destroys that locality:

```
for (int j = 0; j < 3; j++)
    for (int i = 0; i < 3; i++)
        process(a[i][j]);
```

Remember: Access data in the same order it's stored.

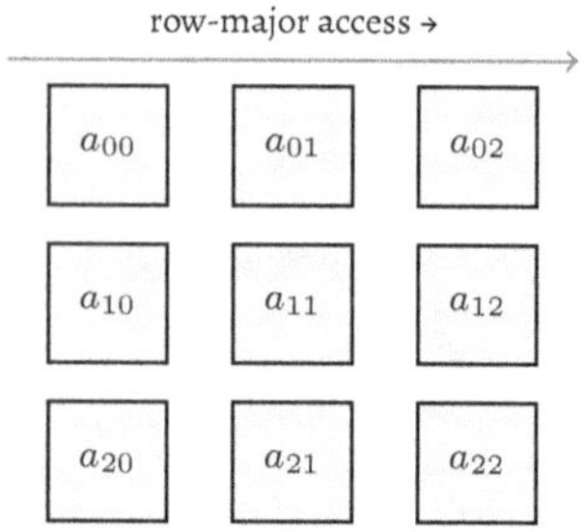

Figure 22.1: *Row-major layout in memory — access rows for best cache performance.*

3. Spatial and Temporal Locality

Spatial locality: accessing nearby data locations. **Temporal locality:** reusing recently accessed data.

Example:

```
int total = 0;
for (int i = 0; i < n; i++)
    total += a[i];      // spatial locality

for (int i = 0; i < n; i++)
    total += a[i];      // temporal locality - cache already
     warm
```

Optimization Rule: Group related data together, and reuse it soon.

4. Struct Alignment and Padding

The compiler often inserts padding bytes in structures to align members to word boundaries. This helps CPU efficiency but can waste space.

```
struct A {
    char  c;    // 1 byte
    int   x;    // 4 bytes
    char  d;    // 1 byte
};
/* Likely size: 12 bytes (due to padding) */
```

Reordering fields can save space:

```
struct B {
    int   x;
    char  c;
    char  d;
};
/* Size: 8 bytes - same data, better alignment */
```

Alignment Tip: Group larger data types first, smaller ones last. It keeps your structs compact and your CPU happy.

5. Arrays of Structs vs Structs of Arrays

In performance-critical systems, layout decisions matter.

```
struct Point { float x, y, z; };
struct Point pts[1000];     // Array of structs (AoS)
```

Pros: easy to read, logical grouping. **Cons:** scattered memory access if only one field is used frequently.

Compare with:

```
struct Points { float x[1000], y[1000], z[1000]; };  //
    Struct of arrays (SoA)
```

Pros:
cache-friendly when processing only one component (like

x). **Cons:** less intuitive.

Interview Insight: When asked about performance in data-heavy code, mention SoA vs AoS — it shows you understand how memory really works.

6. Cache-Friendly Thinking

Always think: "How will memory look to the CPU?"

- Access data linearly.
- Keep hot data together.
- Avoid pointer chasing unless necessary.
- Reuse recent data — don't let it go cold.

Interview Takeaway: Optimization isn't just about reducing instructions — it's about reducing *waiting*. Every cache miss is a pause your CPU didn't need.

22.6 Compiler Optimizations and Inline Functions

So far, we've focused on what *you* can do to make your code efficient. Now let's see what your compiler is already doing — often far better and faster than you can.

Compilers are optimization engines. They don't just translate C into machine code — they analyze, reorder, simplify, and eliminate unnecessary work long before your program ever runs.

1. The -O Levels in GCC/Clang

When you compile your program, you can choose how aggressively the compiler should optimize it.

Listing 22.4: Compiler optimization levels

```
gcc -O0 main.c -o prog    # No optimization (default)
gcc -O1 main.c -o prog    # Basic optimizations
gcc -O2 main.c -o prog    # Recommended balance of speed and
     safety
gcc -O3 main.c -o prog    # Maximum optimization (may
     increase size)
gcc -Os main.c -o prog    # Optimize for smaller code size
gcc -Ofast main.c -o prog # Ignore strict standards for more
      speed
```

Quick guide:

- `-O0`: use during debugging; keeps code readable for gdb.
- `-O2`: safe default — most production builds use it.
- `-O3`: good for computational programs but can bloat binaries.
- `-Ofast`: fastest, but may ignore some floating-point accuracy rules.

Interview Tip: If an interviewer asks, "Which optimization level do you use?", answer: "*-O2 for reliability; -O3 only when profiling shows a clear gain.*"

2. Common Compiler Optimizations

Modern compilers perform dozens of transformations automatically. Here are the big ones interviewers love to discuss:

- **Constant Folding:** evaluates constant expressions at compile time. `int x = 2 * 3;` → becomes `int x = 6;`
- **Dead Code Elimination:** removes unreachable or unused statements.
- **Loop Invariant Motion:** moves calculations outside a loop if they don't change.
- **Common Subexpression Elimination:** reuses results of identical computations.
- **Inlining:** replaces a small function call with its actual body.

All these happen silently, but knowing them helps you write code that the compiler can optimize easily.

Remember: The compiler isn't your enemy — it's your teammate.

3. Inline Functions — When and Why

Every function call adds overhead: pushing arguments, jumping, and returning. For tiny functions that run in loops, this overhead can be avoided with `inline`.

Listing 22.5: Using inline functions

```
inline int square(int x) {
    return x * x;
}

int main() {
    int n = 5;
    printf("%d", square(n));
}
```

The compiler may replace each call to `square(n)` with its body directly — eliminating the call cost.

When to use:

- For very short, frequently called functions.
- When the function is defined in a header file.

When not to use:

- For large or recursive functions.
- When function pointers are involved (cannot inline dynamically).

Quick Note: `inline` is only a *suggestion*. The compiler may ignore it if it decides inlining isn't worth it.

4. Function Inlining vs Macros

Interviewers
often ask this question — "What's the difference between macros and inline functions?"

```
#define SQR(x) ((x)*(x))     // macro
inline int sqr(int x) { return x * x; } // inline function
```

Comparison:

- Macros are preprocessor text replacements (no type checking).
- Inline functions are real functions (type safe and debuggable).
- Inline is safer, cleaner, and preferred in modern C (C99+).

Interview Answer: *"Inline functions combine the efficiency of macros with the safety of real functions."*

5. Profiling Before Optimizing

Never guess what's slow — measure it. Use profiling tools like:

- `gprof` — basic function-level profiling.
- `valgrind --tool=callgrind` — detailed CPU analysis.
- `perf` — low-level performance events on Linux.

```
gcc -pg main.c -o prog
./prog
gprof prog gmon.out > report.txt
```

Key takeaway: Optimization without measurement is just guessing. Professionals don't guess.

6. Pragmas and Compiler Hints

Some compilers allow special hints using #pragma. Example:

```
#pragma GCC unroll 4
for (int i = 0; i < n; i++)
    sum += a[i];
```

This requests loop unrolling — but remember, it's a hint, not a command.

Optimization Principle: Trust your compiler. But understand it deeply enough to know when to intervene.

7. The Real Optimization Mindset

At the end of the day, optimization is a balance:

- Write clean code first.
- Profile and find real bottlenecks.
- Optimize only what matters.
- Measure again.

If your optimization breaks clarity, you've lost before you've begun.

Interview Summary:

- Know what -O1, -O2, and -O3 do.
- Explain inlining and its trade-offs.
- Understand compiler optimizations conceptually.

- Emphasize profiling before performance tweaks.

22.7 Writing Clean, Maintainable, and Interview-Ready C Code

Optimization gets you speed. Good practices keep that speed readable, reusable, and reliable. A well-optimized program that no one understands isn't professional code — it's a future bug report.

This section isn't about clever tricks; it's about discipline. How to write C code that looks like it was written by someone who knows what they're doing.

1. Clarity Beats Cleverness

Write for the next person who will read your code — because that person might be you, three months later.

```
/* Bad */
for (i = n; i--; ) s += *p++;

/* Good */
for (int i = 0; i < n; i++)
    sum += array[i];
```

Interview Insight: If you're asked to "optimize this snippet," you can often impress more by making it clear than by making it shorter.

> **Rule #1:** Readable code is scalable code. If a bug hides behind cleverness, it's not a feature — it's a liability.

2. Consistent Naming and Style

Pick one convention and stick to it. Consistency beats perfection.

```
int get_sum();       // good
int GetSum();        // confusing mix
int getsum();        // inconsistent
```

Use descriptive, intention-revealing names:

- `count`, not `c`
- `total_bytes`, not `tb`
- `MAX_LIMIT`, not `ML`

Use descriptive, intention-revealing names: **Pro Tip:** Align variable names with purpose, not with brevity.

3. Keep Functions Short and Focused

Each function should do one job — and do it well.

```
/* Bad */
void processDataAndWriteFileAndLogErrors();

/* Good */
void processData();
void writeFile();
void logErrors();
```

If you can't describe a function in one sentence, it's too long.

Interview Tip: When asked to "refactor" code, start by splitting long functions into logical units. This shows design maturity.

Do-It-Yourself: Practice Zone

This section transforms what you've learned into performance instinct. Each problem builds a different muscle — reasoning, refactoring, debugging, or analyzing compiler behavior.

Take your time. Write. Run. Profile. This is where good coders become great.

Part A — Optimization Basics

1. Compile the same program with `-O0`, `-O1`, `-O2`, and `-O3`. Record the runtime for each and note differences.

2. Predict how constant folding works:

```
int x = 3 * 4 + 2;
```

3. Identify dead code:

```
if (0) printf("Hello");
```

4. Move loop-invariant code outside the loop:

```
for (int i = 0; i < n; i++)
    total += x * y;
```

5. Spot redundant computation:

```
for (int i = 0; i < n; i++)
    total += (a + b) * arr[i];
```

6. Compare performance of:

```
sum += i * 2;
```

vs.

```
sum += (i << 1);
```

7. Time a function with and without optimization flags.

8. Test integer overflow:

```
int x = 2147483647;
printf("%d", x + 1);
```

9. Identify which expressions compiler can simplify:

```
for (int i = 0; i < 10; i++)
    y = 2 * 3 * i;
```

10. Write an equivalent loop without using multiplication.

11. Compare speed between:

```
arr[i] = 0;
```

and:

```
memset(arr, 0, sizeof(arr));
```

12. Find the redundant variable:

```
int temp = a + b;
c = temp;
```

13. Predict result after constant propagation:

```
int a = 10;
int b = a + 5;
int c = b * 2;
```

14. Rearrange expressions for readability without performance loss.
15. Bonus: find three optimizations the compiler already performs on:

```
for (int i=0; i<n; i++) total += arr[i]*2;
```

Part B — Inline, Macros & Preprocessor

16. Expand this macro mentally and predict output:

```
#define SQR(x) (x * x)
printf("%d", SQR(3 + 2));
```

17. Fix the previous macro so it works correctly for any expression.
18. Spot the problem:

```
#define INC(x) ++x
printf("%d", INC(i) * INC(i));
```

19. Rewrite the above using an `inline` function instead of a macro.
20. Write a macro to compute the cube of a number safely.
21. Compare performance of `inline` function vs. macro using `gcc -E` to inspect expansion.
22. Create a header file with:

```
#define MAX(a,b) ((a) > (b) ? (a) : (b))
```

Then show how missing parentheses can break it.

23. Implement:

```
#define SWAP(a,b) do { int t=a; a=b; b=t; } while(0)
```

Explain why the `do{...}while(0)` wrapper is necessary.

24. Predict the preprocessor expansion:

```
#define ADD(x,y) x+y
printf("%d", 5 * ADD(2,3));
```

25. Write a macro `LOG(x)` that prints both the variable name and its value.

26. Demonstrate the # (stringizing) and ## (token-pasting) operators with an example.

27. Create a macro to generate variable names:

```
/* MAKE(id) -> var_id */
```

Use it to declare and initialize `var_a`, `var_b`.

28. Write conditional compilation for:

```
#if VERSION >= 3
    printf("Modern mode");
#elif VERSION == 2
    printf("Legacy mode");
#else
    printf("Unsupported");
#endif
```

29. Implement a basic debug system:

```
#ifdef DEBUG
  #define TRACE(x) printf("DEBUG: %s\n", x)
#else
  #define TRACE(x)
```

```
#endif
```

30. Challenge: write a macro that safely evaluates an expression only once, similar to inline behavior.

Part C — Memory Access & Cache Behavior

31. Observe time difference:

```
for (int i=0;i<10000;i++)
  for (int j=0;j<10000;j++)
    arr[i][j]++;
```

    Then swap loop order and measure again. *Hint: cache locality loves row-major order.*

32. Predict which access pattern is faster and why:

```
a[i][j]    vs.    a[j][i]
```

33. Initialize a large array twice — once sequentially, once randomly. Measure which is faster and explain.

34. Compare:

```
for (int i=0; i<n; i++) sum += arr[i];
```

    with:

```
int *p = arr;
for (int i=0; i<n; i++) sum += *p++;
```

35. Analyze the difference between:

```
int arr[100000];
int *p = arr;
for (int i=0; i<100000; i++) p[i] = i;
```

and:

```
for (int *p=arr; p<&arr[100000]; p++) *p = p-arr;
```

36. Write a small program that measures the cost of pointer chasing through a linked list vs. sequential array traversal.

37. Predict what happens when array elements exceed cache line size.

38. Explore the effect of loop unrolling:

```
for (int i=0;i<n;i+=4) {
    sum += a[i] + a[i+1] + a[i+2] + a[i+3];
}
```

39. Explain why this code might run slower:

```
for (int i=0;i<n;i++)
  for (int j=0;j<n;j++)
    arr[j][i]++;
```

40. Experiment: compare stack allocation vs. heap allocation speed for a 2D array.

41. Predict output:

```
int a[3] = {1,2,3};
printf("%d", *(a+1));
```

42. Spot the logical error:

```
int *p = arr;
while (*p++) printf("%d", *p);
```

43. Use Valgrind or AddressSanitizer to detect an invalid read beyond array bounds.

44. Explain why accessing memory sequentially improves branch prediction and cache prefetching.

45. Challenge: write two loops — one cache-friendly, one cache-unfriendly — and profile their runtime difference for a large dataset.

Part D — Struct Alignment & Space Efficiency

46. Predict the output:

```
struct A {
    char c;
    int i;
};
printf("%zu", sizeof(struct A));
```

Hint: Alignment causes hidden padding.

47. Rearrange members in the above struct to minimize memory usage.

48. Compare memory sizes:

```
struct X { char c; int i; double d; };
struct Y { double d; int i; char c; };
```

49. Write code using `__attribute__((packed))` and observe how it changes `sizeof()`.

```
struct __attribute__((packed)) Data {
    char c;
    int i;
};
```

50. Why is this code risky?

```
struct __attribute__((packed)) Data {
```

```
    char c;
    int i;
};
```

Hint: Misaligned access can crash on some architectures.

51. Write a struct representing a 2D point and a line segment — compare their memory footprints.

52. Predict result:

```
struct S { short a; char b; short c; };
printf("%zu", sizeof(struct S));
```

53. Compare pointer vs structure size:

```
struct Node {
    int data;
    struct Node *next;
};
printf("%zu %zu", sizeof(struct Node), sizeof(struct
     Node*));
```

54. Align the following manually for optimal packing:

```
struct Data {
    char c1;
    double d;
    char c2;
    int i;
};
```

55. Add padding explicitly and print structure layout using:

```
printf("%p %p %p %p", &s.c1, &s.d, &s.c2, &s.i);
```

56. Observe structure alignment in arrays:

```
struct P { int x; char c; };
struct P arr[3];
printf("%p %p", &arr[0], &arr[1]);
```

57. Predict output:

```
typedef struct {
    unsigned a:3;
    unsigned b:5;
    unsigned c:2;
} BitField;
printf("%zu", sizeof(BitField));
```

58. Experiment: compare access time between bit-fields and normal integers.

59. Create a structure with nested structures and print its total size.

60. Challenge:
    Design a structure representing a "Student Record" with minimal padding, and explain your reasoning.

Part E — Clean Code & Maintainability

61. Refactor this code to improve readability:

```
int f(int a,int b){if(a>b)return a;else return b;}
```

Hint: spacing and naming show professionalism.

62. Identify poor naming practice:

```
int x1,x2,x3;
float y;
```

Hint: choose descriptive, meaningful names.

63. Explain why this design is hard to maintain:

```
int calc(int a,int b,int c,int d,int e);
```

Hint: Too many parameters — consider structs.

64. Split this monolithic function into smaller functions logically:

```
void process() {
    readData();
    validate();
    compute();
    print();
}
```

65. Add comments where necessary — but not everywhere. *Hint: Comment the "why", not the "what".*

66. Predict which version future you will prefer reading in six months.

67. Modularize the following:

```
int main() {
    int arr[100];
    read(arr);
    sort(arr);
    print(arr);
}
```

68. Apply DRY ("Don't Repeat Yourself") principle — refactor any repeated logic into a reusable function.

69. Show why global variables reduce maintainability.

70. Write a function that avoids "magic numbers" by

using named constants.

```
#define MAX_USERS 100
int users[MAX_USERS];
```

71. Compare:

```
#define LIMIT 100
const int LIMIT = 100;
```

Hint: Which is safer and debuggable?

72. Show how consistent indentation improves comprehension.

73. Find the bug hidden by inconsistent braces:

```
if (x>0)
    if (y>0)
        printf("Hi");
    else
        printf("Bye");
```

Hint: Always use braces for nested conditionals.

74. Convert this repetitive code into a loop:

```
printf("%d", a[0]);
printf("%d", a[1]);
printf("%d", a[2]);
```

75. Challenge: review a 50-line program and write three suggestions that would make it easier for someone else to maintain.

Part F — Algorithmic Efficiency & Time Optimization

76. Identify the inefficiency:

```
for (int i = 0; i < n; i++)
  for (int j = 0; j < n; j++)
    if (i == j)
      sum += arr[i][j];
```

Hint: You don't need a nested loop to access the diagonal.

77. Optimize:

```
for (int i = 0; i < n; i++)
  for (int j = 0; j < m; j++)
    for (int k = 0; k < 1000; k++)
        total += data[i][j];
```

Hint: Any work repeated 1000 times unnecessarily is wasted.

78. Predict which is faster:

```
for (int i=0;i<n;i++) a[i]*=2;
for (int i=0;i<n;i++) b[i]*=3;
```

vs.

```
for (int i=0;i<n;i++) { a[i]*=2; b[i]*=3; }
```

Hint: Fewer passes = better cache reuse.

79. Simplify logic:

```
if (x>0) flag=1; else flag=0;
```

Hint: flag = (x > 0);

80. Optimize repeated calls:

```
for (int i=0;i<100;i++)
   printf("%d\n", strlen(str));
```

Hint: Compute once, not every iteration.

81. Remove redundancy:

```
int a = b * 10;
int c = b * 10 + 5;
```

Hint: Store common subexpressions.

82. Improve time complexity:

```
for (int i=0;i<n;i++)
  for (int j=0;j<n;j++)
    if (arr[i] == arr[j]) count++;
```

Hint: Sorting or hashing avoids $O(n^2)$ loops.

83. Predict complexity:

```
for (int i = 1; i < n; i *= 2)
  printf("%d", i);
```

Hint: This runs in $O(\log n)$.

84. Optimize recursion:

```
int fib(int n) {
  if (n <= 1) return n;
  return fib(n-1) + fib(n-2);
}
```

Hint: Use memoization or iteration.

85. Convert to tail recursion:

```
int fact(int n, int acc) {
```

```
  if (n==0) return acc;
  return fact(n-1, n*acc);
}
```

Hint: Tail recursion helps some compilers optimize stack.

86. Optimize search:

```
for (int i=0; i<n; i++)
  if (arr[i]==key) { found=1; break; }
```

Hint: If array is sorted, binary search is faster.

87. Compare complexity:

```
O(n log n) vs. O(n^2)
```

Explain which sorting algorithms fall into which category.

88. Inline optimization:

```
inline int square(int x) { return x*x; }
```

Hint: Reduces call overhead but may increase binary size.

89. Predict which code uses less CPU cache thrashing:

```
for (int i=0; i<n; i++) sum += A[i][0];
```

vs.

```
for (int j=0; j<n; j++) sum += A[0][j];
```

90. Challenge: Rewrite a program that reverses a string, removes duplicates, and sorts characters — all in a single pass if possible.

Part G — Real-World Optimization Scenarios

91. File I/O bottleneck:

```
FILE *fp = fopen("data.txt","r");
while(!feof(fp))
    fscanf(fp,"%d",&x);
```

Hint: Buffered reading (e.g., fread) or batching I/O is faster.

92. Optimize this program that counts words in a large file. Use buffered reading and minimal system calls.

93. Reduce memory footprint:

```
int arr[1000000];
```

Hint: Allocate dynamically or reuse blocks when possible.

94. Avoid redundant recomputation:

```
for (int i=0; i<n; i++)
    result += pow(x,i);
```

Hint: Replace pow() with incremental multiplication.

95. Large-array initialization:

```
for (int i=0; i<1000000; i++) arr[i] = 0;
```

Hint: Use memset() — usually faster and vectorized.

96. Speed up sorting of millions of integers — compare `qsort()` vs. custom quicksort vs. counting sort.

97. Reduce branching:

```
if (x) y = 1; else y = 0;
```

Hint: Use boolean or bitwise tricks: y = !!x;

98. Cache-friendly matrix traversal:

```
for (int i=0; i<N; i++)
  for (int j=0; j<M; j++)
    sum += A[i][j];
```

Hint: Row-major order favors inner-loop on columns.

99. Optimize string concatenation in loops. *Hint: Use a buffer with sprintf or track position manually.*

100. Compiler-level optimization: Compile the same program with gcc -O0, -O1, -O2, -O3. Observe runtime differences and generated assembly size.

Chapter 23

IMPLEMENT WITHOUT LIBRARY FUNCTIONS

If you've reached this chapter, you're already thinking like an engineer — not just someone who uses tools, but someone who wants to understand how they're built.

In C, every library function you call — from `strlen()` to `memcpy()` — hides a tiny algorithm inside it. These functions are written by other programmers who made decisions about how to loop, where to stop, what to check, and how to handle corner cases. And now it's your turn to think like them.

When interviewers ask,

> "Can you implement `strlen()` without using `strlen()`?"

they aren't testing if you memorized syntax — they're testing your *thought process*. They want to see how you think through a problem, how you reason about strings, and how confidently you can navigate through raw memory.

This chapter will help you:

- Understand how common C library functions actually work behind the scenes.
- Build the logic and confidence to write clean, safe implementations yourself.
- Strengthen your understanding of pointers, loops, and array traversal.
- Practice writing robust, interview-ready code from scratch.

Each section will take you one step deeper — from simple string re-creations to memory manipulation and finally to complete utility functions that mimic standard library behavior.

By the end of this chapter, you'll not only know how to use the standard library — you'll know how to rebuild it. And that's the difference between a programmer and a C craftsman.

23.1 String Handling Essentials

If you've spent any time with C strings, you already know they're just arrays of characters ending with a special symbol — `'\0'`. That little terminator gives strings their boundary, and every standard function in `<string.h>` is built around respecting that rule.

In this section, you'll re-create the most common

string functions from scratch. Each task sharpens your understanding of how pointers move, how characters are compared, and how the null terminator decides when to stop.

1. **Implement your own `strlen(const char *s)`.** Count characters until you hit `'\0'`. *Hint: You don't need indexing — pointer arithmetic alone is enough.*

2. **Write `strcpy(char *dest, const char *src)`.** Copy one string into another using a loop. Stop copying when you reach `'\0'`, and don't forget to add it at the end.

3. **Implement `strcmp(const char *a, const char *b)`.** Compare character by character until they differ or both end. Return the difference between mismatched characters.

4. **Re-create `strcat(char *dest, const char *src)`.** Move to the end of the first string and start appending the second. Watch for buffer overflow — make sure there's enough room!

5. **Implement `strrev(char *s)` to reverse a string in-place.** Swap characters from both ends moving inward. *Hint: Use two pointers — one at the start, one at the end.*

6. **Write your own `strchr(const char *s, char ch)`.** Return a pointer to the first occurrence of `ch`, or `NULL` if not found.

7. **Build** `strstr(const char *haystack, const char *needle)`. Search for one string inside another manually. *Hint: Use nested loops — reset the inner index each time a mismatch occurs.*

8. **Bonus: Implement recursive** `strlen()`. If the current character isn't `'\0'`, return `1 + strlen(s + 1)`. *It's elegant, but notice the function-call overhead.*

Each of these tasks teaches you something deeper: how loops stop, how pointers walk, and how invisible terminators control data. The more you write these from scratch, the less you'll fear the word "undefined."

23.2 Memory and Utility Functions

Once you understand strings, you're halfway to mastering memory. Functions like `memcpy()`, `memset()`, and `memcmp()` might seem mysterious at first, but at their core, they're simple loops operating on raw bytes. These exercises will help you re-create them — and strengthen your mental model of how memory really works.

9. **Write your own** `memcpy(void *dest, const void *src,`
   `size_t n)`. Copy n bytes from `src` to `dest`. *Hint: Cast to `char*` before looping — copying works byte by byte.*

10. **Implement** `memset(void *ptr, int value, size_t n)`.
    Set n bytes in memory to a given value. This is great

for initializing buffers or arrays before use.

11. **Write a manual version of** `memcmp(const void *a, const void *b, size_t n)`. Compare two memory blocks byte-by-byte. Stop as soon as you find a difference.

12. **Implement your own** `abs(int x)`. Return the positive value without using `abs()`. *Hint: Use the ternary operator — it's a clean one-liner.*

13. **Re-create integer-to-string conversion —** `itoa(int num,`
`char *str)`. Convert an integer into a character string manually. *Tip: Handle negatives, reverse the digits, and add* `'\0'` *at the end.*

14. **Implement**
the reverse — `atoi(const char *str)`. Convert a string of digits into an integer. *Hint: Subtract* `'0'` *from each character and build the result step-by-step.*

15. **Write a basic version of** `pow(int base, int exp)`. Compute powers using simple loops. *Hint: Use multiplication inside a for-loop — recursion works too, but iterative is faster.*

16. **Implement an approximate** `sqrt(float n)` **using the Newton-Raphson method.** Iterate until the result stabilizes. *Hint: The formula is* `x = 0.5 * (x + n / x)` *— start with* `x = n`.

17. **Bonus: Implement** `swap(void *a, void *b,`

`size_t size)`. Perform a byte-level swap using a temporary buffer. *Hint: This builds the logic behind generic sorting algorithms.*

These utility functions give you low-level control over memory — a skill few beginners truly master. Once you can re-create them, you'll begin to see how every high-level abstraction in C ultimately rests on loops, bytes, and a few well-placed conditionals.

23.3 Advanced Challenges

By now, you've re-created most of C's essential library logic. That's no small feat — it means you understand how bytes move, how strings terminate, and how memory behaves when left unchecked. But to truly think like a systems-level programmer, you need to tackle the functions that combine logic, formatting, and subtle rules.

These next challenges are designed to stretch your reasoning and strengthen your control of flow, edge cases, and performance.

18. **Implement your own** `strtok(char *str, const char`
`delim)`. Tokenize a string by replacing delimiters with `'\0'`. *Hint: Keep track of the static pointer for subsequent calls — exactly like the real one.*

19. **Write a simplified** `printf(const char *fmt, ...)`. Support only %d, %c, and %s. *Hint: Learn about `<stdarg.h>` and `va_list`.*

20. **Build a minimal `scanf()` clone.** Parse integers and strings from user input without the standard function. *Hint: Use `getchar()` and look for whitespace to separate tokens.*

21. **Re-create `fgets()` using `getchar()`.** Stop on newline or EOF and ensure the string is properly null-terminated.

22. **Implement a tiny version of `printf()` that counts characters printed.** Return the number of characters output — interviewers love this addition.

23. **Design your own `strcmpi()` (case-insensitive compare).** Convert both characters to lowercase using arithmetic and compare.

24. **Write a function `trim(char *s)` that removes leading and trailing spaces.** Use pointers to skip whitespace efficiently.

25. **Implement a `replace(char *s, char old, char new)`.** Replace all occurrences of one character with another in place.

26. **Build your own `strdup()` function.** Dynamically allocate memory and copy the given string. *Hint: Combine logic from `strlen()` and `strcpy()`.*

27. **Create a function `reverseWords(char *s)`.** Reverse words in a sentence but not the characters themselves. *Hint: Reverse the entire string first, then each word individually.*

28. **Implement `itoa()` with custom base.** Support binary, octal, decimal, and hexadecimal conversions. *Hint: Use division and modulus — store digits in reverse.*

29. **Re-create `atoi()` with error handling.** Stop when a non-digit is found and return a clean integer result.

30. **Simulate `memmove(void *dest, const void *src, size_t n)`.** Handle overlapping memory regions safely — direction matters here.

31. **Implement a mini `strsplit()` that breaks a line into words.** Return each token via pointer array. *Hint: Combine dynamic memory + pointer arrays.*

32. **Write a `toUpper(char *s)` and `toLower(char *s)` pair.** Convert case manually using ASCII arithmetic (`'A' + 32` and `'a' - 32`).

33. **Bonus: Build your own logging utility.** Create a function `logMessage(const char *level, const char *msg)` that prefixes messages like `[INFO]`, `[WARN]`, or `[ERROR]` and prints them with timestamps.

Once you can implement these, you've crossed a threshold — you're no longer just a user of C's standard library, you're a creator of it. These challenges train your precision, creativity, and coding maturity — exactly what top interviewers look for in system-level problem solvers.

Do-It-Yourself: Practice Zone

Time to put everything into practice! In this section, you'll re-create the logic behind the most-used C library functions — entirely from scratch. Each exercise is a real interview favorite that tests both understanding and precision.

Pro Tip: Don't rush. Implement a few each day, test thoroughly, and write your own test cases before checking against the standard version.

Part A — String Handling Functions

1. Implement your version of `strlen()`.

   ```
   size_t my_strlen(const char *s);
   ```

2. Write your own `strcpy()`.

   ```
   char* my_strcpy(char *dest, const char *src);
   ```

3. Implement `strcat()` — manually append strings.

   ```
   char* my_strcat(char *dest, const char *src);
   ```

4. Write a function to compare two strings — `strcmp()`.

   ```
   int my_strcmp(const char *a, const char *b);
   ```

5. Reverse a string using pointers.

   ```
   void my_strrev(char *s);
   ```

6. Implement your own `strchr()`.

```
char* my_strchr(const char *s, char ch);
```

7. Write a recursive version of `strlen()`.

```
int my_strlen_recursive(const char *s);
```

8. Implement substring search (`strstr()`).

```
char* my_strstr(const char *haystack, const char *
     needle);
```

Part B — Memory and Utility Functions

9. Implement `memcpy()`.

```
void* my_memcpy(void *dest, const void *src, size_t n)
     ;
```

10. Implement `memset()`.

```
void* my_memset(void *ptr, int value, size_t n);
```

11. Write your own integer-to-string converter.

```
void my_itoa(int num, char *str);
```

12. Reverse-engineer `atoi()`.

```
int my_atoi(const char *str);
```

13. Implement absolute value manually.

```
int my_abs(int x);
```

14. Write a basic power function (`pow()`).

```
int my_pow(int base, int exp);
```

15. Implement approximate square root using Newton's method.

```
float my_sqrt(float n);
```

16. Swap two generic variables.

```
void my_swap(void *a, void *b, size_t size);
```

Part C — Advanced Challenges

17. Create your own tokenizer (`strtok()`).

```
char* my_strtok(char *str, const char *delim);
```

18. Write a simplified `printf()` (supporting only %d and %s).

```
int my_printf(const char *fmt, ...);
```

19. Build a case-insensitive compare (`strcmpi()`).

```
int my_strcmpi(const char *a, const char *b);
```

20. Implement a function to remove leading/trailing spaces.

```
void trim(char *s);
```

21. Replace all occurrences of a character.

```
void replace(char *s, char old, char new);
```

22. Duplicate a string dynamically (`strdup()`).

```
char* my_strdup(const char *src);
```

23. Reverse words in a sentence.

```
void reverseWords(char *s);
```

24. Implement `memmove()` safely for overlapping regions.

```
void* my_memmove(void *dest, const void *src, size_t
    n);
```

25. Convert integer to binary representation string.

```
void toBinary(int n, char *out);
```

26. Implement a simple logging function.

```
void logMessage(const char *level, const char *msg);
```

Final Stretch — Mini Project: "Rebuild the Standard Library"

Pick 5–6 functions from above and integrate them into a single file named `mylib.c`. Then include your header file `mylib.h` and test every function thoroughly with unit test programs. The goal isn't speed — it's correctness and confidence.

By finishing this section, you'll no longer rely on standard libraries — you'll understand how they work internally. That's exactly the kind of mastery interviewers look for when they ask: "Can you write `strlen()` without using `string.h`?"

The Minimalist's C Library — Cheatsheet

1. **Strings = arrays + '\0'.** Forget the terminator, invite chaos.
2. **Your loops are your library.** `strlen()`, `strcpy()`, `strcmp()` — all simple loops.
3. **Check memory before access.** Never read or write uninitialized pointers.
4. **Every malloc() deserves a free().** Track your allocations religiously.
5. **Byte logic builds mastery.** Understand what `memcpy()` and `memmove()` truly do.
6. **Conversions build clarity.** Writing your own `atoi()` and `itoa()` sharpens precision.
7. **Group and reuse.** Collect your recreated functions in `mylib.c`.
8. **Readable > clever.** Future-you will thank present-you.
9. **Understand, don't depend.** Rebuilding the standard library is real learning.

Once you can rebuild C's core tools, you're no longer using C —you're mastering it.

Chapter 24

REAL COMPANY QUESTIONS

Part A — Rapid Fire: Conceptual Questions

These questions are inspired by real IT interviews (TCS, Wipro, Infosys, Microsoft, Google, and others). They test your understanding of how C truly behaves — not just what you've memorized.

Each question hides a lesson. Try predicting the output or explaining the behavior before you test it.

1. What will be the output of the following code?

```
#include <stdio.h>
int main() {
    int i = 5;
    printf("%d %d", ++i, i++);
    return 0;
}
```

(Asked in: TCS NQT) — Focus: sequence points and side effects.

2. Differentiate between:

   ```
   char *s = "Hello";
   char s[] = "Hello";
   ```

   (Asked in: Wipro) — Which one can be modified safely?

3. Predict the behavior:

   ```
   int a[3] = {1, 2, 3};
   int *p = a;
   printf("%d", *(p + 3));
   ```

   (Asked in: Infosys) — Is this valid memory access?

4. Evaluate:

   ```
   int a[2][2] = {{1,2},{3,4}};
   printf("%d", *(*(a + 1) + 1));
   ```

   (Asked in: TCS Digital) — Tests 2D array-pointer equivalence.

5. Which is the correct declaration for a pointer to a pointer to int?

   a) `int **p;`

   b) `int *p*;`

   c) `int * * p;`

6. What will this print?

   ```
   char *p = "World";
   p++;
   printf("%c", *p);
   ```

   (Asked in: Accenture) — String literal and pointer arithmetic.

7. Output?

```
#define SQR(x) x * x
int main() {
    int a = 3;
    printf("%d", SQR(a + 1));
}
```

(Asked in: TCS CodeVita) — Macro expansion pitfalls.

8. Explain the difference between `malloc()` and `calloc()`. *(Asked in: Wipro Elite NTH) — Focus: memory initialization.*

9. What happens here?

```
int *p = NULL;
*p = 10;
```

(Asked in: Infosys) — Dereferencing NULL pointer.

10. What's wrong with:

```
main() {
    printf("Hi");
}
```

(Asked in: TCS) — Implicit int return type is obsolete.

11. Find the mistake:

```
int x = 5;
if (x = 0)
    printf("Zero");
else
    printf("Non-zero");
```

(Asked in: Cognizant) — Assignment vs comparison operator.

12. What is the size of `int *` and `int` on a 64-bit system? *(Asked in: Amazon) — Pointer width awareness.*

13. Predict:

```
char c = 300;
printf("%d", c);
```

(Asked in: TCS NQT) — Integer overflow in char type.

14. Output?

```
int a = 10, *p = &a;
p++;
printf("%d", *p);
```

(Asked in: Accenture) — Pointer arithmetic out of bounds.

15. Define a **dangling pointer**. Give one practical example. *(Asked in: Wipro) — Post-free pointer handling.*

16. Output of:

```
int a[] = {1,2,3};
int *p = a + 1;
printf("%d", p[1]);
```

(Asked in: Microsoft) — Pointer arithmetic in array indexing.

17. Spot the issue:

```
char *s = malloc(5);
strcpy(s, "HelloWorld");
```

(Asked in: Infosys) — Buffer overflow due to allocation mismatch.

18. Why should you use:

```
free(p);
p = NULL;
```

(Asked in: TCS Digital) — Preventing use-after-free.

19. Why do macros require parentheses? Show what happens when you omit them.

20. Explain what `restrict` means in C99 and how it helps compilers optimize code. *(Asked in: Google) — Pointer aliasing and optimization.*

Each of these questions is a real interview-level test. Don't just memorize the answer — trace, reason, and explain your logic clearly.

Part B — Core Coding & Logic Builders

These are hands-on logic problems that test both reasoning and clarity of thought. Each problem is similar in difficulty and structure to questions asked in real placement or technical interviews. Try writing the full C code — not just predicting the answer.

1. **Reverse an array in-place without using another array.** *(Asked in: TCS Digital)*

2. **Find the second largest element** in an unsorted array. Optimize it to run in a single traversal. *(Asked in: Wipro Elite NTH)*

3. Write a program to **count the number of vowels, consonants, digits, and spaces** in a given string.

(Asked in: Infosys SP)

4. **Implement your own `strlen()`** using pointer arithmetic. *(Asked in: Microsoft IDC)*
5. **Reverse a string** without using any library functions. *(Asked in: TCS NQT)*
6. **Check if a string is a palindrome.** Avoid using any built-in reverse functions. *(Asked in: Accenture ASE)*
7. **Find the missing number** in an array containing numbers from 1 to N with one missing. *(Asked in: TCS Ninja)*
8. **Rotate an array** to the right by k positions. *(Asked in: Wipro)*
9. **Find the frequency of each character** in a given string. *(Asked in: Infosys SP/DSE)*
10. **Print all duplicate elements** in an array. *(Asked in: TCS CodeVita Prelims)*
11. **Swap two numbers without using a third variable.** *(Asked in: Amazon Technical Round 1)*
12. **Find the factorial of N** using both recursion and iteration. *(Asked in: Wipro Elite)*
13. **Check if a number is prime.** Optimize it to stop at $\sqrt{n}$. *(Asked in: Infosys SP)*
14. **Find GCD (HCF)** of two numbers using Euclid's algorithm. *(Asked in: TCS Digital)*

15. **Find the largest and smallest word** in a sentence. *(Asked in: Cognizant GenC Next)*

16. **Count the occurrences of a substring** within another string. *(Asked in: Wipro Turbo Round 2)*

17. **Sort an array of integers** using bubble sort. Then optimize to selection or quick sort. *(Asked in: TCS CodeVita)*

18. **Merge two sorted arrays** into one sorted array. *(Asked in: Amazon SDE Intern Round 1)*

19. **Find the sum of digits** of a number until a single digit remains. *(Asked in: Infosys Power Programmer)*

20. **Find the intersection of two arrays** (common elements). *(Asked in: Wipro Elite NTH 2023)*

21. **Count total set bits (1's)** in an integer. *(Asked in: Microsoft On-Campus Coding Round)*

22. **Implement binary search** on a sorted array. *(Asked in: TCS Ninja Technical 1)*

23. **Find the maximum sum of a contiguous subarray.** (Hint: Kadane's Algorithm) *(Asked in: Amazon, Google)*

24. **Transpose a 2D matrix in place.** *(Asked in: Infosys SP Round 2)*

25. **Move all zeros to the end** of an array without changing relative order. *(Asked in: TCS NQT Advanced)*

26. **Find if two strings are anagrams.** *(Asked in: Wipro Elite)*

27. **Convert lowercase letters to uppercase** in a string manually using ASCII arithmetic. *(Asked in: Infosys System Engineer)*

28. **Check whether a given matrix is symmetric.** *(Asked in: TCS Digital)*

29. **Remove all duplicate characters** from a string without using extra arrays. *(Asked in: Accenture ASE 2022)*

30. **Count vowels in a sentence using pointers.** *(Asked in: Wipro Elite)*

Remember — most of these questions appear simple. But interviewers look for clean logic, proper edge-case handling, and code that reflects clear understanding, not memorization.

Part C — Debug & Optimization Challenges

These are not just "find the bug" problems — they test whether you understand *why* code breaks. Fixing and optimizing small snippets like these is one of the most common interview patterns in top IT companies. Your job is to identify the logical or performance issue and correct it.

1. **Uninitialized variable problem**

```
#include <stdio.h>
int main() {
    int sum;
    for (int i = 1; i <= 5; i++)
        sum += i;
    printf("%d", sum);
}
```

(Asked in: Wipro) — What should be the initial value of sum?

2. **Infinite loop detection**

```
for (int i = 0; i < 5; i--);
    printf("%d", i);
```

(Asked in: TCS NQT) — Why does this loop never terminate?

3. **Wrong operator in condition**

```
int i = 0;
while (i = 5) {
    printf("%d ", i);
    i++;
}
```

(Asked in: Accenture) — Comparison vs assignment operator.

4. **Pointer bug**

```
int *p;
*p = 100;
printf("%d", *p);
```

(Asked in: TCS Digital) — Always initialize pointers before use.

5. **Memory leak in dynamic allocation**

```
int *arr = malloc(5 * sizeof(int));
arr = malloc(3 * sizeof(int));
```

(Asked in: Infosys SP) — What happened to the first allocation?

6. **Array boundary issue**

```
int a[3] = {1, 2, 3};
for (int i = 0; i <= 3; i++)
    printf("%d ", a[i]);
```

(Asked in: TCS) — Off-by-one errors are the deadliest.

7. **String literal modification**

```
char *s = "hello";
s[0] = 'H';
```

(Asked in: Wipro Elite) — Why does this crash on some compilers?

8. **Incorrect scanf usage**

```
int n;
scanf("%d", n);
```

(Asked in: Infosys) — Missing address operator &.

9. **Forgotten return statement**

```
int add(int a, int b) {
    int sum = a + b;
}
```

(Asked in: TCS Ninja) — What value is actually returned?

10. **Wrong format specifier**

```
float f = 3.14;
printf("%d", f);
```

(Asked in: Accenture) — %d vs %f.

11. **Undefined behavior — modifying and reading same variable**

```
int i = 5;
printf("%d %d", i++, ++i);
```

(Asked in: TCS CodeVita) — What's the output and why undefined?

12. **Segmentation fault**

```
int a[5];
int *p = a + 5;
*p = 10;
```

(Asked in: Infosys DSE) — Dereferencing past the array boundary.

13. **Use-after-free**

```
int *p = malloc(sizeof(int));
*p = 10;
free(p);
printf("%d", *p);
```

(Asked in: Wipro) — Accessing freed memory.

14. **Incorrect macro expansion**

```
#define ADD(x,y) x + y
int main() {
    printf("%d", 5 * ADD(2,3));
}
```

(Asked in: TCS Digital) — Why does this print 17 instead of 25?

15. **Inefficient nested loop**

```
for (int i = 0; i < n; i++)
  for (int j = 0; j < n; j++)
    if (arr[i] == arr[j])
        count++;
```

(Asked in: Microsoft) — Can you reduce the complexity from O(n^2) to O(n)?

16. **Static variable misuse**

```
void count() {
    static int x = 0;
    printf("%d ", x);
}
int main() {
    count(); count(); count();
}
```

(Asked in: Accenture) — Why does it print same or increasing values?

17. **Dangling pointer return**

```
int* foo() {
    int x = 10;
    return &x;
}
```

(Asked in: Infosys SP) — Stack variable addresses vanish after return.

18. **Forgotten file close**

```
FILE *fp = fopen("out.txt", "w");
fprintf(fp, "Hello");
```

(Asked in: TCS) — Why might output not appear in the file?

19. **Integer overflow test**

```
int a = 2147483647;
a++;
printf("%d", a);
```

(Asked in: Wipro) — What happens when int overflows?

20. **Performance optimization**

```
int sum = 0;
for (int i = 0; i < n; i++)
    for (int j = 0; j < m; j++)
        sum += a[i][j];
```

(Asked in: Microsoft) — How can memory access order (row-major vs column-major) affect speed?

Pro Tip: If you can debug confidently, you're already ahead of 80% of candidates. Interviewers rarely care about perfection — they care about your *thought process while fixing the issue*. Always explain what you think is wrong and how you'd confirm it.

Part D — Company-Specific Rapid Fire

These questions are compiled from real technical rounds and coding interviews conducted by major IT and product-based companies. Treat them like mini-interviews — read, pause, think, and explain out loud how you'd solve or reason about each one.

TCS & TCS Digital

1. What is the difference between == and = in C?
2. Predict the output:

```
int a = 10;
printf("%d %d %d", a, a++, ++a);
```

3. Why does this code give undefined behavior?

```
int i = 0;
printf("%d %d", i, i++);
```

4. Write a function to count the number of 1 bits in an integer.
5. Why is `void main()` incorrect according to the C standard?
6. Explain the purpose of `static` keyword in function scope.
7. Why is dynamic memory allocated from the heap, not stack?
8. How does the compiler differentiate between local and global variables with the same name?
9. What happens if you forget to include a header file?
10. Can you modify a string literal in C? Why or why not?

Infosys & Wipro

11. What is the output?

```
int a = 5, b = 10;
printf("%d", a+++b);
```

12. Differentiate between call by value and call by reference in C.
13. Write a recursive function to reverse a string.
14. What is the difference between global and static global variables?
15. Explain how arrays decay into pointers when passed to functions.
16. What will happen if `malloc()` fails to allocate memory?
17. What are wild, dangling, and NULL pointers? Give examples.
18. How can we prevent memory leaks in large projects?
19. What's the difference between `exit(0)` and `return 0`?
20. Why should macros always be written in uppercase?

Accenture & Cognizant

21. Write a program to swap two numbers using pointers.
22. What is wrong with this macro?

```
#define SQR(x) x * x
```

23. Why is it recommended to use `do { ... } while(0)` in macros?

24. Predict the output:

```
char str[] = "C Language";
printf("%c", *(&str[3] + 2));
```

25. How can you dynamically allocate memory for a 2D array?

26. Explain the difference between compile-time and runtime errors.

27. What is segmentation fault? Give one example.

28. Why is using `gets()` dangerous? What should you use instead?

29. What is the difference between pointer to function and function pointer?

30. Why is recursion sometimes replaced with iteration in production code?

Amazon & Microsoft

31. What's wrong with this code?

```
int a = 10;
int *p = &a;
free(p);
```

32. How do you detect a memory leak in C?
33. What is the time complexity of quicksort on average and in worst case?
34. Implement your own version of `memcpy()`.
35. How would you find if two strings are anagrams without using extra space?
36. How does a function call stack frame look in memory?
37. What is the difference between pass by pointer and pass by reference (in C++)?
38. Write a program to reverse a linked list.
39. Why is `volatile` used in embedded programming?
40. Explain how inline functions improve performance.

Google & Advanced Product Interviews

41. Explain undefined behavior with one concrete example in C.
42. What are sequence points and why do they matter?
43. How can aliasing between pointers break compiler optimizations?
44. What is the difference between stack overflow and heap overflow?
45. Why is `malloc(0)` legal and what does it return?

46. What's the difference between shallow copy and deep copy?

47. Predict:

```
int x = 5;
printf("%d", ++x + x++);
```

48. What is tail recursion and when is it optimized by compilers?

49. How do compilers optimize constant expressions?

50. How would you detect memory fragmentation in a large system?

Pro Tip: In real interviews, companies rarely ask for "book-perfect" answers. They want to see how you reason under uncertainty. If you can trace memory, explain behavior, and debug logically — you're already ahead.

The Interviewer's Radar — What They Always Notice

1. **Initialization.** Unused or uninitialized variables are red flags.
2. **Memory pairing.** Every `malloc()` must have a matching `free()`.
3. **Pointer clarity.** Understand `*p`, `&p`, and pointer arithmetic.
4. **Macro safety.** Always wrap parameters in parentheses.
5. **Recursion depth.** Know stack limits and base conditions.
6. **Strings.** Watch for missing `'\0'` and unsafe input.
7. **Operators.** Be ready for tricky ones like `a+++b`.
8. **Efficiency.** Can you reason O(n) vs O(n^2)?
9. **Debugging logic.** Always explain how you'd trace a bug.
10. **Style.** Clean indentation and naming show discipline.

Interviews reward clarity more than perfection — think before you type, reason before you code.

Phase 4

Interview Mindset & Preparation

"Confidence comes from clarity — and clarity comes from preparation."

Developing the mindset, calm, and communication of a true engineer

Chapter 25

THE PSYCHOLOGY OF INTERVIEWS

Take a moment to appreciate how far you've come. From learning your first variable to solving complex pointer puzzles, you've built more than technical skills — you've built the patience, logic, and focus that define real engineers.

Now, it's time to shift gears. This chapter isn't about code or syntax — it's about mindset. Interviews test more than what you know; they reveal how you think, how you stay calm under pressure, and how you turn confusion into clarity.

If the earlier chapters trained your hands to code, this one trains your mind to perform — the way great engineers do when it matters most.

Before we dive into strategies, it's important to understand what an interview truly is — and what it isn't. Many candidates treat it like an exam where there's one right answer, one perfect algorithm, or one ideal way to impress. But interviewers see it differently. To them, it's a window into how you think, how you react under uncertainty, and whether your approach to problems fits the team's rhythm.

So before you practice more code, let's uncover what's really happening on the other side of the table.

25.1 The Real Purpose of an Interview

Most students walk into an interview thinking it's a test of what they know. In reality, it's a test of how they *think*.

Interviewers don't expect you to recall every syntax detail. They're trying to understand:

- How you approach a problem you haven't seen before,
- How clearly you communicate your thought process,
- Whether you stay calm when stuck,
- And how quickly you can reason through your mistakes.

> *"We don't look for people who know everything. We look for people who can learn anything."*

Once you understand this, interviews stop feeling like exams and start feeling like conversations.

25.2 What Interviewers Really Look For

A great candidate doesn't just write code that works — they demonstrate **clarity**, **control**, and **confidence**.

- **Logic clarity:** Do you explain why something works, not just how?
- **Code hygiene:** Do you write readable, consistent, and maintainable code?
- **Error awareness:** Do you avoid undefined behavior and bad assumptions?
- **Resilience:** Do you stay calm when corrected or challenged?
- **Curiosity:** Do you ask insightful questions about constraints or edge cases?

Average Candidate	Standout Candidate
Solves the problem	Explains the approach
Writes code silently	Thinks out loud
Freezes on mistakes	Recovers with reasoning
Memorizes syntax	Understands principles

25.3 Thinking Like an Interviewer

When an interviewer gives you a problem, they're not expecting a perfect solution. They're observing how you think — your process, structure, and reaction to feedback.

They silently note:

- Do you restate the question to confirm understanding?
- Do you break the problem into smaller parts?
- Do you use examples or test cases before coding?
- Do you fix your mistakes with reasoning or panic?

When you pause to think, you project confidence. Silence with focus is better than speed with panic.

25.4 Emotional Control During Interviews

Even the best candidates experience anxiety — blanking out, forgetting syntax, or misreading a question. The difference lies in response, not perfection.

Practical ways to stay calm:

- Breathe before answering — it resets your focus.
- If you forget syntax, explain the logic first.
- When stuck, talk about your assumptions.
- Smile. It signals confidence even when thinking.

Mental checklist:

✓ Restate the problem in your own words.

✓ Identify input, output, and constraints.

✓ Plan the approach verbally.

✓ Handle edge cases.

25.5 The Four Layers of Confidence

Confidence in interviews isn't a mood — it's a structure built over time.

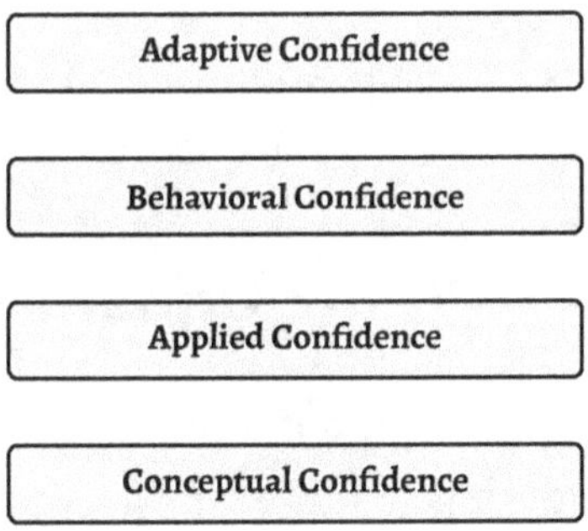

Build from bottom to top — every layer reinforces the next.

1. **Conceptual Confidence:** You understand the *why* behind each topic.
2. **Applied Confidence:** You've practiced real coding questions.
3. **Behavioral Confidence:** You can articulate your reasoning calmly.
4. **Adaptive Confidence:** You handle surprises without losing composure.

25.6 Common Interview Mindset Traps

Myth	Reality
"They expect perfect answers."	They assess approach and reasoning.
"Forgetting syntax is failure."	Explaining logic matters more.
"Speed is everything."	Accuracy and composure count more.
"Saying yes to all helps."	Admitting "I don't know" earns trust.

25.7 How to Think Under Pressure

In real interviews, pressure is a constant companion. The best way to handle it is to make *thinking* your habit.

- Break big problems into smaller parts.
- Speak your thoughts clearly — it shows awareness.
- Verify edge cases before compiling.
- Treat mistakes as feedback, not failure.

> *Interviews aren't about eliminating fear — they're about performing calmly in its presence.*

25.8 The 5-Minute Reflection Ritual

Right after your interview, take five minutes to reflect — this is your personal debugging time.

- What did I explain clearly?
- Where did I hesitate or panic?
- Which concepts felt weak?
- What will I improve before the next one?

Every interview, even the failed one, teaches you something valuable — each mistake is rehearsal for your best version.

The Calm Coder's Manifesto

1. Think before you code.
2. Explain before you execute.
3. Pause before you panic.
4. Debug before you doubt.
5. Reflect before you move on.

Calm isn't a personality trait — it's a skill you build one interview at a time.

Chapter 26

COMMUNICATION SKILLS FOR ENGINEERS

26.1 The Hidden Superpower of Every Engineer

By the time you've reached this chapter, you've already solved logic puzzles, debugged memory leaks, and handled complex code. You've sharpened your technical mind — but here's the truth: **the ability to communicate that knowledge clearly is what sets real professionals apart.**

In interviews, meetings, or even project discussions, the best engineers aren't just the ones who can write code — they're the ones who can *explain it*. If a brilliant solution stays trapped in your head, it's as good as not existing.

This chapter is your guide to expressing your technical ideas with clarity, confidence, and credibility. Not like a public speaker — but like an engineer who communicates logic.

26.2 Why Communication Matters More Than You Think

You might have heard this: "I know people who speak really well but can't code." True — but that's not the full story. In most interviews, **both skill sets are judged together**. Communication doesn't replace coding skills — it amplifies them.

Consider this:

- You're given a coding problem and you freeze — not because you don't know the logic, but because you can't express it.
- You explain your solution, but the interviewer can't follow your structure.
- You complete the task — but you never communicated your thought process, so the interviewer assumes you just guessed.

Sound familiar? It happens all the time — and it's not about intelligence, it's about expression. **Communication is the bridge between what you know and what others understand.**

26.3 The Three Dimensions of Technical Communication

In engineering contexts, communication has three pillars. Once you master these, every interview and discussion becomes smoother:

1. **Clarity** — Speak simply, not vaguely. Avoid filler words like "basically" or "sort of." Replace them with direct expressions like "Here's what happens step by step."
2. **Structure** — Organize your thoughts logically: *Problem → Idea → Approach → Result.*
3. **Empathy** — Understand who's listening. Tailor your explanation for your audience — whether it's an interviewer, a teammate, or a non-technical manager.

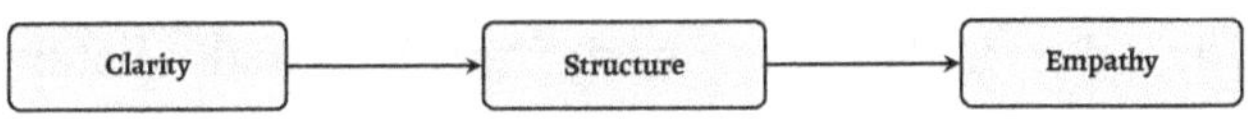

Master all three for complete communication.

26.4 Speaking Like an Engineer (Not a Textbook)

Engineers often think "clear communication" means "using big words." But in real interviews, clarity comes from simplicity — not complexity.

Example:

- ✗ "The issue arises due to an anomalous dereferencing of memory allocation."
- ✓ "The bug happens because we're using a pointer after freeing it."

Another example:

- ✗ "I optimized the function using a recursive traversal of the binary structure."
- ✓ "I used recursion to visit every node in the tree — it made the code cleaner."

Remember: In interviews, you're not trying to impress — you're trying to be understood.

26.5 Listening — The Silent Superpower

Most engineers think communication means "talking better." But half of communication is actually **listening intelligently.** In interviews and team meetings, great listeners often leave stronger impressions than great talkers.

When an interviewer explains a question, don't rush to answer. Pause, listen carefully, and confirm your understanding. It's a subtle sign of maturity that immediately builds trust.

Example:

- ✗ Jumping in immediately: "Yes, yes, I got it — you mean the array problem, right?"
- ✓ Pausing first: "So if I understand correctly, you want a solution that works for any array size, right?"

The second version does three things:

1. Shows you actually listened.
2. Buys you time to think.
3. Makes the interviewer feel respected.

Listening isn't silence — it's **processing.** In technical conversations, this habit makes you stand out as calm, composed, and analytical.

26.6 Writing for Clarity (Emails, Reports, and Documentation)

Writing is another form of engineering. It's how you debug human misunderstanding.

Every engineer eventually writes:

- commit messages
- emails explaining bugs
- documentation for future teammates

Your goal is not to sound "formal." It's to make your message readable, even to a tired developer at 11 p.m.

Example of poor communication:

- ✗ "We need to resolve the deployment discrepancy due to environmental misconfiguration."

Improved version:

- ✓ "The app failed because the test environment used an old config file. I've fixed it and redeployed."

Pro Tip: Before you send or submit anything you write, do a 10-second "clarity test." Ask yourself: *Can someone new to the project understand this without asking me twice?* If not — simplify it.

26.7 Handling Miscommunication Gracefully

Even the best communicators get misunderstood. The difference between an amateur and a professional is how they respond when that happens.

Scenario: You explain your logic in an interview, but the interviewer disagrees or misunderstands.

How many do this:

- ✗ "No, that's not what I meant."

What a good engineer does instead:

- "I see where you're coming from. Let me rephrase that — I meant that we allocate memory dynamically so it adjusts at runtime."

You didn't lose confidence; you adapted. That's what interviewers are really testing — not whether you're perfect, but whether you can stay calm under small communication breakdowns.

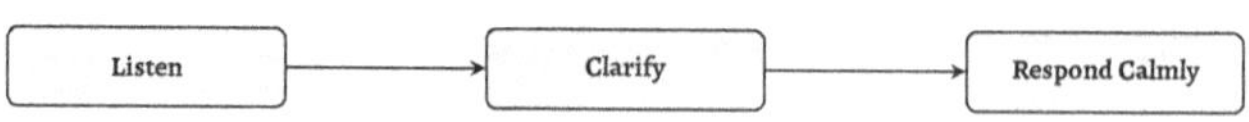

The engineer's cycle for clear communication.

Golden Rule: Clarity + respect = confidence. You don't need to "win" every conversation. You need to stay professional in every one.

26.8 How This Affects Your Interviews

When candidates are technically equal, communication becomes the deciding factor. Many recruiters quietly mark candidates higher for:

- structured explanations
- confidence without arrogance
- thoughtful pauses
- and clear, honest acknowledgment of mistakes

These are the habits that make an interviewer think, *"I'd like to work with this person."*

You don't have to speak like a TED-talk presenter. You just have to communicate like someone who loves solving problems — and knows how to explain them clearly.

26.9 Handling Technical Discussions in Interviews

In a technical interview, communication isn't about talking nonstop — it's about thinking out loud in a structured way. Interviewers don't just want the right answer — they want to see your **reasoning process**.

Try this structure whenever you face a technical question:

1. **Restate the problem** — "So the goal is to find duplicates in the array, right?"
2. **Outline your approach** — "I'll first use a hash table to track occurrences."
3. **Walk through an example** — "Let's test it with [2, 3, 2, 5]."
4. **Discuss complexity** — "This runs in O(n) time, but uses extra memory."

This turns your answer into a conversation rather than a monologue. It shows the interviewer you're not just coding — you're thinking like an engineer.

Example:

- ✗ "We can use a loop and check duplicates."
- ✓ "We can use a hash table — it'll help us find duplicates in one pass instead of nested loops."

See the difference? One answers the "what." The other explains the "why." Interviewers always remember the "why."

26.10 Group Discussions and Collaboration Skills

In the IT industry, almost no project is solo. You'll always collaborate — whether in code reviews, team discussions, or agile meetings. That's why communication isn't just about explaining yourself — it's also about making others feel heard.

Here's how strong communicators stand out in group settings:

- **They don't interrupt.** They wait for a pause and then add value.
- **They summarize others' points.** "So you're saying we can cache the response to reduce API calls?"
- **They connect ideas.** "Building on what Priya said — if we also use pagination, we can save bandwidth."

Interview Tip: In group discussions, interviewers observe how you *build on others' ideas,* not how loudly you speak. Confidence is quiet; aggression is noisy.

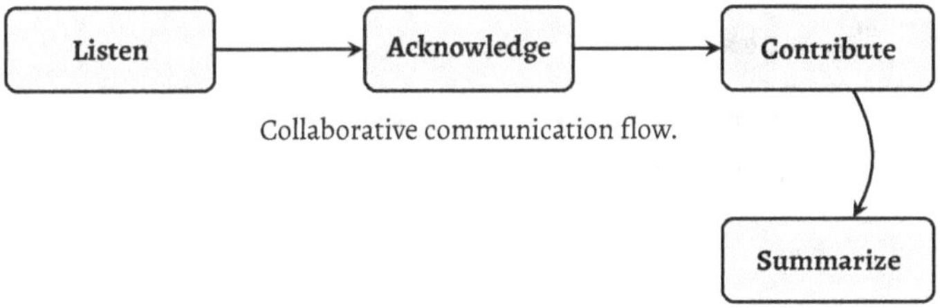

Collaborative communication flow.

26.11 Communicating Under Pressure

Every engineer, at some point, faces this: the interviewer interrupts, time is short, and your code isn't compiling. At that moment, your ability to **stay calm and communicate clearly** matters more than your syntax.

Here's how to handle pressure situations like a professional:

- **Pause instead of panicking.** Take a deep breath and restate what's working so far.
- **Narrate your thought process.** "I think the issue might be with the array bounds — I'll check the loop condition."
- **Ask for a hint respectfully.** "Would you like me to optimize this further or continue with the current logic?"
- **Stay solution-oriented.** Don't defend mistakes; fix them confidently.

Example:

- ✗ "Oh no, I think I messed up — wait, wait, let me try again."
- ✓ "I see the logic failed for an edge case — let me handle that before continuing."

That one sentence can completely change how the

interviewer perceives you. Grace under pressure is a rare and powerful skill.

> **Pro Tip:** If your brain freezes, verbalize your thoughts. Interviewers can guide you only if you keep communicating.

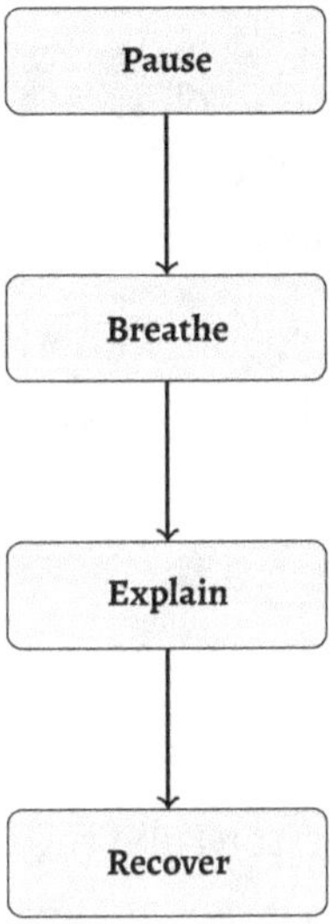

The mental flow for calm communication under stress.

26.12 The Takeaway

You don't need to be a public speaker. You just need to communicate your logic like a builder explaining their design.

Great communication = Structured thinking + Calm expression. That's the formula interviewers remember long after your code fades from the screen.

Do-It-Yourself: Practice Zone

Part A — Speaking Confidence

1. Explain your favorite coding project to a non-technical friend in under 60 seconds. Focus on clarity, not code.
2. Pick a LeetCode problem you solved. Record yourself explaining the approach as if in an interview. Then listen back — did you sound clear and structured?
3. Practice saying, "I don't know that yet, but here's how I'd find out." This single sentence builds interviewer trust.

Part B — Listening Exercises

4. Watch a technical talk or YouTube tutorial. Summarize it in 3 sentences. (No jargon allowed!)
5. During a mock interview, repeat the question back before answering: "So just to confirm, you're asking about memory allocation, right?"
6. In a group discussion, paraphrase someone else's point before adding yours.

Part C — Writing for Engineers

7. Write a short email explaining a bug to your team lead. Keep it under 80 words. Include what

happened, why, and the fix.

8. Rewrite this unclear message: "System broke yesterday due to some config thing." → Make it sound professional and precise.

9. Write a one-line commit message for each of these changes: fixing a typo, adding input validation, improving performance.

Part D — Interview Communication Drills

10. Simulate a coding interview. Verbally describe every step of your solution. Ask a friend to interrupt you with clarifying questions.

11. Practice the "calm reset" — intentionally make a small mistake, then correct it gracefully.

12. Join a coding community or forum. Explain answers to others in plain language. Teaching is the best communication practice.

Final Reflection — The Engineer's Voice

Write a short paragraph (4–5 lines) starting with: *"Good communication makes me a better engineer because..."* Be honest — this reflection often reveals what you truly value in your work.

Communication Cheatsheet for Engineers

- ✓ **Explain your thought process aloud.** Interviewers evaluate how you think, not just what you type.
- ✓ **Keep it simple.** Replace jargon with clear, logical language.
- ✓ **Listen before answering.** Confirm your understanding before responding.
- ✓ **Organize your responses.** Use the structure: Problem → Idea → Approach → Result.
- ✓ **Stay calm under pressure.** Think, breathe, and talk through your reasoning.
- ✓ **Show empathy in collaboration.** Acknowledge others' ideas and build on them.
- ✓ **Clarity beats vocabulary.** Technical communication is about precision, not decoration.
- ✓ **Confidence ≠ arrogance.** Be assertive, not aggressive.
- ✓ **Write like an engineer.** Every email or comment should be clear, short, and testable.

Communication turns knowledge into influence and logic into leadership.

Chapter 27

COMMON HR AND MANAGERIAL QUESTIONS

A surprising number of interviews are decided long after the coding round finishes — in a short conversation where the laptop is closed and the interviewer listens. This chapter helps you prepare for that conversation. Here we focus on what HR and managerial interviewers are actually testing, how to tell your story authentically, and practical exercises to make your responses clear, honest, and memorable.

27.1 The Real Purpose of HR Interviews

At a glance, HR interviews may seem soft and vague compared with technical rounds. That's intentional. HR's role in the hiring process is to evaluate things that *cannot* be verified by running code:

- **Personality fit.** Would you work well within the team and company culture?

- **Communication style.** Can you explain your thoughts clearly and professionally?
- **Attitude under stress.** How do you behave when you don't know an answer or when plans go wrong?
- **Long-term stability.** Are you likely to stay, learn, and grow with the company?

HR Insight: HRs don't want perfectly rehearsed scripts. They want consistent people — the same message in your words and in your tone.

When HR asks the usual opener, *Tell me about yourself,* they aren't asking for a curriculum vitae. They're checking whether you can summarise yourself confidently and succinctly.

27.2 How to Tell Your Story — Authentically

Your personal story is your simplest and strongest asset. A clear structure helps you deliver it without sounding robotic.

Answer Framework (Present → Past → Future):

- **Start with the present:** Who are you today? (student, intern, final-year project, current role)
- **Move to the past:** What experiences, projects or skills brought you here?

- **End with the future:** Why this role, and how does it fit your next step?

Good vs. Poor examples

✓ *Good:* "I am in my final year of Computer Science and I've spent the last year building a small REST API for the college library using Node.js. Through that project I learned to design endpoints and handle concurrency; now I want to join a backend team where I can deepen those skills and contribute to production systems."

✗ *Poor:* "I love coding, I learn fast, and I like working hard." (Vague, cliché, unverifiable.)

Tips:

- Keep the 90-second and 30-second versions ready. Use the 30-second answer for short screens.
- Use specific, recent examples (projects, internships). Specificity is credible.
- Avoid long lists of buzzwords; explain one or two points well.

27.3 Understanding Behavioral and Situational Questions

Behavioral questions ask *what you did*. Situational (or hypothetical) questions ask what you *would* do. Both measure thought process and judgement.

The simplest

structure for answering behavioral questions is the **STAR** method:

S — Situation: Brief context and background.

T — Task: Your responsibility or the problem to solve.

A — Action: What you did, step by step.

R — Result: The outcome, what you learned, and ideally measurable impact.

Sample behavioral prompts (use STAR):

1. "Describe a time you worked effectively in a team."
2. "Tell me about a challenge you faced and how you overcame it."
3. "When did you disagree with a manager or teammate? How did you handle it?"
4. "Describe a situation where you had to learn something quickly to deliver a result."
5. "Talk about a failure and what you learned from it."

Practical note: Focus on your role — be honest about the extent of your contribution. If the result wasn't perfect, show learning and follow-up.

27.4 Handling Managerial Rounds with Confidence

Managerial rounds mix technical thinking with leadership, ownership and prioritisation. While HR checks fit and tone, managers test higher-level judgement.

What managers are listening for

- **Decision-making:** Can you choose a reasonable approach and stick by it with justification?
- **Ownership:** Do you take responsibility and communicate clearly when things go wrong?
- **Prioritisation:** Can you balance multiple tasks and explain trade-offs?
- **People sense:** Do you show empathy and clarity when discussing team interactions?

Common managerial prompts:

- "How will you prioritise these tasks under tight deadlines?"
- "Explain a time you led something from idea to delivery."
- "How do you decide between building a quick workaround and designing a long-term solution?"

Example answer structure for prioritisation:

1. Assess impact and urgency (customer-facing, blocker, low-priority).
2. Communicate assumptions and constraints to stakeholders.
3. Break tasks into deliverable slices and set checkpoints.

4. Re-evaluate and re-prioritise as data appears.

27.5 Top HR and Managerial Questions (With Guidance)

Below is a compact table of common questions, what interviewers are really asking, and how to answer.

Question	What They're Really Asking	How to Approach It
Tell me about yourself.	Are you clear and confident?	Use Present → Past → Future; keep both long and short versions ready.
Why do you want to join us?	Do you know the company?	Mention alignment with your goals and one specific company detail.
What's your strength and weakness?	Are you self-aware?	Share one real strength with an example. For weakness, show growth and reflection.
Describe a time you failed.	Do you take responsibility?	Use STAR — emphasize what you learned and how you improved.
Where do you see yourself in 5 years?	Are you stable and ambitious?	Show realistic long-term goals that align with the company.
How do you handle tight deadlines?	Do you plan effectively?	Explain prioritization, progress tracking, and communication under pressure.

Question	What They're Really Asking	How to Approach It
Tell me about a conflict at work.	Do you manage relationships well?	Show empathy, professionalism, and resolution steps.

Short advice: Keep the list compact and conversational — save deeper practice for the workbook section.

Quick Recap Before You Move On

The HR Interview Mindset

- Be honest, not humblebragging.
- Prepare stories, not scripts.
- Pause before replying — a short pause signals reflection.
- Confidence is a habit built through preparation and small wins.

Do-It-Yourself: Practice Zone

This section is designed like a workbook. For each prompt, write your answers in the spaces provided and practise them out loud. Aim to convert each STAR story into both a 90-second and 30-second version.

1. **Tell me about yourself.**
   Task: Write a 90-second version and a 30-second elevator version. Keep the present, past, future flow.
2. **Describe a time you failed.**
   Task: Use STAR. What happened? What did you learn? How did you follow up?
3. **Whatś your greatest strength and a weakness?**
   Task: For strength, pick a concrete example. For weakness, pick a real non-critical skill and explain how youŕe improving.
4. **If you had a conflict with a team member, how would you handle it?**
   Task: Briefly write the steps you would take to resolve the conflict.
5. **Why did you choose your field of study?**
   Task: Connect motivation to skills youv́e built and possible career routes.
6. **What motivates you at work?**
   Task: Be specific: solving edge cases, building user-facing features, mentoring juniors, etc.
7. **Describe a time you worked in a team to meet a**

deadline.
Task: STAR + describe how you communicated and handled scope changes.

8. **Give an example of a decision you made with incomplete information.**
Task: Focus on assumptions, risk mitigation, and follow-up checks.

9. **How do you prioritise tasks when everything seems urgent?**
Task: Write a short checklist you would follow in such a situation.

10. **Why should we hire you?**
Task: Combine one technical strength, one behavior trait, and one company-specific reason.

11. **Walk me through a project on your resume.**
Task: Describe the goal, your approach, your contribution, and the impact in three short paragraphs.

12. **Describe a leadership moment.**
Task: Even a small example counts — mentoring a peer, coordinating tasks, or taking the initiative.

Practice schedule suggestion (for printing):

- Day 1: Write 3 stories in STAR format (30–40 minutes)
- Day 2: Record and listen to your 90s and 30s versions (20–30 minutes)
- Day 3: Mock interview with a friend or mentor (30–45

minutes)

Chapter 28

RESUME BUILDING FOR TECH INTERVIEWS

Your resume is your first line of communication with an employer — the six-second story that determines whether your profile moves to the next stage. In this chapter, we'll explore how to write, structure, and refine your technical resume so that it speaks your language: results, clarity, and impact.

28.1 Why Your Resume Matters More Than You Think

A resume is not a formality. It's your professional advertisement — the bridge between your academic life and your first offer letter. Recruiters spend an average of 6–10 seconds scanning each resume, searching for specific keywords, clarity, and measurable results.

Recruiter Insight: A resume doesn't get you the job — it gets you the interview.

The resume should highlight what matters most for the role. Use it as your spotlight: pick 4–5 achievements that best showcase your value, not a list of everything you've ever done.

✓ Focus on achievements, not responsibilities.
✗ Avoid dense text or decorative templates — simplicity wins.

28.2 Understanding How Recruiters Read Resumes

Recruiters often scan resumes in an "F-shaped" pattern: left to right, top to bottom, pausing on keywords and metrics. The most visible parts are:

- Top one-third of the page (your summary and skills)
- Bold keywords like technologies or languages
- Quantifiable achievements
- Clear headings and whitespace

A technical recruiter typically looks for:

- Languages and frameworks (C, C++, Python, React, etc.)
- Project impact — measurable improvements or results
- Internships or internships with relevant tools
- Clean formatting and zero spelling errors

Recruiter Insight: A clean resume is subconsciously read as a well-organized mind.

28.3 Structuring a Technical Resume

Your resume should be one page long (two only for professionals with multiple years of experience). Structure it logically:

Recommended Resume Sections:

1. Header (Name, Contact, LinkedIn, GitHub)
2. Summary / Objective
3. Education
4. Technical Skills
5. Projects
6. Experience / Internships
7. Achievements / Certifications

Each section should earn its space. If you can't explain how a line adds value, remove it.

Pro Tip: Arrange sections by relevance. For students, put projects before experience; for working professionals, the reverse.

28.4 Writing Each Section Effectively

1. Header

Keep it minimal:

> **Aarav Nair**
> `aarav.nair@example.com |`
> `github.com/aaravnair |`
> `linkedin.com/in/aaravnair`

Avoid adding personal details like age, gender, or photo.

2. Summary or Objective

Make it concise, impact-driven, and role-aligned.

> *Good:* "Final-year Computer Science student with a strong focus on system design and backend development. Experienced in C, Python, and database optimization through hands-on projects."
> *Poor:* "Seeking a challenging position in a dynamic organization to enhance my skills."

3. Education

List in reverse chronological order. Include degree, institution, and percentage/CGPA (if strong).

> **B.Tech — Computer Science and Engineering**,
> XYZ University (2021–2025)

CGPA: 8.6 / 10

4. Technical Skills

Use categories for readability:

Languages: C, C++, Python
Frameworks: Flask, React, Node.js
Databases: MySQL, MongoDB
Tools: Git, Docker, VS Code

Tip: Tailor this section to the job description — don't list every skill you've ever tried.

5. Projects

Every project must demonstrate measurable impact. Use the "Action → Result" pattern.

Library Management System — C, MySQL
Built a command-line library management tool that reduced manual record-keeping by 70%. Implemented error handling and search optimization.

Portfolio Website — React, Node.js
Created a personal website hosting resume and blog; integrated GitHub API to dynamically fetch project cards.

✓ Use verbs like "Built", "Developed", "Optimized", "Implemented", "Reduced".
✗ Avoid "Was involved in" or "Worked on".

6. Experience / Internships

Focus on your contributions, not job descriptions.

Backend Intern, ABC Tech Pvt. Ltd. (June–August 2024)
Developed API endpoints using Flask; reduced response latency by 30%. Wrote unit tests and contributed to database migration scripts.

7. Achievements / Certifications

Qualified in Google Kickstart Round H — 2024
Completed Coursera Certification: "Machine Learning by Stanford University"
Top 10 finalist, Hackathon 2023 at IIIT Hyderabad

28.5 Formatting, Design, and ATS Compatibility

Applicant Tracking Systems (ATS) parse resumes before humans see them. That means your design must be machine-readable.

Formatting Guidelines:

- Use fonts like Calibri, Lato, Helvetica, or Source Sans Pro.
- Maintain font size between 10–11.5 pt.
- Keep margins between 0.5 and 0.7 inches.
- Avoid tables, images, and columns that break parsing.

- Save as PDF unless otherwise mentioned.

Recruiter Insight: Simplicity and clarity always beat creative chaos.

28.6 Top Resume Mistakes to Avoid

✗ Using paragraphs instead of bullet points.
✗ Listing responsibilities instead of achievements.
✗ Ignoring measurable metrics.
✗ Forgetting GitHub or LinkedIn link.
✗ Spelling or grammar errors — instant rejection.

✓ Use numbers wherever possible: "Reduced load time by 40%."
✓ Include strong project links (GitHub, portfolio).
✓ Ask a peer or mentor to proofread.

Quick Recap Before You Move On

Tech Resume at a Glance

- One page, clean layout, consistent spacing.
- Every bullet starts with a strong action verb.
- Quantify achievements wherever possible.
- Include links (GitHub, LinkedIn, portfolio).
- Save final draft as PDF and test on multiple devices.

Do-It-Yourself: Resume Workshop

Now it's your turn to create or refine your technical resume. Use the prompts below to structure your own version:

1. Write your one-line summary: Who are you and what's your focus?
2. List your top three projects and their measurable outcomes.
3. Write two bullet points under each project using the Action → Result format.
4. Create your "Technical Skills" list under clear categories.
5. Add achievements, certifications, and relevant links.
6. Review: Can a recruiter skim it in 6 seconds and remember three key points about you?

Final Checklist:

- Resume fits on one page.
- Clear section headings and alignment.
- Consistent font sizes and spacing.
- Impact-driven, quantified achievements.
- Proofread — zero typos.

Remember: Your resume tells your story before you enter the room. Make sure it speaks confidently and clearly.

Ending Note: From Learner to Engineer

"The journey doesn't end with the interview — it begins with curiosity."

As you reach the end of this book, take a moment to look back at how far you've come. You started by learning syntax, built logic step by step, and understood how to think like an engineer — not just a programmer.

The goal of this book was never to fill your mind with code alone, but to help you *think in C*, reason through problems, and grow the kind of mindset that companies truly value.

Remember, interviews are just checkpoints — moments that measure where you are, not who you are. The real journey begins when you continue to learn, explore, and stay curious long after you close this book.

Keep experimenting, keep failing, keep learning — that's how you transform from a learner into an engineer.

"All the best for your journey ahead!"

www.ingramcontent.com/pod-product-compliance
Lightning Source LLC
Chambersburg PA
CBHW062132160726
48282CB00027B/798
* 9 7 8 9 3 5 4 6 9 4 5 8 5 *